Take Freedom

THE JOHN HOPE FRANKLIN SERIES IN
AFRICAN AMERICAN HISTORY AND CULTURE

Waldo E. Martin Jr. and Patricia Sullivan, editors

The best scholarship in African American history and culture compels us to expand our sense of who we are as a nation and forces us to engage seriously the experiences of all Americans who have shaped the development of this country. By publishing pathbreaking books informed by several disciplines, the John Hope Franklin Series in African American History and Culture seeks to illuminate America's multicultural past and the ways in which it has informed the nation's democratic experiment.

A complete list of books published in the John Hope Franklin Series in African American History and Culture is available at https://uncpress.org/series/the-john-hope-franklin-series-in-african-american-history-and-culture.

Take Freedom
Recovering the Fugitive History of the Denmark Vesey Affair

James O'Neil Spady

The University of North Carolina Press CHAPEL HILL

This book was published with the assistance of the John Hope Franklin Fund of the University of North Carolina Press.

© 2026 The University of North Carolina Press
All rights reserved
Manufactured in the United States of America
Set in Merope by Jamie McKee, MacKey Composition

Cover art: *Marshland Landscape*, 2000. Oil on canvas, 60″ × 48″ © Jonathan Green.

Library of Congress Cataloging-in-Publication Data
Names: Spady, James O'Neil, 1968– author
Title: Take freedom : recovering the fugitive history of the Denmark Vesey affair / James O'Neil Spady.
Other titles: John Hope Franklin series in African American history and culture
Description: Chapel Hill : The University of North Carolina Press, [2026] | Series: The John Hope Franklin Series in African American History and Culture | Includes bibliographical references and index.
Identifiers: LCCN 2025037601 | ISBN 9781469686363 cloth alk. paper | ISBN 9781469686370 paperback alk. paper | ISBN 9781469686387 epub | ISBN 9781469687902 pdf
Subjects: LCSH: Vesey, Denmark, approximately 1767-1822. Official report of the trials of sundry Negroes, charged with an attempt to raise an insurrection in the state of South-Carolina | Black people—South Carolina—Charleston—Social conditions—19th century | Antislavery movements—South Carolina—Charleston—History—19th century | Charleston (S.C.)—History—Slave Insurrection, 1822 | BISAC: SOCIAL SCIENCE / Ethnic Studies / American / African American & Black Studies | SOCIAL SCIENCE / Black Studies (Global)
Classification: LCC F279.C49 B5376 2026
LC record available at https://lccn.loc.gov/2025037601

For product safety concerns under the European Union's General Product Safety Regulation (EU GPSR), please contact gpsr@mare-nostrum.co.uk or write to the University of North Carolina Press and Mare Nostrum Group B.V., Mauritskade 21D, 1091 GC Amsterdam, The Netherlands.

To community organizers

Contents

List of Illustrations ix

PROLOGUE
Sunday, June 16, 1822 1

CHAPTER ONE
Amaritta's Yard 4

CHAPTER TWO
Take Freedom 45

CHAPTER THREE
The Workhouse Fight 83

CHAPTER FOUR
Burials and Aftershocks 125

AFTERWORD
The Story of the Papers 141

Acknowledgments 159

Notes 161

Index 207

Illustrations

FIGURES

1.1 A Charleston windmill, 1799 10

1.2 The *Fredensborg*, built in 1778 22

2.1 Map of Charleston environs, 1825 65

2.2 Lucas's house, 2021 78

3.1 Receipt with Christopher Jeannerett's handwriting, 1823 88

3.2 Social network flowchart for testimony in the 1822 uprising movement 101

4.1 1837 potter's field plat overlaid on a 2024 map of Charleston 127

4.2 *Slave Sale, Charleston, South Carolina* by Eyre Crowe, 1856 137

5.1 Lines from House and Senate copies of investigatory records, 1822 153

MAPS

1.1 Charleston, South Carolina, 1822 9

1.2 East side wharves and Finance and Insurance District 27

2.1 Weapons caches 62

2.2 Mill complexes 73

For the latest versions of the maps in this book, go to mappingblackcharleston.org.

TABLE

5.1 Handwriting samples: The investigatory record copies and four clerks with similar handwriting 146

Take Freedom

Prologue
Sunday, June 16, 1822

Midnight was moonless. The night patrol was unable to see into the marshes, across the fields and yards, or down the streets and alleys. Rebel detachments moving nearby, seeking their positions for timed and coordinated attacks, would have been almost invisible. Patrollers would not even see silhouettes. The rebels would commandeer guns and gunpowder from the city's public and private weapons caches in surprise assaults. Within minutes they would wield the slavers' arsenal against slavery. Demonstrating their new power by destroying whoever would continue to oppose their freedom—white or Black—they would march through the city gathering new adherents from among people choosing freedom in this night of reckoning. The Black community would outnumber and outgun the whites. The first skirmishes—lopsided in their favor.[1]

This revolutionary scenario was a vision of a secret movement within part of the Black community of Charleston, South Carolina, in 1822. Denmark Vesey has become the most prominent name associated with the events, but the movement was bigger than him. There were several leaders. There was a diverse following. Indigenous African knowledge influenced it, and Africans were among the most active leaders. Certain movement leaders—especially Gullah Jack, Peter Poyas, Monday Gell, Denmark Vesey, and a few others—planned an uprising that became a pivotal event in an ongoing, hemispheric pattern of war against slavery and slavers. Their organizing demonstrated African and African American willingness to take freedom by force from people who would not give it peacefully.[2]

Though Denmark Vesey was already free in 1822, he and other free Black people were part of the movement. His wife Susan may have been part of it, too. She was almost certainly aware of the planning, having been present in their little house with a group of women while Denmark led a large planning meeting in other rooms. The Veseys' interests were not entirely different from those of the masses of enslaved people. Both Denmark and Susan had friends and loved ones in the city who were still enslaved, and when part of a kinship network is property, no part of it can be entirely free. Enslavement harmed and humiliated all free Black people, who had to worry about what slavers could do or were doing to people they loved. Slavery attached a racial stigma to Blackness that stole resources and opportunities from free Black people such as Susan and Denmark. The whites' government harassed the free Black population with targeted regulations, fees, licenses, and taxes that they did not apply to whites. Free Black people could not vote. Their children did not attend the state-funded free schools. They could not leave the state and return. They could not expect equal rights in court. And what anemic freedoms remained whites critiqued in the local press as excessive.[3]

The primary cause of antislavery rebellion was slavery. Slavery meant that whites took profits from the labor of enslaved people and from the bodies of their children, who were also saleable property for the slavers. For financial benefit, whites separated Black families and friends for their own interests whenever they wanted. Even when they did not sell or rent out people very far, kin might live in different parts of town. Permanent separations occurred. Acquaintances, friends, and family of both the free and the enslaved were callously—even contemptuously—marketed for profit. Such suffering motivated enslaved people's desire for freedom, so they became like fugitives, metaphorically and sometimes actually running from white power. Experiencing or witnessing this running was a common part of life. Across the city, people devised fugitive strategies to safeguard relationships, protect places of solace, and conserve available resources to try to thrive. They would have considered divulging unauthorized visits, meetings, or conversations to whites to be condemnable if it could be avoided. The community might, for example, disparage someone who, in order to curry favor with whites, reported people for taking food or using a horse without permission. In other words, slavery birthed an ethics of silence. Silence could be power. Domination and inequality created the need for this discretion.[4]

Slavers in South Carolina became significantly more aggressive during the late 1810s and early 1820s. They took regulatory, legislative, and private action to deepen the slaving, racial order. It became all but impossible to buy one's freedom or the freedom of family members. A faction of whites used government and vigilantism to harass the Black-led church in the city. By the summer of 1821, some Black Charlestonians could see the danger in the new repressiveness. They knew slavers well. Hundreds of Black Charlestonians were indigenous Africans who had been trafficked into Charleston during a reopening of the slave trade in 1804–8. They could remember losing everything but life itself to slavers. The American-born enslaved also knew that even their personal, affectionate relationships were not respected as loving relationships by slavers. They knew slavers might continue to develop an even crueler spirit. Whites declared that there were too many enslaved Black people in Charleston. They asserted that free Black people had too much freedom. Many Black Charlestonians understood the implications of such statements for their future, and a few began to believe that a more radical response was necessary. "We forget," writes Tiya Miles, "that love is revolutionary." Some Black Charlestonians became unwilling to wait and see what white Charleston would do next. They found allies who also believed that they could not continue to live this way and revived years-old discussions about rising up.[5]

CHAPTER ONE

Amaritta's Yard

> Runaway... Mary, about 30 years of age.... She has been seen frequently about the Planters' Hotel where she has a husband; probably she may go to Sullivan's Island now... as the family has gone there.
>
> —Ad to capture Mary Woods, Charleston, 1822

> I had outwitted him.... It is the only weapon of the weak and oppressed against... their tyrants.
>
> —HARRIET JACOBS, on successfully escaping slavery

When Mary Woods's slaver advertised for her capture in 1822 in the epigraph above, he was engaged in a struggle with her. She or her recent ancestors had arrived in Carolina involuntarily, and he was trying to prevent her from willfully taking back some of her freedom. The origins of that fugitive will, in nearly all of Charleston's African American community, were ultimately in homelands in various parts of Africa. They or their ancestors had been captured by African enemies working to satisfy the demands of European and American slave traffickers on the coasts. Their arrival in Charleston was pivotal because their labor would build the colony. But Black Charlestonians were neither settlers nor the colonized Native Americans—they were trafficked arrivals from another continent. They came to outnumber whites by three to one in the greater Charleston area. In the rural and coastal neighborhoods, the numerical superiority of the Black population over the white was sometimes as high as eight to one—a ratio almost as lopsided as Haiti's nine-to-one Black majority on the eve of its revolution in 1791. In 1820, there were 57,000 enslaved people and 3,500 free Black people living in and near Charleston. These Africans and African Americans were ubiquitous in the economy, culture, and society of the region. Daily life in the city was suffused by their work, knowledge, and relationships.[1]

A significant proportion of this Black majority had arrived quite recently. Warm feelings of affinity connected places in Africa to the settler places in which they were forced to live. Knowing who the people were in Charleston who came from one's indigenous region in Africa was vital in 1822. Africans from the Dakar region, from the Akan states, from Igboland, and from the Kongo and Tanzania highly valued closeness with people from their ancestral homes. Charleston's diverse Black population also had hundreds of enslaved people who had formerly been settled in other slaving colonies in the Americas. These people, too, often sought acquaintances and friendships with one another, such as the "French Negroes" who had arrived from Haiti and other Caribbean colonies. Those who had been born in greater Charleston often maintained multigenerational networks of beloved friends and kin. Enslaved people in the city sometimes had relatives on plantations in the countryside, including grandparents who raised the children of the city dwellers. All these Africans and African-descended Americans formed social ties of affection and support—created despite the captivity of enslavement.[2]

Relationships were nourished in yards all over the city. They were the site of labor, meals, and social interactions in the open air and the light of day. An extension of a house, a yard was a space where women did much of their labor. In a mild climate like Charleston's, people could work in the yard most of the year. From the yards, women could learn about the activities of their household and neighbors. The yards were where enslaved women and men shared news and sustained friendships. Conversation, labor, and shared meals created intimacies we can only glimpse. In Amaritta La Roche's yard, her former and her current husband met to eat the meals she provided. Sometime around 1821, she left the first husband—with whom she had two children—and married Rolla Bennett. The slavers' laws did not recognize marriages among the enslaved, but the Black community respected them. Her first marriage had been to Joe La Roche, and it had produced at least two children. Amaritta's and other enslaved women's labor, from birthing children to preparing food and more, made them critical to the social reproduction of the city's enslaved labor force. Her and Joe's two children, as was true for all children of enslaved women, inherited her status as enslaved from birth. They were the exclusive property of Amaritta's enslaver. But Amaritta was not powerless. Though we do not know what happened to her children, we know she facilitated a relationship between Joe and Rolla. The men were *intimate* friends, it was said. Amaritta, Joe, and Rolla navigated personal relationships and the almost impossible daily life of the enslaved with a dexterity that exemplified personal affection and mutual support.[3]

The social attachments among Black Charlestonians were as ardent as those described by Frederick Douglass, who wrote that during his enslavement in Maryland he "had a number of warm-hearted friends" whom he "loved almost as I did my life." The mere thought, he continued, of "being separated from them forever," by escaping slavery without them, "was painful beyond expression." Such bonds were fugitive. People were always running from white power, and it separated loved ones. Mary Prince, a former slave from the Caribbean, declared that even her freedom was tinctured by sadness "while separated from my dear husband" and all her "old friends and connections." It might seem like an unpardonable abandonment to leave loved ones behind, but slavery made this fugitivity necessary. Otherwise, unacceptable choices might have to be made for the benefit or survival of oneself, loved ones, friends, or community. Harriet Jacobs wrote about the remorse she felt for leaving her children in her flight from slavery, but she always insisted that her escape was necessary for her freedom and, ultimately, for theirs too. If there was a fault, she argued, it belonged to the slavers. It was also the fault of slaving tyrants that she and friends and family broke the law to hide her when she fled. Her family and friends valued her as a person over and above any claim her slavers asserted to her body as a profitable commodity. That ethic of secrecy and other covert assistance was among the most important everyday resistance techniques Black Charlestonians needed. This ethic surely aided Mary Woods when she fled in 1822 to the Planter's Hotel in Charleston, where her husband worked. That same year, many of the women in yards and houses likely overheard conversations about an uprising, but none talked to whites about what they heard while the plans were still secret. Secrecy had a high value. It facilitated survival of themselves, beloved friends, and kin even when maintaining secrecy was formally illegal.[4]

Douglass, Jacobs, and Prince wrote retrospectively from a place of greater safety. From freedom they could more readily describe their affection for loved ones during their enslavement. They could tell their wrenching stories about momentous choices to leave them all behind. Amaritta, Joe, and Rolla were never able to tell their own story freely. Their enslavement is part of why we know so little about them. Slavery required tact about what one said and to whom, when, and how one spoke. Amaritta was in greater danger than Mary Prince, who was free in England when she published her story. Proof of how meaningful the difference was is available in the fact that Amaritta's marriage with Rolla ended when he was executed alongside Denmark Vesey for participating in the 1822 uprising movement.[5]

Charleston women's labor enriched slavers while also producing some small portion of a more desired life. Sarah Paul and Susan Vesey, the former enslaved and the latter free, cooked and did laundry in the community. We know little about them before 1822 beyond these facts and that they were related to Denmark Vesey. Like Amaritta's relationships with Joe and Rolla,

Sarah's and Susan's relationships with Vesey reflected a pattern of social change and continuing attachment. Sarah was a stepchild of Vesey's, and although they lived apart because she was still enslaved, he visited her and she cooked for him. Susan was Vesey's second or third wife, and she, too, had other relationships. When Rolla and Vesey and other men secretly discussed rebellion, these personal relationships must have been among their foremost concerns. The political economy of slavery, capitalism's antinomy of love and exploitation, was a problem seemingly without a solution. A rebellion could revolutionize their situation or lead to death. Choosing was agonizing and fearful. If an uprising seemed less like a chance for freedom and more like a futile, immanent risk to loved ones, would people betray each other to white authorities? Doing so would break the ethic of keeping each other's secrets. And it might mean betraying beloved friends to the hangman.[6] Painful, potentially life-changing decisions were made in yards throughout Charleston, a city that had been transformed by Black laborers who were intimately familiar with its geography.

For the bare life they lived, Black Charlestonians supplied the great majority of the labor the city needed. Black laborers transformed the land and the waterways for whites such as Rolla Bennett's slaver, Governor Thomas Bennett. They made the millponds and built the lumber mills that were among the most impressive industrial facilities anywhere in the South at the time. For capitalists in Charleston's agriculture-related industries, Black labor was a capital good. These laborers filled in marshes, cleared ground, and built dams, causeways, sheds, bridges, wharves, docks, and other structures. They also operated such facilities, working under white direction, loaded and unloaded ships, and farmed the cleared land. Black people did all these things and more for the white population, especially for its wealthier classes. They worked wet-nursing babies, preparing meals, serving personal needs, carrying messages, and making all manner of craft items, from mantuas to barrels. They built the public infrastructure, too, by constructing and maintaining everything from streets to seawalls and more. Enslaved labor made it possible for whites to direct the reshaping of the peninsula during the 1810s and 1820s.[7]

As they expanded their dominion over the land of the peninsula, white Charlestonians committed to expanding slavery's dominion over the economy too. In 1803, South Carolina became the only US state to reopen Atlantic slave trading after having closed it in the wake of the American Revolution. Once the US government banned the transatlantic slave trade into the United States in 1808, Charleston became a significant port in a thriving domestic slave traffic. The city's interstate trafficking in people contributed to the expansion of both slavery and colonial settlement westward, where Cherokees, Creeks, and other Native nations sought to resist US colonial appropriation of their land. These two elements—settlement and slaving expansion—yoked indigenous North Americans and the enslaved to the growth of capital in Charleston. This capitalism made race central to its profitability strategies, and its political and social arrangements reproduced the conditions of its success. In 1822, Cherokee and Muskogee people within a few hundred miles of Charleston still governed themselves autonomously. White Carolinians, like other white settlers in the United States, could still imagine using slaves to clear freshly colonized Native land to expand their production. During the 1810s, they could still speculate on colonial plantations as long as they were willing to go to the very northwestern corner of South Carolina or—much more likely—cross into Georgia. Alabama and Mississippi or places farther west that Carolina settlers sometimes deemed ideal. Projectors wanted the cheapest possible labor to ensure the quickest, maximal profitability they knew how to produce on the indigenous land they intended to possess. Charleston remained a significant center for such speculation because it was a port and mart for trafficked labor and other commodities. The docks and wharves of Charleston's East Bay Street together with the banking and insurance district near Broad Street and East Bay made the city a key port in the colonization and slavery expansion into Georgia and the Mississippi River Valley in the 1800s (see map 1.1).[8]

By 1822, Charleston had long been a good site for the hand manufacture of craft goods to export inland via rivers and estuaries. Enslaved and free Black workers had been an integral part of the industrial labor pool for these crafts. In the last years of the eighteenth century, at least half of Charleston artisans worked in facilities with at least ten other workers, free and enslaved. In John Wyatt's lumber operation in the 1790s, as many as seventeen workers filled out time cards and were paid hourly wages. The most powerful factories were dedicated to processing Southern agricultural products for market. Situated on a peninsula formed by rivers that extended into the countryside and in possession of a deepwater port, Charleston received rice, lumber, foodstuffs, and other commodities by water. These and other products were processed to be used locally or shipped out to other places in the world. Governor Thomas Bennett was a leading figure in the development of commerce, both as a businessman and a politician. His lumber mills on the Ashley River were a prominent landmark.[9]

Black workers labored in Bennett's and several other milling establishments in Charleston. There was an industrial sawmill on the west side along

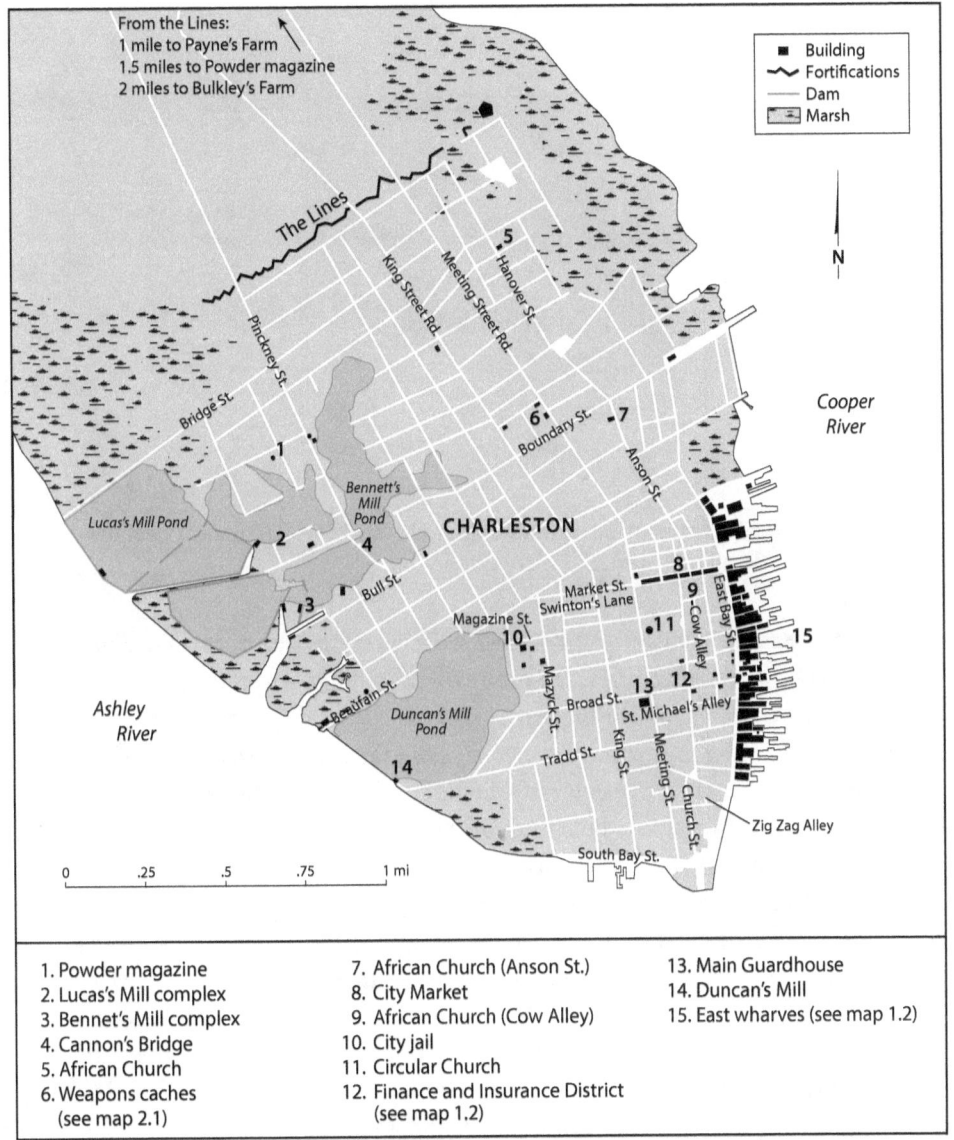

MAP 1.1 Charleston, South Carolina, 1822. See mappingblackcharleston.org for updates.

FIGURE 1.1 A Charleston windmill and neighborhood in 1799. From the collections of the South Carolina Historical Society, Charleston.

Beaufain Street that used teams of enslaved laborers in place of steam-, wind-, or water-powered machines. The groups of men stood in a pit to process raw logs using a giant saw. The biggest, oldest mechanized facilities were those powered by tides and wind. Several of these facilities were on the Ashley River in an area that was partly outside the city limits on "the Neck," a region north of Boundary Street but south of the 1812 fortifications known as the Lines (see map 1.1). Along the Ashley in the city and on the Neck in 1822, from Tradd Street to near the Lines, there were windmills, steam mills, and tidal mills. One of the most significant of these was Wyatt's Windmill, which was an imposingly tall, round foundation structure made partly from brick (see fig. 1.1). Wyatt and a partner—both tradesmen—had established a carpentry and building partnership in the late eighteenth century that exemplified the city's growing industrial sector. The windmill represented a form of vertical integration, giving them an advantage over competitors through a more reliable supply of high-quality lumber. In the 1790s, the operation was led by as many as three master tradesmen partners. It owned eleven slaves who were used in operations and employed seventeen free carpenters and a white accounting clerk.[10]

Charleston's industrialists used slave labor to reshape the land and the marshes for profit. Over time, one of their highest priorities was the enhancement of transportation by land and water. They invested in ferries, bridges, and wharves. The tidal marshes that formed the entire west side of the peninsula had discouraged deepwater shipping navigation for generations and kept traffic across the Ashley River to the slow pace of light boats. In the 1810s, a private company built a bridge, but a storm destroyed it. The company replaced it with a costly and fast ferry. Fully operating by 1818, the ferry was an eight-horse team boat with enough power to traverse the Ashley River's currents and distance with speed and confidence.[11]

Traveling south along the river from the ferry, the first set of mills one encountered were owned and operated by the Lucas family (see map 1.1). Their mills lay just outside the city limits in 1822, but the suburb was intimately intertwined with the city's economic, social, and political life. Bram and Richard Lucas were brothers who were enslaved to the Lucas family and worked in their industrial rice-milling facilities. Their work made them closely familiar with the neighborhood, the Lucas rice-milling facility, and its several millponds. Their enslaver, Jonathan Lucas, had created some of the earliest mills in the state and established for himself a leading reputation as an engineer and mill designer. By 1800 he had his own rice mill complex just north of Boundary Street, which grew into one of the largest such operations in the South. He became a prominent individual in Charleston, with significant roles in the militia. In the first decade of the nineteenth century, Jonathan Lucas began expanding his mills. He enclosed the marshy lowlands on the western edge of the Charleston peninsula using earthen and fill dams to create tidal ponds. As the tide came in, water flowed into the pond through floodgates. At high tide the floodgates were closed. As the tide flowed out, water could only escape the pond by flowing through the water courses that powered Lucas's Mill.

By about 1811, Lucas had expanded these ponds upstream from Boundary Street as far as the Charleston Bridge Ferry. Technically beyond the city limits, Lucas's Mill frequently sent smaller boats filled with barrels of processed rice downriver into the city and around the peninsula to the east-side wharf complex where the deepwater ships docked. His mill was described as "one day" or "six hours" away from Charleston's wharves by boat. He sometimes sent multiple boats of milled rice a day for months at a time, delivering scores of barrels a week. On the docks, draymen would move rice across shorter distances between ships and warehouses. One of these might have been William Garner, an enslaved drayman who, in the late 1810s, was hiring out time to save money and buy his and his family's freedom in an agreement with his owner. He was a skilled drayman. He was also persuasive and enjoyed a rapport with other draymen in the city, making him a good candidate for recruiting teams of drays if Lucas needed them. Lucas's rice-milling enterprise brought draymen such as Garner into regular contact with other workers. The rice process often required cooperation between different classes of enslaved and free workers: millers to process the product on-site, carpenters and blacksmiths to maintain the mill, coopers to make and maintain the barrels, and stevedores, boatmen, sailors, and laborers to move and load the cargo on the docks. Such laboring networks were also possible organizing networks.[12]

For a generation, the Bennett family had been building, expanding, and rebuilding their own mill complex just south of Lucas's. In fact, the Lucas family was often part of the Bennett family's expansions. Bennett's was probably the most prominent industrial milling operation in the city. Anyone crossing his millpond on the public Cannonsboro Bridge beside it got a view of the facility to the west with the Ashley River in the background. In 1822 his primary business was lumber, which eliminated competition with Lucas's rice milling. Between 1811 and 1818, Thomas Bennett's enslaved laborers expanded his tidal mills for him. He also had a wind-powered "Old Saw Mill" nearby (not to be confused with Wyatt's Mill). These facilities were operated and maintained by Bennett's mill slaves, such as Rolla, Peter, Ned, Batteau, and Mathias, alongside whatever free people also worked there. During the 1810s, slaves also rebuilt mill dams to create a vast expansion of the former millponds. When completed, the Bennett's Mill Pond extended into the Ashley River marshes south of Lucas's expanded pond (see map 1.1).[13]

To the south of Bennett's, across Beaufain Street, a third tidal pond powered Duncan's Mill. Its millhouse was at the far western head of Tradd Street, with a dock on the river. Duncan's Mill competed with Bennett's in processing lumber, and it struggled in these years. It seems to have been starved for capital and business after the expansion of Bennett's Mills and perhaps especially because of the financial panic of 1819. In early 1819, Mr. Duncan's mill business seems to have shut down completely. It was up for sale in June, together with a stock of unsold lumber and blacksmith tools. The city intervened to keep the millpond water from remaining stagnant and becoming a public health hazard. However, the facility gradually recovered, seemingly under new ownership. By the beginning of 1821 a large fresh-lumber inventory was being sold on behalf of the mill at Edmonston's Wharf, though the lumber itself was viewable "at Duncan's Mill." A year later a significant inventory of lumber on rafts had drifted away from "Duncan's Mill Pond," and a reward was offered to anyone who would return it to "Steele's Lumber Yard," a facility on the north rim of the pond, near the head of Beaufain Street. Even though Steele appeared to control the facility, the former name was still used repeatedly.[14]

All of these water-powered facilities had new competition emerging across town. On the east side of the city there were a few steam mills along East Bay Street. Because they were adjacent to the Cooper River wharf complex, they had better access to deepwater shipping than the tidal mills on the west side, which saved money and enhanced the chances of profitability. In the years immediately preceding the 1822 uprising movement, several of these enterprises advertised in the local papers. They were clustered south of Boundary Street near Gadsden's Green. John Egleston and a partner ran a sawmill in 1820 that they claimed was the only one in the South that could make fine mahogany veneers. Nearby, Chieffell's Steam Mill operated near Gadsden's Wharf. Coats' and West's Steam Mill was probably located along East Bay near Boundary beside Gadsden's Green too. In 1821, Egleston expanded his milling enterprises by adding a steam-driven cornmill operation to his mahogany veneer business. All of these steam mills would have been quite audible on the street, and enslaved workers, such as the enslaved African named Gullah Jack, who worked nearby and would become a leader of the uprising movement, would have passed them regularly. He was a craft woodworker, witnessing early mechanization.[15]

Draymen such as Ceasar Smith likely visited these mills on the east and west sides as part of their labor. Ceasar was an African who was tall and had a dark complexion. He stayed close to friends and acquaintances among other indigenous Africans when he could, and kept a dray horse at a stable worked by another African named Perault Strohecker. As a drayman, Ceasar's daily rounds carting goods around the city probably often started at Perault's stables near Second Presbyterian Church and proceeded directly to the wharf complex south of Hassel Street on the Cooper River. He might often have had errands in the East Bay Street industrial area's mills too. For the steam factories, being near the wharves was an advantage over the tidal mills and windmills on the west side, as they were closer to abundant labor. A large proportion of the wharf, craft, and industrial workers of the city lived in the southeastern portion of town. The area south of Boundary Street on both sides of East Bay was sometimes known as Gadsdensboro. The part of Gadsdensboro on the inland side of East Bay Street had seen significant draining, clearing, and housing construction by enslaved workers. The part of the land closer to the river was still called a "green" probably because of flood-prone grounds and the minimal construction of the planned and approved street layout. Only Concord Street appears to have been opened by 1822. Nonetheless, the proximity to newly built and actively planned worker housing was probably explains the density of steam mills in this section of East Bay Street.

Impoverished enslaved and free Black workers lived here in housing that was sometimes cited as a "nuisance" by the city but generally tolerated, because it was profitable for the lot owners.[16]

For the enslaved who were building this city, their labor taught them the lay of the land and about the marshy borders of the city's neighborhoods. They were more intimately familiar with the water and the ground than much of the white population was. They learned about the Carolina waterways in different tides and seasons. They learned how to use the estuaries and coasts for the fish and game living there. Ads seeking to recapture escaped slaves frequently mentioned fugitives' use of the water for food and transportation or of the swamps for hiding or even creating small camps. Denmark Vesey probably became quite familiar with the tidal marshes, creeks, and rivers as part of his daily affairs. His former master, Joseph Vesey, had a farm on high ground beside a marsh on the Ashley River above the Lines on Charleston Neck. Though there were roads nearby, the quickest and most direct route was probably in a skiff or canoe. Local water travel like this was common. Indeed, enslaved men such as Gullah Jack and Peter Poyas sometimes used boats to get around.[17]

These men might have sometimes joined others on the mudbanks collecting oysters at low tide. In this labor, they observed waterways, mills, and whites' comings and goings. In 1818, a wealthy visitor to Charleston observed groups of Black people oystering as he crossed into the city on the Ashley River ferry at low tide. The ebb tide had exposed "many oyster banks." With the crabs having scurried deep into their burrows, the oysters "stood straight up" out of the mud and close together like the bristles of an upturned hairbrush. The visitor watched the gatherers "taking them out of the mud" and putting them into baskets. The community also became familiar with the pathways through the changing marshes and currents at high tide and low. They learned when they could get food or when one could depart or enter the city undetected by whites.[18] The water created a shifting mass of routes and possibilities for Black as well as white people. Knowledge of it was power.

Indigenous Africans in Charleston

The last years of the legal transatlantic slave trade, which federal law terminated on January 1, 1808, saw a rush of human trafficking into Charleston. In that mass of final victims, Monday Gell (a harness maker), Gullah Jack (a healer and ship carpenter), Perault Strohecker (a drayman), and many other women, men, and children were trafficked into the city. They joined Denmark

Vesey (a carpenter), who had been trafficked decades earlier. Monday Gell was an Igbo, Gullah Jack was probably from part of what is now Tanzania, Denmark Vesey appears most likely to have been from the Gold Coast, and Perault Strohecker was from Senegal. They were indigenous Africans, and their indigeneity mattered in Charleston's daily life.[19]

Gullah Jack's odyssey into enslavement began sometime in 1805 or perhaps even earlier. He was an adult when Zephania Kingsley gained possession of him at Zanzibar, in modern Tanzania. However, Jack was not from Zanzibar. Kingsley said Jack's native country had been called "M'Choolay Moreema." Euro-Americans such as Kingsley frequently butchered the sounds and spelling of native African languages. It may also be that Kingsley only partially remembered the name of the place seventeen years later. Regardless, scholars have never precisely established the location of M'Choolay Moreema. Zanzibar lay at the end of a set of long slave trading routes extending hundreds of miles west into Tanzania and south into Mozambique. These paths suggest many likely places potentially hundreds of miles inland. Kingsley claimed that Jack spoke the "Angola" language spoken across the center of the African continent. But "Angola" was not a language. It was not a country at the time, either. It was a term for a broad group of related languages widely spoken in most of Central Africa. Modern Africanists roughly identify this "Angola" language group with the word "Bantu." Bantu speakers in the East who lived within a few hundred miles' proximity of Zanzibar increasingly experienced slave raids in the 1790s to 1800s. Jack was most likely one of these people. He may well have been trafficked along the Bagamoyo slave and ivory trading route that traversed eastern Tanzania and ended on the Mrima Coast across from Zanzibar, where we know Kingsley acquired him. Most people so captured were destined for Oman or French plantations on Mauritius, but a few went elsewhere. Statistics show that almost all the East Africans who arrived in the United States came in these last years before 1808. Jack was most likely one of these people and not a man from the Kongo or other places 1,000 miles away in West Central Africa, as has been argued in the past.[20]

Gullah Jack's traffickers might have brought him along the routes that terminated at Bagamoyo or Dar es Salaam, across the channel from Zanzibar. One possible location of "M'Choolay Moreema" is on one of these routes about a hundred miles south. One town of the Bantu-speaking Ndengereko people is Mchukwi, a small rural community on the slaving route and road to Bagamoyo. "M'Choolay" is certainly a possible mangling of the word "Mchukwi." Moreover, this region of the coast west of Zanzibar and extending south to the Rufiji River near Mchukwi was often referred to as the Mrima Coast. To an inexperienced Anglo-American ear in the early 1800s, the words "Mchukwi" and "Mrima" spoken together may have sounded quite like "M'Choolay" and "Moreema"—however incorrect such a crude spelling would have been. Kingsley did not know any Bantu languages, and when he described Jack's origins in 1822 he was recalling the names after seventeen years. His memory might have faded, but pronunciation would have been terrible. The scribe's comprehension may have further confounded the words.[21]

Regardless of which specific eastern Tanzanian town or region Jack came from, he already was an adult with indigenous carpentry and healing skills when he was taken up. He was wearing his medicine bag around his neck. He had his distinctive long whiskers when he was loaded onto the slaving vessel at Zanzibar. Ngoni men have been documented as sometimes using facial hair for marks of distinction. Items Jack used for healing in Charleston, such as ground nuts, parched corn, and crab claws, were all familiar food products in eastern Tanzania. Crab species similar to those found in Charleston are common in Tanzania's rivers and on the coast and were sometimes part of ritual traditions.[22]

Jack's medicine bag and whiskers help us understand his power. They were so important to him that his African captors and two successive white masters had decided against trying to take them away. Jack used them and his skills to build a reputation for specialized knowledge in Charleston. Whites who commented at all apparently regarded his knowledge of conjure as harmless superstition, but many of the Black people who mattered most to Jack paid closer attention. It is in this context that the African gained an American name. His name might be a reference to connections with the Gullah community in Charleston and all along the coast from Florida to North Carolina. He learned to speak the Gullah language. Some of the Christians and members of the Brown Fellowship Society in the Black community were probably trepidatious about him. However, both respect and fear would make him a person of significance. Gullah Jack presumably felt confident as a result. That he succeeded in keeping the medicine bag when he arrived probably enhanced his faith, suggesting a pathway to protect himself in this enslaving world.[23]

Jack's woodworking and medicinal skills were appropriate to life on the Mrima Coast and along the Rufiji River. There, a mangrove wood industry was centuries old, concentrated in the Matumbi Hills around Mchukwi. Crabs abounded in local waters, which local people incorporated as symbolic animals in songs and rituals.[24] Jack's healing skills might mean he'd been a *mganga*, adept in *ngoma* medicine and ceremony. *Ngoma* assisted with psychological disturbances, such as fears and anxieties, by getting patients to express them. In eastern and southeastern Africa, drums and vocals were also common elements in medicinal performances directed to assuage psychological difficulties. Ceremonies could go on for hours or all night. A major purpose was emotional: People would perform, speak, or express their anxieties and fears. *Ngoma* healed fears.[25]

Jack's knowledge and practice cemented his reputation in the Black Charleston community as a healer for ailments of the body and spirit. Through the knowledge that his medicine bag and practices offered, Jack found social belonging among the Charleston-area enslaved. His experience was not unique in the Americas. In Jamaica, some enslaved people carried an obeah, a material object such as a "bundle" that might encompass materials such as blood, feathers, beaks, aquatic or land-dwelling animal teeth, broken bottles, grave dirt, alcohol, or eggshells—in other words, items of animal origin or human manufacture. Obeah men were socially significant healers and consultants within the slave community. Jack attained such status in greater Charleston among the Gullah and the non-Gullah enslaved in the city.[26]

The Black community in Charleston gave Jack two names. One name survives in the records as "Gullah Jack." It was his most common name. Historians generally consider it a reference to the enslaved Gullah community in the Lowcountry. It suggests how closely associated with the rural Gullah people Jack became. Though he was a carpenter forced to live in Charleston, he became so closely associated with rural plantation workers that other enslaved craft workers took to naming him after the Gullah. It is possible that the "Gullah" in Jack's name also incorporates a reference to the crab claws Jack gave out as part of his healing practice. In some East Central African Bantu languages, a crab claw is a *nkala*. The African enslaved man Yorick Cross said that he and Jack called his crab claws "cullah"—easily recognizable as a possible imprecise representation of the sound of the word *nkala* when written down by Anglo-Americans ignorant of the original language.[27]

Town slaves also called Jack "Cooter Jack." Two common species of turtle in South Carolina now bear the name "cooter," but "Cooter Jack" seems to have had two quite different African roots. In Tanzania, like in South Carolina, there are several species of both freshwater and sea turtles that are sometimes used ceremonially. And the word "cooter" seems possibly related to the word *kuta*, a word for turtle among many Bantu speakers. Jack likely got this community alias in Carolina because he worked with turtles in his healing practice—as he might have in Tanzania. Similarly, brackish-water and saltwater crabs abounded in both South Carolina's marshes and coastal Tanzania's estuaries. Jack's names betoken his experience that mixed Black

Charleston's blend of African knowledge and practice with the new geography the Africans and other enslaved people were remaking with their own hands. Whether Cooter Jack or Gullah Jack, he was a person with skills among both the Gullah people and city-based Africans. His names signaled that he belonged, that he had power in the local waters.[28]

Monday Gell seems to have had none of Gullah Jack's spiritual or medicinal training, but he was a talented politician and organizer. He came from the Igbo homeland in modern Nigeria, in West Central Africa. Igbos were a central cultural force in many parts of the Atlantic world's slaving societies, including in Virginia. They were also numerous in Charleston in the early nineteenth century and were influential enough that they would form their own contingent in the uprising movement. Monday Gell—and all Igbo people in Charleston—would have known diviners like Gullah Jack back home. Practices such as Jack's were among the most common religious practices from West Africa to East Central Africa. The Igbo called such diviners *dibia*, a role within the Obia religion. "Obia" became "Obeah" in parts of the Americas. Obeah divination communicated information from ancestors or gods and spirits and promised protection from danger and harm in this life. One practitioner in Charleston seems to have had divination powers of second sight, an old blind man who was able to sense and address the psychological condition of people he met. To the extent that Monday recognized Gullah Jack as a healer and ceremonial leader, he probably would have noticed familiar skills in Jack's practice. Certainly, it was easy for Monday to understand Jack as comparable to an Igbo *dibia*. Recognition of knowledge and practices in each other that were indigenous to Africa may have helped facilitate respect between Monday and Jack. It helped that they also lived next door to each other.[29]

That indigenous African divination techniques may have been important to Monday and in Charleston in general is suggested by the fact that even Islamic or Christian conversion failed to dislodge divination from local cultures. It has remained a vital part of African and diaspora religious systems into the twenty-first century. We can therefore reasonably conclude that the evidence of it in Carolina means the practices had real meaning and influence in the lives of some of the people. Divination in Carolina, as in most cultures of Africa, made information from ancestors or gods available that could not be attained by empirical means. Spiders or crabs might reveal information based on how they moved across specially marked and placed cards. Specially cut cowrie shells might communicate information from spirits based on how they fell when thrown for the purpose. Fox tracks might be the mechanism of spirit communication to the living. Some of these techniques might be combined. Part of the reason these practices persisted even where Islam and Christianity had made significant inroads was that the newer religions often did not address people's fears, anxieties, and desires as well as the older knowledge did. The new religions mainly promised peace *after this life*, especially the kind of Christianity Charleston-area slavers taught, in which slaves were encouraged to imagine that their obedience in this life would be rewarded with salvation in the hereafter. In contrast, indigenous African divination provided techniques to assuage the daily fears of the living. Divination promised therapy in this life.[30]

Monday Gell's Igbo political practices of decentralized leadership and community contributed most meaningfully to how he lived in Charleston. Many, if not nearly all, of the enslaved Igbo in Carolina, including Monday himself, would have come from stateless Igbo communities. These communities were often weaker militarily because they were smaller than the states in the region. As Europeans built enslavement into a vast Atlantic trafficking empire, these communities became subject to ever more raiding. Nonetheless, Igbo communities such as the one Monday likely came from governed themselves through hundreds of autonomous villages in close communication and coordination. In local Igbo politics, elder men usually were the leaders. However, though Igbos would have deferred to elders, they would not be dictated to. Coercion was not respected. Additionally, men who distinguished themselves economically or socially through personal talents and skills—such as Monday—were also leaders, even when they were younger. In South Carolina, Monday got married, learned to read and write, and attained a measure of distinction as a hired-out craftsperson living on his own as the proprietor of a craft shop. The Charleston Igbos respected him in ways no outsider could expect to fully even understand. Gullah Jack and Denmark Vesey both had also distinguished themselves in Charleston, but they could not supplant a person like Monday with fellow Igbos. They simply would not have been as skilled in negotiating Igbo politics. Monday often invited people to his shop to share news (and they came). He socialized with Africans (at least one called him "Pa" and his wife "Ma"). He communicated with prudence and care—urging people to mutual regard and tact. He would value an ensemble of leaders who led by persuasion and mutual respect. He would not likely respect a strict social hierarchy and would not be voluntarily subservient. His indigenous political knowledge would lead him to expect reciprocal loyalty, with only the most sensitive things subject to secrecy oaths in which gods were called upon to punish tale-tellers.[31]

In strong contrast to Monday, Perault Strohecker was accustomed to giving and receiving commands. Perault was born in West Africa "about a week's travel" from the slave trafficking island fort of Goree. His father was reportedly named "Mamadu," but that spelling is probably an inaccurate transliteration. Perault's family was wealthy. Among other property, he owned sixty workers (presumably people enslaved in the West African manner). His family's core business was buying tobacco and salt with gold they brought from inland. He had made the trip to Dakar and Goree at least a half dozen times for the family business. He also had combat experience as a subaltern commander. When he was captured in battle and sold as a slave, his family tried to ransom him but were too late to stop the slave ship, which departed and ultimately ended up in Charleston. Perault was first put into service as a slave of James Delaire, the ship's owner. In 1814, Perault was sold to the Strohecker family. All indications were that Perault had always been of a "very tenacious" and bluntly spoken character—especially when he thought himself in the right. Whites regarded him as someone who would rather die than lie. They contrasted Perault's indigeneity with Gullah Jack's quite starkly, viewing Jack as "barbarous" and Perault as honest, almost noble, like a gentleman. His family's wealth and slave owning seems certainly to have been a reason for the difference in whites' perceptions of him.[32]

Though historians have debated Denmark Vesey's origins, advances in the available evidence strongly suggest that he was from the Gold Coast in West Africa. Capt. Joseph Vesey declared in April 1782 that a cargo of enslaved people he had purchased on St. Thomas, which included Denmark, was from the Gold Coast. Joseph Vesey did not hedge the description. This declaration would later be independently and directly confirmed as applying to Denmark. A white Charlestonian minister who was twelve years old in 1822 remembered that Denmark was from "Africa." More precisely, Thomas Brown, a fellow free Black carpenter who was an adult when he knew Denmark in Charleston, also independently corroborated Denmark's Gold Coast origins when he remembered Denmark as a "Coromantee" who "was brought from the coast." "Coromantee" refers to a region of the Gold Coast. It derived from the name of the Gold Coast town of Kormantse, which had slave trafficking forts nearby. Though it was customary in the Americas to refer to Coromantee as if it were an ethnicity, it was not an ethnicity. Coromantee was most likely just Denmark's final departure point from the continent. His birth and childhood had probably passed in one of the inland village societies, perhaps as far away from the coast as the great northern swath of terrain called the Saheel that stretched all the way across the top of West Africa along the southern boundary of the desert. People from these inland village communities often found themselves battling raiders and resisting being captured and trafficked to the coast by Fante or Asante.[33]

Denmark Vesey was about fourteen years old when he found himself on a ship—quite possibly the *Fredensborg*—being carried to the Danish West Indies (see fig. 1.2). Never having quite come to full adulthood in his birth community, his education with his home community was perhaps incomplete. Nonetheless, he might have had memories and skills related to fishing, hunting, and fighting that he carried with him all his life. The use of guns might well have been a part of his early life. Like all other regions of Africa south of the Sahara, the Gold Coast was home to socially complex societies that had long possessed advanced metallurgy, textiles, and other technologies. Long before Denmark's birth, people in the region had become adept in the use of firearms. On the Gold Coast, one Englishman observed that the Fante and "most of the other nations in this part of Africa" expected all adult men to keep a musket ready for battle at a moment's notice. The *Fredensborg* arrived in the Caribbean on November 19, 1781. Denmark was barely a teen when he was purchased by Joseph Vesey at St. Thomas in late 1781 or early 1782. He lived in Saint-Domingue (later Haiti) for a short while. But Joseph Vesey ultimately brought him to Charleston, where Denmark later bought his freedom after winning a lottery in 1799.[34]

Even though he was free and about fifty-five years old in 1822, there were aspects of Denmark Vesey's life situation that would have facilitated relationships of trust with some of the enslaved. Slavers brought a lot of enslaved Gold Coast people into South Carolina. Well over one-third (38.2 percent) of all enslaved people arriving in 1776–1800 were from the Gold Coast. Vesey should have had community among others of his home ethnicity, but he was enslaved to a ship captain (Joseph Vesey) and disappeared on voyages periodically. If he was from Africa, this would help explain why he was part of the early group of organizers of the uprising, several of whom were also African. Scholars have sometimes wondered that his age and accomplishment as a free man didn't make it odd for him to be among the planners. Whites would represent Vesey as a bully, domineering, and not really a trusted part of the Black community. But looking at Vesey from the perspective of indigenous Africans, we can see that because he was an aged African-born man of free status in a slaving society, with a trade, and having acquired some modest property, others would have had reason to hold him in high regard as a distinguished elder capable of leading the community.[35]

FIGURE 1.2 The *Fredensborg*, built in 1778. Photo by Pernille Klemp. Courtesy of the Maritime Museum of Denmark, Helsingør.

Denmark Vesey had important interests and problems in common with the enslaved in 1822. His family members were still enslaved. They were owned by different white people around the city. Moreover, he was forced to live with racist regulations, taxes, and social values. Vesey's was a life in which the best years of youth had been spent as an enslaved person, followed by a middle age in which white racism meant enslaved family members could never be freed. This loss of the fruits of his labor and family reduced his chances of ever being able to support himself in his fast-approaching old age. Without access to the labor and aid of his children, Vesey's prospects were fairly bleak. When any Africans thought about him, they would have to realize that his hamstrung freedom was their best-case scenario if they remained slaves. In fact, his model of attaining freedom might well have been an ambition for some of his friends and acquaintances: They all perhaps knew that Denmark had purchased his freedom.[36]

All Black lives in Charleston were lives of exploitative labor that did not end until a person's productive and reproductive capacities wore out. This economy was the defining constant of racialized capitalism in Charleston, whether the workers were free or enslaved, men or women. As many as 80 percent of free Black women may have worked outside of their domestic lives, and all enslaved women worked for their slavers as well as their own families. Enslaved women worked in public markets and hired out their services. Skilled, resourceful, and determined to thrive, not merely survive, these women lived no version of white middle- or upper-class domestic privilege. Susan Vesey was free, but she cooked and did laundry for money. Sarah Paul was enslaved and cooked for her mother's former husband Denmark Vesey, as well as completed whatever other duties she was assigned by her slaver. They were workers outside the home as well as in it. Amaritta was an enslaved worker of the La Roche family, who had a plantation twelve miles south of the city. Amaritta went there often to labor and to visit family, but she appears to have lived mainly in Charleston, apparently at her slaver's urban property. She was a cook in the La Roche yard, and she perhaps hired out as well. Like many other enslaved women, she was probably active in the Charleston City Market, certainly as a customer and possibly as a seller. The social reproduction of daily life in the city—how people ate and domiciled—was profoundly more reliant on the Black population than the three-to-one ratio of Black to white people in greater Charleston implied. Nearly all enslaved and free Black men and women worked outside their homes, while a large proportion of white women did not work outside the home. The economy of Charleston was therefore even more reliant on the labor of its Black residents than their overall population supermajority suggested. The city was utterly reliant on Black labor.[37]

The lives of enslaved women in 1822—even harder to document than those of enslaved men—demonstrate the interwoven networks of social life and labor in Black Charleston. Women were at the center of information networks. One of the few ways to see these networks is to notice women's marriages and social labor. Beck Barker was the first woman to marry Denmark Vesey. Her slaver was a white man named Barker. Because Denmark had been able to buy freedom for himself, Beck must have wanted him to pay for her freedom or at least buy her from Barker as soon as he could get enough money. But if he did try, it seems that Barker either would not let Beck go or that Denmark could not negotiate a price that he and Beck could pay. In the meantime, Beck gave birth to at least three children. She also had children from a previous marriage, and she was sold repeatedly. As a result, she had a network of children and spouses in various households. She likely kept tabs on as many family members as possible as frequently as possible. Denmark at the time of his death was married to Susan Vesey, a free Black woman. Susan was a laundress, and she ironed with groups of women in her and Denmark's house on Bull Street as part of a laundry business. Beck and Susan, through their children scattered across other households and their public labor for money, had numerous opportunities in any given week to hear (or overhear) news of the community.[38]

These women did much of their laundry and cooking labor in the yards of the city and its suburbs. These spaces were sites for expression and maintenance of commitments and attachments, for mutual support and affection. Probably few things of major significance could develop without the women knowing something of it—even if they knew few or none of the details. Prudence Bussacre had no blood relationship or familial-marital relationship with the enslaved man Julius Forrest. Yet she had raised him as if he were her own child, and he was frequently in her yard. Sally Howard had an in-law relationship with the enslaved man Jesse Blackwood, and he was often in her yard seeking his brother, who lived in the same household as Sally. The yards reproduced community over and against the centrifugal forces of slavers' demands, which were at best indifferent to relationships among the free and the enslaved. Sarah Paul was Denmark's stepdaughter (one of the children of Beck Barker). She earned wages cooking for Denmark. Because she was enslaved, this may have been the primary way to maintain the familial tie. She fed her stepfather in John Paul's yard and at Denmark's own home. She might also have worked elsewhere in the city for wages to give her owner. Many enslaved and free Black women probably experienced variations on such alienating and exploitative arrangements. It was a poor simulation of freedom, but the sociability made for a potent information network.[39]

The Fugitive Geography of Charleston

Because of the white domination of the city, yards were also stopping points on Black people's routes of surreptitious mobility. The enslaved and free Black community had to create a discreet, if not secret, map of the city for themselves if they wished to build and protect meaningful lives. The city's layout and the ways Black Charlestonians experienced it in 1822 is vitally important context for understanding their lives and their opportunities for resistance.[40]

Twenty-first-century Charleston, with its large blocks of densely built and imposing stone and brick architecture, is not the city that Black Charlestonians knew in 1822. It was not as heavily built in stone and brick as it is today. It was becoming increasingly ornamented, but in many places it had lightly populated urban blocks, open yards and unbuilt fields, and informal alleys and paths that probably allowed off-street, surreptitious mobility. Although in one section "every street" seemed to have chinaberry trees "in full flowery perfection" arranged like a lilac colonnade on both sides of stone-paved streets with brick sidewalks, most of the city streets were unpaved and probably undecorated.[41] Even a crowded area such as the City Market and its neighborhood still featured large yards, marshy and muddy ground, and unbuilt plots in some places. Fencing enclosed many blocks, but others were open.

The city's geography was a peculiar amalgam of genteel exhibition and theater of power. As Adam Hodgson remarked on a visit, after landing at Gibbs and Harper's Wharf and "entering the city" in one of its more densely built districts, he felt he had been "transported into a garden." He was amazed by trees "laden with ripe oranges" and peach trees "covered with blossoms." Everywhere out in the open he encountered "flowering shrubs of a description which I had been accustomed to see only in hot houses." And yet walking on one such "fashionable promenade" that was "enlivened by gay parties and glittering equipages," he turned a corner and discovered how the geography could hide people and events. He was shocked to walk right into "a sale of slaves." About 100 disconsolate people were being actively auctioned in the "public street." The city's physical layout contrasted affluent abundance with normalized exploitation, and just as the narrative of Hodgson's stroll could be interrupted by the drama of human trafficking, so too could the story of any given errand being run by Black Charlestonians. The geography offered such narrative of discovery or a reminder, and it also offered both surveillance and escape.[42]

At the start of the 1820s, tides still flooded much of the town daily. On the west side especially, the creeks, marshes, and millponds penetrated the peninsula almost as far as the College of Charleston.[43] The almost ubiquitous water challenged all development ambitions—not least white control of enslaved people, who could use the water to move about the city in secret. Every day, sections of existing streets were flooded by vast millponds that covered significant portions of the city's unrealized street plan. Flooding repeatedly damaged housing, businesses, and infrastructure. A storm destroyed an East Bay Street landfill and extension project. Charlestonians frequently pursued their own landfill projects, dumping any refuse or materials they had on hand in order to raise or level out their lots. In the early 1820s, the city ordered a specific schedule for draining Duncan's Mill Pond because stagnant water would become a threat to public health.[44]

Even in difficult economic times enslaved labor helped keep the infrastructure from deteriorating, and in general slave labor helped insulate the city's economy against the worst effects of deep recessions. From 1819 to 1822, while other parts of the United States experienced economic setbacks, Charleston saw notable expansion, and not just in milling operations. William Gadsden opened a new and far larger wharf and shipyard on the east end of Boundary Street. William Smith Jr. expanded his wharves, also adding shipbuilding capacity. For years Smith had just one wharf, near Broad Street along East Bay. Known generally as Smith's Wharf—and described by one enslaved person as a site from which the uprising was supposed to start—by 1820 it was becoming too small for Smith's business, so he took steps to expand his facility. He acquired marshland north of Boundary Street and Gadsden's Wharf, in Mazycboro to build a much larger wharf complex. As early as May 1820, his wharf in Mazycboro was operating, suggesting that the financial panic had not delayed his expansion for long, if at all. Records of the construction do not survive, but if he followed the conventions of rice planters, slaves did the dangerous and miserable trenching and dam construction required to drain the land and sink the pylons for the wharf and dock.[45]

The reconstructed map of Charleston in 1822 (see map 1.1) reveals a city with infrastructure that was strikingly more extensive than it had been on maps published in the 1780s. King Street and Meeting Street still ran north-south and roughly parallel to each other and became King Street Road and Meeting Street Road north of the city. However, in 1822 the two roads were becoming more densely populated north of Boundary Street to the Lines. By 1822, more of the planned cross-streets were open than had been in the 1780s. King Street had more stores and homes than Meeting. North of the Lines, both avenues became farm roads and may have been little more than compacted dirt roads. By contrast, south of Boundary Street, King and Meeting Streets were quite urban. There was more density and more use of stone and brick than there had been in the 1780s. Within the city limits, the same three thoroughfares crossed the entire peninsula from east to west in 1822 as they had in the 1780s: Boundary Street, Broad Street, and Tradd Street. On the west side, the ground was lower and still less densely occupied, because the lower flood-prone and marshy ground was more difficult to build on. On the east side, higher ground supported the city's greatest building density. Parts of the east side were honeycombed with warehouses and other buildings, especially in the city's wharf and dock complex, which stretched for at least a mile along the Cooper River. All this expansion had been accomplished using mostly Black labor, and Denmark Vesey had witnessed it—and had been part of the labor—over his entire adult life in the city since arriving in the early 1780s.

In 1822, Gibbs and Harper's Wharf was part of a neighborhood that was a practical and symbolic center for Black Charlestonians. The Circular Church drew a large following, even though it was white led. Nearby, the Cow Alley

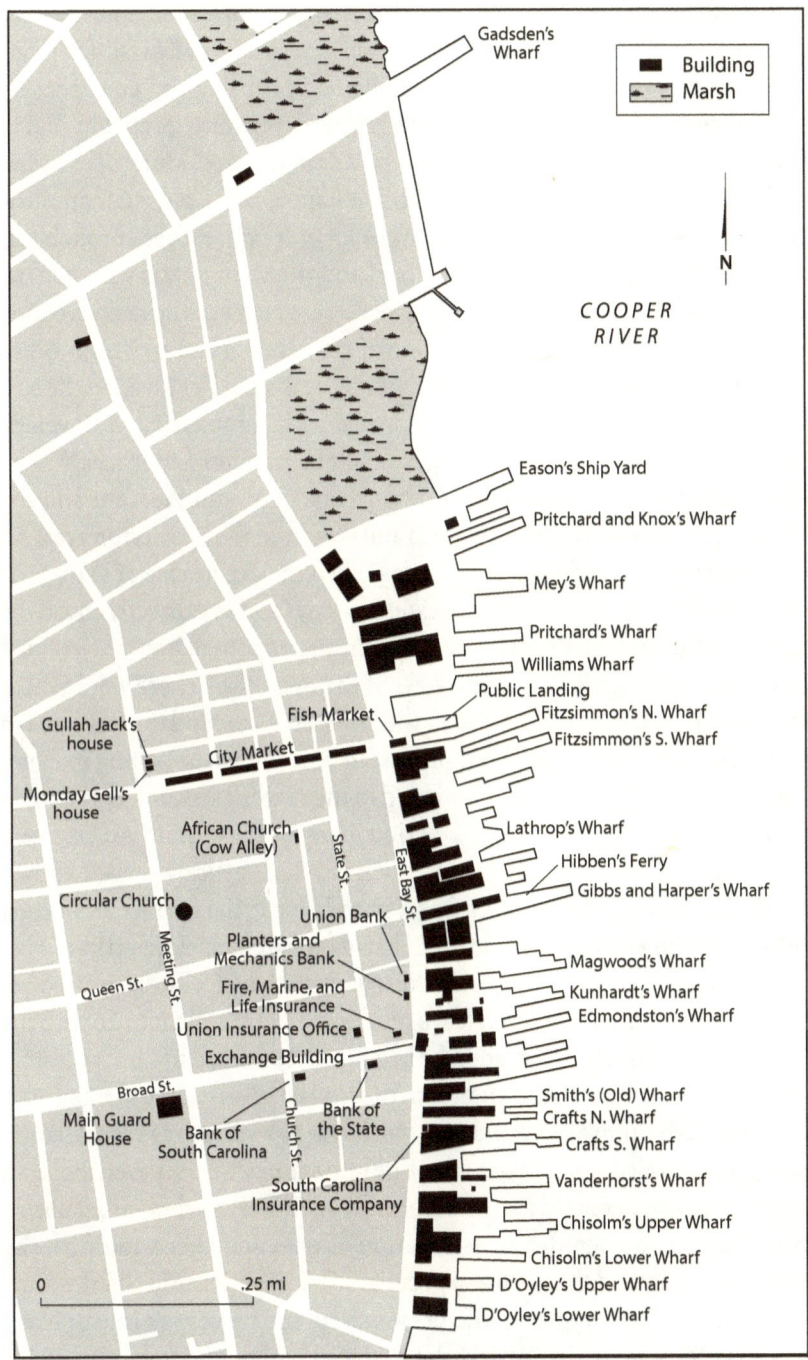

MAP 1.2 East side wharves and Finance and Insurance District. See mappingblackcharleston.org for updates.

praise house of the Black-led African Church was a hub for religious services (see map 1.2). The City Market was probably an almost daily visit for many people—certainly weekly. This neighborhood probably had an especially high concentration of enslaved laborers. There were also, probably, just as many informal residences for enslaved people in the area. Much of the slave auctioning occurred close by—on Vendue Range, at the old customhouse, and in a variety of other establishments. A lot of freight moved through this small district. Gibbs and Harper's Wharf and the vicinity was where many passenger ships departed. Like the Bridge Ferry, which was the main crossing on the Ashley River on the western side of town, Hibben's Ferry from Gibbs and Harper's Wharf was the primary crossing of the Cooper River on the east side of town. But the east side was crowded with commerce and travelers. There would have been many strangers and many countryside faces.[46]

Hibben's Ferry linked the city to the village of Mount Pleasant and the mainland road network heading north and east from the Charleston area. An English visitor to Charleston in 1820 described the experience of taking the ferry on a clear day: "We crossed an extensive bay" and saw directly ahead the buildings and landmarks of Charleston, "the metropolis of South Carolina." To the left, passengers had "a fine view of the open sea." There were visible "several ships riding at anchor," laden with freight. All around the ferry, ahead and to the sides, there was also a profusion of small boats "sailing in every direction." Though they go unmentioned in the visitor's account, Black pilots and watermen would have been steering many of these craft. An enslaved mulatto man named Patrick was one such person. Patrick was well known around Gibbs and Harper's Wharf, as he had been a pilot in the harbor for a few years. In his early thirties, he could navigate the channel expertly. But his experience of the waters was quite different from that of whites. He used his knowledge to break the law and leave his city master. He did it to be with his wife, who was still at the plantation he had formerly worked in Christ Church. White visitors also would not know that the Hibben's Ferry route merged with the route from Sullivan's Island, on which the last victims of transatlantic slaving had traveled from their quarantine into the city. But enslaved men and women who had taken this route as recently as fourteen years earlier surely sometimes remembered. The association of pain and alienation with the beauty of the city and the bay was a peculiar Black experience in Charleston.[47]

Not only in memory but in the present, too, the cityscape's role in Black lives was often agonistic. Patrick, the enslaved harbor pilot who fled to his wife in Christ Church, had probably been "hired out" by his slaver. As one writer bluntly described, "hiring out" in 1820 resulted from a slave owner having "more negroes than he can employ." Such labor was frequently either rented out on contract, or if no contracts were available, an owner might give a man, woman, or child papers and order them to go to town "to seek employment, bringing him a portion of what they earn." While it could lead to new freedoms, it was a command serving the white slavers' interest that also meant an enslaved worker's forced separation from friends or family in or near their usual household. The enslaved worker might have to pay only a prearranged sum to the master and "keep the remainder" of their wages. But if the worker did not find work, they might not be able to buy food and presumably would not have access to the supplies of their parsimonious slaver either, given the physical distance that hiring out could require. And the work conditions were sometimes very poor. Black children worked as chimney sweeps—among the most hazardous of jobs—because it offered them more pay than other work available to them.[48]

Both hired-out people and urban enslaved workers working for their owners often lived on their own. Noah Davis—an urban enslaved person in Virginia around 1820—slept in the shop where he worked. He did not live at his master's home. For Davis, sleeping apart from the master meant that he came and went as he pleased because he could not easily be surveilled. He and his colleagues drank in the shop and on the job, even though it was forbidden. But Davis's work was good and he earned the confidence of the shop owner. This good standing, together with the urban environment, created opportunities for him to learn to read and write. He began writing by copying his boss, who wrote his customers' names into the shoes they had ordered. Later, Davis learned to read through more formal methods. In his *Narrative*, Frederick Douglass discussed similar workplace imitating as his first stage in learning to read and write. Only later did he receive direct instruction. Such approaches were probably fairly common and partly how Monday Gell and others learned to read and write too.[49]

Like Davis, Monday Gell and Gullah Jack also lived beyond the supervision of their slavers. Their residences were in the center of the city. Monday's owner, John Gell, ran his livery stable and residence at 127 Church Street, but Monday lived and worked blocks away on Meeting Street. Gullah Jack's slaver, Paul Pritchard, lived near his wharf off East Bay Street at 6 Hasell Street, but Jack lived next door to Monday on Meeting Street. So neither of these men lived with his master.[50] The exact location of their sleeping quarters was likely in a section of Meeting Street very close to the City Market, close enough to be within easy reach. It was also in the heart of a bustling biracial marketplace, which made inconspicuous the outdoor gatherings of groups of slaves that

Monday and Jack hosted during the uprising. Records claim that Monday's shop and quarters were next to a cabinetmaker and a mahogany shop. This is most likely the block defined by Market, Meeting, and Elery Streets and Maiden Lane (see map 1.2). There was a cabinetmaker on the east side of Meeting Street on this block and a lumber merchant on the north side of Market Street who had large quantities of lumber for sale in early 1822. Being near the northeast corner of Meeting and Market Streets placed Monday's and Jack's residences in what was certainly one of the busiest corners in the city.[51]

The City Market in 1822 consisted of five rectangular buildings along the middle of "a long street ending upon the harbor." It attracted droves of people. Across East Bay Street from the market stall was a fish market on the wharf that featured a live fish pen sunken into the waters of the Cooper River. Here, too, crowds gathered. Regularly, the market had "the most beautiful tropical fruit," raised locally or imported from around the South and the Caribbean, such as oranges and pineapples. Among other products there were pistachios and a variety of other nuts, many sorts of potatoes, cabbages, white and red radishes, and a variety of fish. One visitor saw only one type of shellfish: oysters. The oysters, roasted in the open air at the market, were popular with Black Charlestonians, who consumed them "with great avidity" in the streets.[52]

In the City Market, and in other places in the city, turkey buzzards did much of the work of cleaning up rotting meat left over from butchering. They became a ubiquitous part of local lore: their sensitivity to the smell of rotting meat was said to be so good that if they perched near the house of a sick person, it was because they could smell death. They were officially protected from harm by the city. Useful and controllable, the city allowed them to watch over the market and keep it clean. Gullah Jack left the City Market area daily and probably avoided most of the buzzards' gaze whenever he cut across open lots northeast of his lodgings to reach his master's wharf efficiently. Monday, however, both lived and worked beside the City Market. His constant presence there would prove pivotal for the movement. Nearly every Black person in the city probably came through the market area of the wharf complex daily or at least weekly. Ever the astute indigenous Igbo politician, Monday claimed that he told people to come to him whenever they *wanted the news* about planning. It would have been easy to do so; in fact, it was among the safest places in the city to gather in public because white people expected to see gatherings of Black men near the market. It was unremarkable.[53]

Many other Black Charlestonians both lived and worked near the wharf complex. They lived with family or friends wherever an affordable living opportunity arose. At the northeast corner of Lynch's Lane and Zig Zag Alley near

East Bay Street there was an example of such housing. One landlord owned five lots. The neighborhood had been excluded from recent improvements made to East Bay Street, which appears to have left it relatively unprofitable. All five lots were rented by Black people and families, because the landlord considered that to be "as profitable as the situation and unimproved state would permit." To make the lots affordable for themselves, the Black residents subdivided the lots repeatedly. The city declared the "profitable" site a public health hazard. It was a "peculiar accommodation" on a collection of "irregular lots" with haphazard drainage and grading. Probably because of standing water, the site was ordered to be demolished entirely and rebuilt with proper drainage connected to the city sewer system. Similar poor people's housing developments existed in Bedon's Alley and Stoll's Alley, along Church Street, and in the vicinity of East Bay and Boundary Streets. Christopher Gadsden filled in land beside his new wharf south of Boundary Street along East Bay Street and sold smaller-than-normal lots for worker housing, probably mostly as rentals. Many of these workers were likely enslaved and free Black men, women, the elderly, and children.[54]

Not all of the Black population lived in the most cramped and dilapidated quarters. The free Black family of Daniel Payne lived on Swinton's Lane (see map 1.2). His family prospered. The lane was probably crowded with people and businesses, but it was close to the City Market and the Cow Alley and Anson Street branches of the African Church. Little Daniel learned the basics of reading before he was five. To provide a kind of picture book, his father carried him through the streets after dark, "with my feet straddling over his shoulders," to learn to properly identify "every object" by the light of the newly installed streetlamps.[55] Denmark Vesey also lived in a somewhat wealthier part of town, even farther west than the Paynes. Out on Bull Street toward the millponds, housing seems to have been more dominant than in the wharf district and the City Market. Vesey lived on Bull Street. As a carpenter, it gave him better access to Bennett's Mills, Steele's Saw Pit, and Duncan's Mill—all of which specialized in lumber processing. But meetings of large numbers of slaves who did not otherwise have business or a residence in the neighborhood were more likely to attract unwanted attention—especially if they were outside. Thus, uprising planners met inside at Vesey's. However, these appear to have been prearranged and planned gatherings held inside behind a gate that locked. Vesey himself would get better general information at Monday's shop—in the center of what has been called the "motley crew" of urban American seaports in the era of enslavement. Unlike his own home, Monday's place was safe for random street encounters and spur-of-the-moment inspiration and conversation, which might have drawn too much attention at Vesey's. As one man described it, there were *meetings* (plural) in the back lot of the mahogany shop behind Monday Gell's shop. These were very likely meetings in which indigenous African political practices—perhaps Igbo—determined the procedures that guided outcomes. Because Monday was Igbo and was slated to lead an Igbo group in the uprising movement, they probably sometimes spoke Igbo.[56]

Despite the unauthorized freedoms that living in one of the largest urban concentrations of free and enslaved Black people in the United States might seem to allow, whites still dominated and controlled the Black community. Work schedules, regulations on their movements, and penalties and punishments to discipline noncompliance were common. Resistance was common, limning the contours of the constant racial power struggle in Charleston. One traveler claimed in 1820 that when he toured the city jail, most of the Black inmates were hired-out slaves who had not paid their wages to their masters. The enslaved woman Maria Lucas was once sent to the Workhouse merely "to be kept from drinking." The Workhouse attendant was asked to be sure that she "take care of her child and keep it and herself clean." She was "not to be punished," though confinement itself must have felt like punishment.[57] Some of the enslaved were hired to hunt down others in the city. Smyth, an enslaved man, carried a paper granting him authority to move about the city to pursue a "fellow servant" and to "procure such aid as may be requisite" for his quarry's apprehension.[58] Gullah Jack's owner, Paul Pritchard, sometimes threatened to shave off Gullah Jack's long and distinctive whiskers to control him. Benjamin Hammett chastised an enslaved man for presuming to talk about religion with his enslaved man Bacchus. Peter Prioleau would take a break and stroll through the fish market and loiter at the waterside only when his master was out of town.[59]

White surveillance and domination dogged the lives, relationships, and mobility of Black Charlestonians. In Charleston, even prosperous free Black people "having horses and carriages," such as Jehu Jones, could not lawfully ride them for pleasure in the city. After curfew, free Black people could not "be seen outside of [their] house." At 10 p.m. "a thundering drum" from the city guardhouse at Meeting and Broad Streets announced the release of the night patrol to "clear the streets of all [Black] men, women, and children" regardless of freedom status. Even whites who did not own a particular person were allowed to police the Black population. If they caught an enslaved person in the street after curfew, they could seize them and take them to the Workhouse at their discretion. Newspaper ads sometimes reported people seizing property from enslaved people in the street on suspicion of theft.[60]

The Workhouse was central to this struggle to control the Black population. A visitor in 1819 was shown an enslaved Black man incarcerated for fleeing his slaver to be with his wife and children. He and his partner had been "married according to the church," but heedless of that sacred fact, his master sold him to a man who took him to Columbia, over 100 miles from his wife. Explaining his marriage to the new owner, he realized the man "would not give me up." So he left the new owner without leave and returned to Charleston, where he was captured and imprisoned. Among the women the traveler met in the Workhouse, he was shocked to find that there were some who were "beautiful." When one looked at him in a way he considered conceited and impertinent, he concluded blandly that "such manners" were the "feminine faults for which" she and the other Black women "feel the lash or suffer confinement." He also met an incarcerated group of Black crew members "of a privateer." The men were over six feet tall and tattooed on their faces with their country marks and spoke in strong accents, indicating they were African. They had been imprisoned on suspicion that they were not really part of the crew but were instead part of the cargo being "smuggled into the country for sale." The resolution of these cases is unknown, but enslaved people could sometimes just disappear through these buildings—all but permanently separated from loved ones. Even discussing the Workhouse must have awakened feelings of sorrow, terror, and resentment at the role the place played in breaking up lives.[61]

When the enslaved left their owners, they often were accompanied by friends and family or were headed to reunite with them, like the man in the Workhouse who fled Columbia to reunite with his wife in Charleston. The period from the early 1810s through the 1820s in South Carolina saw an increase and then a peak in mass maroon or fugitive activity by the enslaved. Scholars have argued that the efforts of the British military to foment slave flight and rebellion during the War of 1812 played a part, but the full set of contributing factors are unknown. It is possible that dislocations from family and friends helped fugitive groups form. The peak of such fugitive activity came in the early 1820s, both before and after the uprising movement in Charleston. There is some evidence, too, that enslaved people in the city of Charleston were aware of the scale of fugitive groups in the countryside. For example, the enslaved man Jack Cattell in 1822 noted that a rebellion based in the city might be of great benefit if it could *obtain the assistance* of the substantial numbers of fugitive slaves outside the city among the country people.[62]

People who left their owners often went to Charleston, and if Amaritta La Roche or anyone else in the Black community encountered them randomly, their communications would have been cautioned by fear of betrayal. Moses, for example, was a young man born in Virginia who walked away from his master and was presumed to be hiding in "some of the wood boats about Charleston."[63] Living among unoccupied boats along the wharves would have required assistance to avoid capture, get food, and keep warm on the cold water. Satisfying all these needs could easily bring Moses into contact with shipbuilders and repairers on the wharves, and perhaps he passed Perault Strohecker and Naphur Yates as they talked beside the scale house near Smith's Wharf. Prudence Bussacre might have supplied a man like Moses with food if asked. Any of these people could have felt sympathy for someone like Moses. Much like Moses, they all moved around the region surreptitiously sometimes or knew people who did so. Both an unauthorized trip across the city or region by someone such as Beck Barker or a more permanent departure by someone running away from an owner necessitated not getting caught. If caught, both might end up in the Workhouse. To evade the Workhouse, one needed the help of strangers—at least in their willingness to keep secrets from whites. An ethic of mutual assistance held the slavers' assertions of property rights in abeyance in general, but especially so whenever beloved friends and family were concerned.[64]

The ads that owners placed to recapture people they considered runaways all were designed to try to enlist the public in apprehending fugitives. On just one day in August 1822, ads in the *City Gazette and Commercial Daily Advertiser* sought help capturing several men and women. Owners offered rewards for anyone who would place the fugitives in jail, return them to their owners, detain them privately, or aid in the conviction of possible accomplices. Sometimes ads ran for so long that they might seem a little desperate.[65] The people pursued this way were of particular value to their pursuers. Sometimes they were tradespeople who left their masters despite their "privileges." In other cases, no great skills are mentioned, but the person is either of special interest to the owner or recapturing them is so difficult that the pursuers need help. Owners also offered cash rewards, such as five or ten dollars. Sometimes the reward could be as much as $100 (equal to several thousand dollars in 2023).[66]

Efforts to reestablish social bonds that had been disrupted by slavers gave direction to people's flight. Abram left his owner and traveled nearly 150 miles to Charleston using forged free papers and the alias William Wilson. He had numerous acquaintances in the city. On the run, he rarely smiled to avoid displaying his large front teeth, including a plainly visible missing tooth that his pursuer made certain to describe to all of the readers of the *City Gazette*. Even so, he was distinguishable. He was a carpenter, and his status was displayed by what he wore: a small black cap, a blue jacket with a velvet collar, and blue pants. He was also taller than most men. He stood out. Recognized by a white person at Chisolm's Wharf who did not realize he was a fugitive, Abram pretended to have been hired out by his master to work on a boat nearby. The deception worked long enough to prevent his arrest, and he fled the city. He sailed in a sloop to Georgetown, where he also had friends who could help him.[67]

Others also planned well, had help, or were lucky and—like Abram—were able to travel long distances and evade recapture for long periods of time. Massa left her master near Columbia in September 1819 and was still uncaptured a year and a half later. She made the approximately 120-mile trip to Charleston because she had been raised nearby on Daniel Island and had lived in the city.[68] Another person, Watson, left his enslaver in Georgetown to be with his wife in Charleston—a sixty-mile journey along a route that one of the uprising organizers would later travel. When the patrols were out on the roads, it was dangerous. He and the 1822 uprising movement might have made the journey by water through Christ Church Parish rather than risking the roads. Jacob, a carpenter, left his master on an even more challenging route. He left Charleston and had last been seen on the road near Columbia. He carried a forged paper pass—with a seal—authorizing him to travel to Delaware, apparently by stagecoach. Practiced at flight, he had sometimes left his owner pretending to be a free man named Jim Hadden. He was a tailor who could make or modify garments for disguise. When his owner advertised for him, "Jim Hadden" had been successfully away from him for about ten months. As Jim, he might finally have made his escape permanent.[69]

Fugitives needed people's help and could find it if they went to family, friends, and acquaintances. Fanny left her owner to return to an old neighborhood with her child Juliana, who was only about four years old. For a long time, she had been held as property by a family on King Street in Charleston. A return to that neighborhood would be a return to loved ones and acquaintances. Isaac was a good boat hand who escaped his master to fish around Sullivan's Island and live nearer his father on Charleston Neck in Radcliffboro.[70] Ruth was eighteen years old when she ran away to Charleston, possibly, as cover, pretending to still belong to a family in the city where she'd been enslaved for years. At eighteen years old, she must have made numerous acquaintances in Charleston. She almost certainly had family. Margery also left for Charleston, where she had a large group of acquaintances and friends to help hide her and her husband, Thomas. Forty years old, bright, and clever, she probably had the skills to remain out for some time.[71]

Some passed themselves off as free people or hired-out workers very successfully because of help from the community. Pompey Watson was an enslaved man who escaped his master by climbing out of a second-story window in the city. He was very well known around town as a sawyer, especially by cabinetmakers—so well known that his owner said he needed little description to be identifiable. His would-be captor feared that his extensive network of friends would help him and employ Pompey, so he warned against anyone employing him on threat of being prosecuted. Pompey is a person that Denmark Vesey could have recognized. The Black Charleston community included many thousands of people, but Pompey was a sawyer and Vesey was a carpenter. A business acquaintance was possible. One can imagine the literate Vesey reading the runaway ad for Pompey in the newspaper or hearing of it from a mutual acquaintance. The point is that running away was intelligible to and within the experience of even those Black Charlestonians who had perhaps never done it themselves.[72]

Dye fled her master to return to family relatively nearby, and she took her four daughters with her. Though she had been living on a plantation in the countryside, she was very well known in Charleston. Describing her, her owner reminded Charlestonians that they knew her well from market days. All of his theories about the location of Dye and her children presumed that reassembling family would be her only motive. He surmised that the group may be with Dye's husband, who lived on a different plantation outside the city. Or she might have found refuge with her father, who worked at a brickyard outside the city in Goose Creek. However, her eldest daughter Lydia was hired out to a Mrs. Jones at her Charleston shop—possibly a grocer listed at 83 King Street. The scattering of the family to at least four regional locations was a special hardship of the Black community regardless of freedom status. Enslaved people often shared this specific kind of suffering with free Black people such as Denmark Vesey. Despite his personal freedom, the mothers of Vesey's children and the children themselves seem to have belonged to at least two or three different masters. The enslaved man William Garner had at least one free relative (a brother) and was actively trying to buy his freedom and the freedom of his family.[73]

The case of Charlotte demonstrates the fugitive dynamics affecting mixed free and enslaved families. Charlotte missed people in Charleston. In July 1821, she left her enslavers to return to her people. In her late twenties, she was bright and had numerous social connections in a variety of places in coastal South Carolina. But she had lived in Charleston for some time and had been trained to be a good cook and pastry chef. Her former owner speculated that she was probably working in that industry somewhere in either Georgetown or Charleston—harbored by friends and relatives, several of whom were free people of color, including her father. Despite knowing where she had likely gone, her owner had failed to recapture her as of August 1822, over a year later.[74]

Such success in escaping and creating a free identity on one's own authority may well have given whites incentive to target the free Black community in their aggressive eagerness to capture people and gain the advertised rewards. Lucy, approximately twenty-five years old and an uncommonly skilled housekeeper, left her master in January 1819 and was still being pursued in 1823. The hunt went on so long and she was considered so valuable that a speculator was able to purchase her in absentia from her former owner and begin pursuing her himself. The speculator-hunter believed that she was in or around Charleston because, though born in Virginia, she had grown up in Charleston. He believed that she was hiding in plain sight either there or in Georgetown and passing as a free person. He speculated that she had possibly changed her name or perhaps had acquired free papers, because she was "very artful." The questions and suspicions that must have fallen on free people of color in Charleston and Georgetown from any white person trying to attain the reward for her capture must have been intimidating, insulting, and humiliating. Interrogations might have begun with assertions that a person's name, story, and even freedom papers were lies and forgeries. White reward-hunting within Black Charleston posed a danger to the free and the enslaved.[75]

To hide, many fugitives mingled with the large Black population in the Cooper River wharf district along East Bay Street below Hasell. The bustle of the market area and the wharf complex was reassuring. Large numbers of Black men and women came to the city weekly for Sunday Christian prayer services. The Circular Church was very close to the wharves and had a large Black following, including Amaritta's husband Rolla Bennett. The African Church had praise houses on Anson Street and in Cow Alley (also called Philadelphia Alley), close to the City Market and the wharf complex.[76] Located centrally, these meeting places grounded the African Church in the city's largest concentration of enslaved people and free Black people. Enslaved and free people came through the neighborhood often from the countryside on errands for masters generally—and secretly on their own account. The resulting near-constant infusion of relative strangers to the local people meant that the wharf area was a uniquely effective place for fugitive slaves to attempt a new life or return to an old one. Fugitives would not stand out.

The enslaved and the free created their own fugitive geography on the water and the land of the white city. White people were, at best, dimly aware of the full scope of Black knowledge, but Black Charlestonians produced networks that successfully supported forays across a wide territory, day and night, despite the risk of capture and punishment. They learned the weaknesses in their masters' surveillance abilities and readiness. They shared such information with each other, and they almost never revealed fugitives or unauthorized activities to whites. They sometimes coordinated with others as far as 100 miles away. The basis of knowledge for such extensive networks was established through ordinary daily activities. Slaves learned things about the slavers—from literacy to livery—and that learning provided them power when they chose to use it. For many, there was a lot of waiting to use what they knew. There was likely nothing unusual about waiting long periods of time to find an opportunity for flight. Enslaved people merely seeking passage on a boat or ship might wait years, eavesdropping or observing in order to find the right people and the right moment. But Charleston was always beckoning as a destination or a waypoint.[77]

Outwitting the slavers, as Harriet Jacobs declares in the second epigraph to this chapter, was the tactic. Networks of trust, acquaintance, and affinity were the first resources of logistical power. The fugitive geography of the Black community required networks of trust that would keep dangerous secrets and support vital deceptions, the only weapon they had to resist their tyrants. But deception was about more than resistance. It was also about surviving and even thriving, if possible. Perhaps not all Black resistance relied on such networks, but it seems likely that all organized social movements did. Michael Nicholls has argued that intimate human relationships shaped Gabriel Prosser's 1800 rebellion in Virginia. Those events focused on a neighborhood called the Brook, which was "framed by a watershed north of Richmond" that was the focal point of the "physical and human connections these men had with other parts of central Virginia." Slavery was the primary reason behind the desire to escape, but social networks and affinities provided the relative safety, logistical resources, and sense of power and possibility that attempting escape or revolution required.[78]

Trying to Solve a Problem without a Solution

Between 1817 and 1822, two entirely nonviolent social movements of enslaved and free Black Charlestonians emerged from these networks of friends, acquaintances, and family. The first was a mass church movement, and the second was a much smaller effort to emigrate to Liberia and Sierra Leone in West Africa. Both movements addressed the central problem of Black Charleston: the white slaving and racism that actively threatened their lives and relationships.

In 1817 the Black community launched the African Church, led by Rev. Morris Brown. It is significant that the church started as a dramatic walkout during a dispute with the white leadership of the Methodist church in Charleston over Black members' authority to manage their own donations. The walkout was large. Hundreds of Black members left the white Methodists' church. Their formation of the African Church was an assertion of their will for greater autonomy. It was bold in the suppressive racial environment of Charleston, but the movement grew, garnering significant support within the first year. According to Methodist Church records, 4,367 Black, Charleston-area Methodists left the white church in 1818 and joined Brown's congregation. With 75 percent of greater Charleston's Black Methodists, the movement formed three new congregations: one main church in Hampstead with a purpose-built building, a missionary house on Anson Street just south of Boundary Street near an older African burial ground, and a missionary house in Cow Alley near the Circular Church and the City Market. The walkout was momentous for the Black community, no doubt, and a discomfiting surprise to whites, who repeatedly harassed the congregation with violence, intimidation, and at least one petition to the state to shut the Hampstead church down.[79]

In the African congregation, the free Black family of Daniel Payne built and sustained affective ties and a spiritual community of belonging. Daniel, a future minister in the city, was just a small boy in the late 1810s. Born in the heart of Charleston about 1811, his parents were free people and from 1817 until 1822 they were devoted participants in the African Church's Cow Alley congregation. The Paynes had many relations and friends in the city because of their labor and their religious affiliations. His father had been born free in Virginia and was kidnapped as a child and enslaved in Charleston until he purchased his freedom in adulthood. He became a Methodist class leader who led two classes, and he and Daniel's mother emphasized education in their home. Daniel's mother was born in South Carolina and was of African and Catawba ancestry. She regularly took her "little Daniel" by the hand with her to Methodist class meetings, having him sit with her throughout. When he was eight years old, Daniel remembered years later, he walked to and from the Cumberland church with his mother, once weeping over the sermon on the way home. He prayed often. He prayed in the street, in gardens, and in the dark of the city at night under "a moon-lit sky." When both of his parents died before he was ten, the larger family and social networks that had created the church and that the church nurtured showed themselves. His grand-aunt, a Mrs. Sarah Bordeaux, took custody of him. The Minor's Moralist Society—a free Black charity in the city—assisted his education for a total of five years. He began working as an apprentice carpenter—Vesey's trade, though there is no direct evidence he ever knew Vesey. Later, he worked a stint as a carpenter with his brother-in-law that lasted "four and a half years." This was the conventional program of the church community that certain elements among the white politicians in Charleston attacked as radical from its inception in 1817.[80]

Denmark Vesey seems to have had an awakening because of the church movement. He had gone through the staid, bookish, and exacting process of attaining full Communion in the white-led and white-dominated Second Presbyterian Church. On April 12, 1817, he had been admitted to full Communion for the first time. This was a rare achievement. Most people in the congregation did not get as far, regardless of whether they were white or Black. Success marked Vesey as an intellectually curious, textually informed, and academically accomplished evangelical. Nonetheless, sometime after achieving full Communion at Second Presbyterian, he appears to have become drawn to the breakaway, Black-led African Church. He also began to associate with attendees of the Circular Church, which was white led but had a lot of Black members. Though no church membership rolls show that he formally withdrew from Second Presbyterian or that he formally joined the African Church, he definitely became associated with members of the African Church at some point between 1817 and 1822. At the African Church, he would have met families who were free, united, and prosperous. The Paynes were an example. The Payne family members were no longer separated by slavers' property interests as Vesey's own family was. Perhaps he retained formal membership at Second Presbyterian and attended the African Church often enough that regular congregants thought of him as a member. Black membership at the African Church seems to have been fairly fluid and informal because of its rapid growth and its missionary focus. If Vesey wanted to be among the most assertive and progressive Black Christians, he would want to know members of the African Church. The dramatic movement of hundreds and then thousands out of the white churches might have awakened him anew and drawn him into its pews or into some form of close association with its members as early as 1818.[81]

A second movement emerged and tried to resolve the problem, the contradiction of love and slavery in Charleston. A group of approximately forty free Black Charlestonians expressed an interest in emigrating to Sierra Leone, the British colony for freed slaves and African American emigrants in West Africa. Sierra Leone was well known. It was promoted as having a civil appearance, public buildings, and schools. A visitor to Mesurado, the site that would become Liberia and Monrovia (the US colonial answer to Britain's Sierra Leone colony), described it as "picturesque." These colonial projects were set "on the very borders of [the] benighted heathen" and inspired whites to want to rid themselves of freed Black people. Though there were free Black people who went voluntarily—occasionally returning with highly critical accounts of the colonies—other free Black commentators were critics from the beginning. However, if discomfort and disgust about gaining freedom through exile was present in Charleston, only implicit evidence exists. Most important, a significant motivation for emigration was the prospect of bringing a majority of close family and, if possible, friends along to get them out of the reach of slavers.[82]

In late 1821, James Creighton sailed for Sierra Leone and Liberia in West Africa with his own family. He had just a dozen other emigrant passengers on board, far fewer than the forty families who had once considered going. Colonization in Africa could not solve the core problem of how slavery separated people and ruptured cherished and life-sustaining relationships. Creighton himself owned several slaves that he hoped to free in West Africa, but only one of his enslaved people agreed to go. By law he would be unable to free those who stayed behind in South Carolina. Nonetheless, all but one of Creighton's slaves chose to remain enslaved rather than leave their Charleston relations and friends behind. Creighton had lived in Charleston a long time, and he surely understood how slavery tortured families. Nonetheless, his solution was a bad compromise. Leaving to escape slavery was a little like becoming a refugee to escape a war: even though you could maybe take everyone with you, inevitably some kin, friends, and remembered places and memorials get left behind at the mercy of enemies and exploiters. Charleston, as a known geographical place that offered resources for survival, would be lost utterly in the new country. Like refugees, they would become complete strangers in a new place.[83]

Staying, however, was not much of a solution either, given slavery's racism. Daniel Payne learned to read at the African Church in the 1810s and eventually became a minister and a schoolmaster in Charleston. He fled the city in 1835 out of fear of white hostility to his school. The trauma of the experience is palpable in the autobiographical account he wrote many years later. It speaks to both the loving relationships Payne had known in the 1810s and the traumatic fear engendered in the 1820s. After departing Charleston for good, he missed his people and home so much that he suffered "sad reflections about my native city" and especially "about the loved ones I had left behind me." He mourned leaving not only his "only sister," whom he never saw again, but the children in his school as well. Nightly, for "many years after leaving," he dreamed about Charleston. In his dreams he went "wandering over its streets, bathing in its rivers, [and] worshiping in its chapels." The potential for such affections to produce a radical antislavery stance can be overestimated but only with difficulty. Payne's feelings about "unjust" and "cruel" laws got their outrage from the violation he experienced of his love of home, his livelihood, and his people. His belief that God had made all people of "one blood" was gored by the horns of the impossible dilemma of how to thrive while racial chattel slavery existed.[84]

The antislavery and antiracist African American writer David Walker visited in Charleston in 1821 and gained further perspective on the same unresolvable problem. He had left his native Wilmington, North Carolina—like a fugitive, despite being free—in the hope that Charleston could become a new home. He does not seem to have had friends or relatives in Charleston, but the free Black community of the larger Charleston District was larger than Wilmington's entire population. And it was close to Wilmington. Schooners and other vessels regularly transited the roughly 130 nautical miles between the two cities. Walker was only in his early twenties, and a change of residence might have seemed strategic. Like a fugitive slave fleeing to Charleston, he might have hoped that the larger Black community would help him.[85]

Walker gave up on Charleston, however, and left abruptly after attending a proslavery sermon at a camp meeting in April 1821 at Goose Creek (across the Ashley River, outside the city). The steam-powered boat *Columbia* picked him up at Gadsden's Wharf and sailed all the way around the tip of the peninsula and up the Ashley River to Goose Creek. That the meeting was quite large is attested by the fact that two other boats joined *Columbia* in shuttling passengers to and from the camp all day, each day of the revival. Prayer and sermons continued for days. Walker did not camp at the site, but he wrote that the large gathering included masses of Black Carolinians. He was shocked to hear a white preacher tell the enslaved people present that they should be joyfully obedient to their masters or else accept whippings contritely. Walker was a devoted Methodist, and this sermon's slaving ideology offended him. Disgusted, he left the city. Neither the large numbers of Black people who attended the Circular Church nor the members of the Black-led African Church congregation were enough for him to stay. Awakened as he was becoming to the injustice of slavery and slavery's racism, he was also free enough, young enough, and iconoclastic enough to be able and ready to wander. His example throws into relief the fact that the majority of Black Charleston could not just leave as he did. They remained rooted in the city and stuck with slavery's dilemma: if you stayed, you could not protect your people from separation by sale, and if you became a refugee you probably had no choice but to live with separation, because you could not take everyone with you.[86]

Conclusion

Free and enslaved Black Charlestonians were part of an ethnically diverse community, the origins of which lay in thousands of unwilling arrivals. The colonialism of this enslavement created the Black position in the city's culture, and it echoed symbolically in both the nightly curfew warning drums from the city guard and unauthorized Black mobility. Black culture in Charleston was fugitive. Neither European settlers nor indigenous Americans, Black people built the material infrastructure and the economy of a city that did not regard them as people who belonged. They built lives in this colonizing society. Yet their closest relationships were always under threat. Whites policed the activities of both enslaved and free Black people.

Amaritta La Roche, traveling back and forth with her slaver's family between town and plantation and trying to preserve her relationships under the watch of the mistress and master, might wonder whether she would always live that way. Peter Poyas, an enslaved ship carpenter working on the wharf on South Bay Street and constantly needing to evade white power while trying to cultivate love and meaning in life, might wonder whether he would always be on the run. Even free Black people had few resources—beyond their intelligence, hard work, and community assistance—with which to defend their relatives, interests, and needs against Charleston's powerful white minority. Enslaved people, men and women, might be sent to the Workhouse merely for "moral" infractions or simply for being on the streets after the 10 p.m. curfew drums sounded. Whites used members of the Black community as informants. Free people could be hassled in the street, too. Would they always be running and hiding from slavers and other white supremacists?

Probably all free and enslaved Black people in the city learned to trust their social networks for survival. Their networks shaped who they were as people, and they in turn shaped the networks with their skills and knowledge. These bonds created pathways for confidentiality, despite white people's power to police them. People might speak Gullah or an African language; they might meet to talk in noisy public places like streets or yards in the vicinity of the City Market; and they might meet secretly in the private homes of free Black people. Inside and outside these networks, they often practiced a social ethic of tactful assistance and nondisclosure of each other's unauthorized activities. One could expect close friends, family, and coworkers to keep mum about unauthorized activities as long as they were not endangering the person. One could hope for aid sometimes, even perhaps from strangers. Fugitives from plantations frequently demonstrated these networks and ethics when they ran to allies in the city—people who kindly hid and helped them at their own risk. But trying to build this socially networked and mutually assisting Black community in slaving Charleston was exceedingly difficult. In fact, without respect and belonging instead of the alienation of slavery's racism, making community was like building a house while someone else tries to dismantle it. There were two meanings of belonging among people in Charleston: as beloved friends and family or as property. The latter was always leeching the former. Persisting under such conditions was an act of love with revolutionary potential.

CHAPTER TWO
Take Freedom

We can't live so.
—PETER POYAS

[We] live such an abominable life . . . [we] ought to rise.
—DENMARK VESEY

[We are] beaten, cuffed, and abused.
—MONDAY GELL

Take the country from the whites.
—GULLAH JACK

Fight the whites—as the poor negroes suffer dreadful slavery.
—A group of unnamed movement participants

Poverty, suffering, fear, and abomination is how the rebels described urban slavery in the epigraphs above. As medicine, Gullah Jack gave them crab claws to put in their mouths for courage when the moment came to begin their war against enslavement. Jack called the crab claws "cullah," and he sourced them in local waters. Crabs were as abundant in South Carolina as they were in Tanzania. Around Charleston, Jack could catch them in the tidal marshes in the city and countryside. His practice with them resembled *ngoma* practices that were indigenous to large parts of eastern and southern Africa. Somewhere near the Mrima Coast, Jack had often observed crabs. He had learned to understand them. He saw how they maneuvered the constantly moving tidal boundary between the land and the water. The tide gave the crabs cover under the water, and then it exposed them on the mudbanks and among the marsh grasses. Crabs learned to use the land and the water to wait for the right moment to strike prey or predators. They learned decisiveness and tact. Jack told would-be rebels that putting his medicinal crab claw in their mouth as they commenced fighting would make them invulnerable. It was a remedy for their fears about injury and death. It was a token of his concern for both the feeling and the safety of his fighters. Jack's recruits were probably all East

Central Africans and Gullahs who more often understood the potency of the crab claw. Because of this shared way of knowing, unspoken instructions were possibly also clear to them: Wait until the proper moment, then act quickly and decisively in an instant. But Jack knew the recruits had to choose for themselves and he was haunted by a fear of his own. Would they accept the power he offered them? He could not be certain, but he knew the uprising depended on their choice.[1]

As long as the 1822 uprising movement continues to be described as a conspiracy inspired and led solely by Denmark Vesey, its meaning to participants such as those most drawn to Jack will be obscured. For the Gullahs and East Africans, Jack was the leader. That stature means that Gullah Jack worked in coordination with Vesey, not as Vesey's subordinate. The term "conspiracy" also obstructs understanding. This seemingly objective legal term, applied in this instance, badly misdescribes the movement. To whites, as the victors, any movement for the freedom of slaves was just a nefarious "plot" or "crime." Slave law allowed slavers the discretion to punish anything less than eager acceptance of servitude. It was illegal to rebel. It was also illegal to make any effort to rebel—even just conversationally. The law insulted the sanity and morals of such "conspirators" and "plotters." South Carolina termed delusional and unlawful the simple act of encouraging people to try to escape. Actual attempts at escape could be punished with a death sentence. To the enslaved, their movement was not a crime. They wanted to rescue themselves from the thrall of their exploiters, their tormentors, their oppressors. Violence was their last, dreaded means. It was about freedom, not crime.[2]

Understanding what the rebels' desire for freedom might have meant to them requires an emphasis on the relationships among the rebels and in the Black Charleston community. The events of 1822 cannot be explained fully as a lone hero's tale, though there is heroism in the story. The uprising's leaders were coequals who suffered more fear, uncertainly, and hesitation than mythic heroes do. Their story is not a nationalist narrative of progress toward a more perfect union, though the fact that such a movement could happen challenged US activists and policymakers. Rather, it is a local story with diverse African dimensions. The movement's members apparently described it as a *rising*. This term preserves meanings missed by terms such as "conspiracy" and "plot." The rebels knew their uprising movement might be exposed and prosecuted. They knew they might die. People they loved might die. But by calling it a rising rather than a plot or conspiracy, they asserted an all-encompassing vision. Their purpose was freedom for as much of the community as was willing to take it together. We can trace the possible meaning of the desire expressed in the epigraphs for this chapter by noticing the rebels' relationships with acquaintances, friends, and relatives. These relationships created a kind of counterstructure to slavery and racism in which commitment to and affection for each other mattered nearly as much as self-preservation—and sometimes more than personal survival.[3]

Black Charlestonians knew how brutally whites punished rebellion. They had seen how runaways were treated. Those who could read, such as Monday Gell, might have remembered newspaper reports of the 1816 proceedings against an enslaved rebellion effort in Camden, South Carolina. In that incident, the attempted insurrection resulted in several hangings even though nobody had been harmed and no property damaged. Vesey may have personally witnessed the hangings of several men who tried to start a rebellion in Charleston in 1797. In this case, too, it had not mattered that no insurrection had commenced. Whites aggressively suppressed all signs of Black attempts to regain the freedoms they or their ancestors had known.[4]

Why would anyone in 1822 make the dangerous decision to start a revolution against slavery that was so violently entrenched? Monday Gell answered this question when he told Smart Anderson that the reason for the movement was slavery itself. They were treated as chattel, not people. Peter Poyas and Denmark Vesey also understood that slavery itself was the problem, as seen in this chapter's epigraphs. Their exploitation in Charleston was more intensively reductive than any slavery in the parts of Africa where slavery existed. In Charleston, the enslaved were commodities. They were capital. They were like things. They and all their descendants were to be human livestock, forever. The law cared not a whit for their affectionate relationships with their children, parents, friends, or spouses or any other social relations.[5]

Because Charleston's economic development employed all Black workers together according to skills, regardless of freedom status, ethnicity, or religion, the diverse crowd of Black workers was able to build familiarity with each other. Then they talked with each other in the streets, in social settings, at the market, and at church. We will never know the topics of conversation specifically because they did not tell us in their own words, but we can describe this uprising movement's dilemmas and challenges better than almost any other in the era of African enslavement in the United States. Statements attributed to the rebels—as quoted in the epigraphs to this chapter, for example—suggest the movement's debates, if not its consciousness. In sum, movement participants characterized being enslaved to whites as a life of execrable abuses. They declared they couldn't continue to live so. They wondered aloud about their dreadful condition under white domination. They discussed whether they ought to attempt to rise and see what they could do to free themselves and their people. They feared the whites, but they thought spiritual forces were with them and that they could fight and succeed. To the most convinced, it was clear that begging and praying would not protect either them or their beloved friends and family. The movement members surely did not share all these feelings or agree on all these propositions all the time, but they resolved to take their freedom from the whites. We can partially recover the process and the planning.[6]

The talk among Peter Poyas, Denmark Vesey, Monday Gell, and others they were convincing to join in the rebellion is reported in some detail in the records. However, because the records were written by their enemies, white slavers, we have a hard time hearing the movement's recruitment rhetoric well. We might learn more by comparing what we know of the 1822 rebels' discussions with the statements of other enslaved people who got to tell their story more completely. Frederick Douglass's resolution to resist began with private thoughts. The actions followed long after: he talked with others, he fought back against a beating, and finally he planned and executed an escape with the collaboration of sympathizers. Harriet Jacobs, too, resolved privately what she was going to do before seeking help from others. Then she hid and escaped to protect herself and try ultimately to free her children. The 1822 organizers appear to possibly have had a similar process of thought, talk, planning, and execution. But even merely escaping was a collaborative act. As in those other narratives, all resistance relied on help and one could not easily know who to trust. Reaching out to others was fraught with fear and a real danger of betrayal. Like in Douglass's and Jacobs's communities, Black Charlestonians practiced an ethic that discouraged snitching on people. Whenever the Charleston enslaved decided to depart from their masters without permission, their efforts were shaped by their relationships: Who would help them, who could be trusted, and whom could they run to without being caught? Ardent affections guided agonizing moments of decision.[7]

How to Trigger an Uprising

It is not surprising that enslaved people decided to fight back. What needs some explanation is the timing. Why did these particular Black Charlestonians act when they did? If one believed that beloved friends and family were safe from slavers' worst acts for the moment, if one felt able to meet one's most basic needs in daily life despite hard exploitation, and if one felt the weight of the slaving society's surveillance and believed it was impossible to overturn, then one might refuse to risk even greater misery or death in a struggle for freedom. But what if whites upturned this bare life? The protests as summarized in this chapter's epigraphs could apply to any time in the history of slaving, but they were all apparently voiced at this particular time. Why? The timing becomes clearer when we look at the changing conditions of slavery, racism, and the Black community in Charleston in 1817–21.

There were at least two churches in Charleston that mattered to the Black community and to uprising movement members. One was the Circular Church on Meeting Street. It was white led and had a white minister, the Reverend Benjamin Palmer. The other, the African Church, was more important. It was Black led and had a Black minister, the Reverend Morris Brown (a future head of the entire African Methodist Episcopal Church). The African Church was larger than the Circular Church, and it had missionary houses on Anson Street and Cow Alley. In fact, the Cow Alley site was barely two blocks from the Circular Church. On Sundays that immediate neighborhood must have been crowded with Black churchgoers. That proximity might be why some of the 1822 organizers were associated with both the Circular Church and the African Church. But the African Church was special. It was the result of a community movement, and a significant proportion of Charleston whites resented it. Whites' violent persecution of the church movement was the first of several triggering events driving the timing of the 1822 uprising. The white violence was an insult. Apparently, to Peter Poyas, the white assaults on churchgoers were like an act of war.[8]

Direct assaults on the African Church occurred almost as soon as the church began operating in 1817. Harassment reached a peak in 1818 and seems to have continued into the 1820s. The church had white allies, such as the thirty-two whites who signed a petition in support of it in 1820, but they apparently could not or would not fully protect the congregation. Nonetheless, the church became vital in the life of Black Charleston. The church's Cumberland Street missionary house (in Cow Alley), like the Anson Street branch near Boundary Street and the main church on Hanover Street in Hampstead, cultivated community, family, and spirituality among Black Charlestonians, both free and enslaved. Eleven-year-old Daniel Payne and his mother—part of a small free family—regularly walked hand in hand to the congregation's class meetings. She made him sit with her throughout the discussions and prayers. He learned to read in the church and became an avid reader. He developed an affection for biblical scholarship. He read about Scottish partisans' rebellions against English rule, and aware of "Hayti and the Haytiens," he developed a short-lived desire to become a soldier and "go to Hayti." He long remembered an affecting sermon in 1819, which sent him "home crying through the streets." Later, when his mother suddenly died, Daniel, still a child, practiced prayers he had learned from her. Always sensitive and spiritual, he enjoyed praying in Charleston's streets and gardens under "a moon-lit sky." This was the church that certain factions of the white populace aggressively harassed, beating and jailing its congregants, breaking up its worship services. The violence directed toward the city's only Black-led church was a threat against the Black community's aspiration for a peaceful future. It taught a lesson about the boundlessness of white aggression: even churches were not sacred.[9]

A second proximal cause for the timing of the uprising movement was a financial panic in the United States created by a rapid decline in cotton prices on the global market in 1818–19. In Charleston, economic recessions might force smaller businesses to fail, but larger entities such as Bennett's Mills were probably able to weather downturns more readily. For generations, larger enterprises, which owned many of their workers as slaves, had possessed extreme labor supply flexibility. They could degrade the living standards of their laborers or forcibly extend work hours to save on costs and increase productivity. Such larger businesses could try to undercut the prices of smaller businesses. If that failed, they could reduce or shut down their operations and hire out the enslaved portion of their workforce. Through hiring out, a cotton shipper could make money off the business of other operations, even in different industries or markets. They could also simply sell their enslaved workers to raise cash, liquidate debts, or reduce costs. On the Perry plantation just north of Charleston, there were almost no taskable adults left in the early 1820s, "the prime hands" having been told to "come to town [Charleston]" to look for wage work. Other plantations sent workers to Charleston to be sold in the thriving domestic slave trafficking markets.[10]

The result of hiring out and selling people was family separation and the fragmentation of friendships in the Black community. Even just a few miles would become prohibitive for the enslaved, who were denied free movement and transportation. Mary Prince, enslaved in Bermuda, recounted the memory of her separation from family and friends as a child, when her slaver, her mistress, "became poor" and sold her to another nearby plantation. Prince remembered the separation as a trauma even after a harrowing life of physical and psychological abuse. Her loved ones left behind, especially her mother, "could only weep and lament" over her and others sold at that time. Similarly, in the Charleston area, the plantation enslaved were sent to the city when cotton prices plummeted, and doubtlessly some city workers were sent back to the country as town-based business slowed. Painful separations probably attended all such forced relocations. Yet sometimes, planters complained that their enslaved workers who had been in Charleston and returned had become more resistant due to direct exposure to free Black people's ideas. In doing so, they pinned on free Black people a reality that was the slavers' own responsibility: people systematically separated from family and friends as chattel develop resistance ideas and strategies.[11]

At the start of the 1820s, white people eliminated the most important legal pathway to freedom, too. In 1821, the path to freedom that Denmark Vesey had followed by purchasing himself in 1799 became all but illegal. This change formed the third proximal cause for the uprising movement's timing. In December 1800, the South Carolina legislature had enacted its first limitations on whites' ability to free enslaved people. The measure impeded manumissions but did not slow them much if at all. In the 1810s, an enslaved Charleston woman in her forties named Catherine got a chance for freedom under this law. Antoine Plumet bought her around 1812 from Peter Catonet, partly on the promise that he would take on the difficulty of freeing her under the 1800 statute. She had agreed to repay Plumet the $300 he paid for her to facilitate her freedom. She saved her wages and may have paid him, but Plumet refused to free her. Because there was no written agreement, he easily kept her and her wages in his pocket. Then, he unexpectedly and prematurely died in 1816, and Catherine briefly became de facto free at the age of forty-six. She ignored the executor of the estate, who insisted she was still property, and lived as a free woman for two years until a court battle reenslaved her. She sued for breach of contract to restore her freedom. Her legal counsel filed suit in early 1820 but the proceedings were delayed. While she waited months for her case to proceed, the state made it unlawful to emancipate slaves without an act of the legislature. Her case—and every other hoped-for emancipation—was taken out of the hands of judges and property owners. Every case would have to be decided individually by legislative vote. The judge in Catherine's case had no choice but to dismiss her suit in 1821. The new law seemed likely to block all efforts of enslaved people to attain freedom by self-purchase.[12]

Nearly simultaneously with this ominous tightening of the manumission law, a movement for the colonization of freed slaves and free Black Charlestonians to Africa commenced. Colonization offered a little more freedom for some people but only at the price of losing connection to friends and family in South Carolina, probably forever. In the autumn of 1821, Black Charlestonians watched such an emigration happen. Some of the enslaved and free Black population, including well-known people, made the decision to depart for Sierra Leone. In October, James Creighton, a free Black Charlestonian, departed on the *Calypso* with a group of emigrants. Some of the emigrants had family and friends leaving with them, and others left people behind in slavery. The dilemma of whether to accept such losses for freedom must have featured significantly in every decision to depart. Jack Lopez, a freeman, had a brother who was enslaved. If Lopez emigrated, his brother could not go with him. Departure would also mean exchanging friends and support networks for places and people unknown to them in a colony controlled by white US philanthropists. As the ship left, many of the people on board and onshore must have grieved a separation that was likely permanent. As if to aggravate the wound, a gale forced the *Calypso* to return to Charleston just a few days later. Its passengers temporarily disembarked. Having said goodbye, the departed were suddenly back. Three weeks later, the scenes of farewell repeated themselves as the ship left again.[13]

Days after the *Calypso*'s final embarkation in November 1821, the unstoppable Catherine Catonet petitioned the legislature for her freedom under the new law. Her petition was one of dozens of such petitions received that year—all from people desperately trying to secure the freedom they had thought would eventually be granted by their owners. All of their petitions were rejected. The year 1822 began with dozens of Black South Carolinians and perhaps hundreds more of their acquaintances, friends, and relatives discovering that the narrow legal door to freedom in the state had closed completely. The enslaved drayman William Garner had been actively saving money to buy his and his family's freedom through an arrangement with his owner. There was no hope left for him.[14]

As November became December, the days got shorter and the nights got longer and Peter Poyas, Denmark Vesey, and others pondered their dilemma. Denmark Vesey, according to witnesses, declared that he would not leave for Africa with Creighton, because he preferred to stay and help the people and his own enslaved family members and friends. Peter Poyas and others among the enslaved had reportedly considered rebellion before, because of the white assaults on churchgoers in 1817 and 1818. Now, pleading with slavers seemed more clearly revealed as futile than ever. There seemed to be only one way left to attain freedom for themselves and their people and potentially stay together. Sometime before Christmas 1821 these men—possibly with the knowledge of at least some of the women of Black Charleston—agreed to the dangerous idea of an uprising. They knew they would need lots of people.[15]

Organizing a Movement

They needed more people. However, they did not limit their recruiting to African Church members. They did not trust the church leadership. Instead, most of the organizers' recruiting happened at random in the street, at night on the margins of town, or in private quarters in the city. They focused on finding the most useful people who could best be trusted to keep the secret. As they looked for allies, they knew they had to be careful. They called it "the rising," but that phrase was dangerous in public. A group of enslaved people talking about a *rising* in public would certainly attract attention and investigation. "The rising" was a term to use in more secure spaces, tactfully. In public and with people whom it was hard to trust, they spoke in more coded language. The rebellion was sometimes called *the business* and the planning meetings a *society*. Terms such as these made their organizing sound like a social club or commerce. Anyone overhearing them on the street would think little of it.[16]

A tradition in memory and among historians holds that Denmark Vesey was the overall commander, that he inspired and instigated the effort, and that other prominent individuals were his subordinates. However, Gullah Jack, Peter Poyas, and Monday Gell are among others who at various times were identified as either the overall leader or part of the leadership. This indicates that the movement's leadership was more of a group in coalition, and it had to be. The movement they built was diverse, with English, Igbo, Gullah, French, and other languages spoken. The movement had Christian and non-Christian sections. No accounts suggest that Vesey had the language, spiritual, or cultural skills to persuade so diverse a group. Monday Gell, Peter Poyas, Gullah Jack, and Perault Strohecker—all Africans—had indigenous African knowledge, spiritual authority, and language skills that Vesey did not possess. Though Vesey seems to have been born in West Africa, in 1821 that life was over forty years past. Though he had once been enslaved, he had been free for two decades. Nonetheless, he was useful. His literacy, his courageousness, and, most important, his free status were valuable for the movement. Because he was free, he could carry letters without much fear of being discovered. He could host meetings in his house without fearing the city guard. He could move around the city with greater safety than any enslaved person.[17]

Freedom had gradually made Vesey socially distinguished from the masses of enslaved workers in both his spiritual life and his home life. In April 1817, he completed the long and demanding process of becoming a full communicant member of the Second Presbyterian Church, a prestigious white-led and white-majority church in the city. This membership set him apart from the Black masses. He may have left Second Presbyterian to join the African Church sometime in 1817, but there is no direct evidence of that. He may have continued as a member of Second Presbyterian into 1818 or into the 1820s. We just do not know, because the church records are lost. He was not, however, a member of the Brown Fellowship Society—which was dominated by free people of color, born in the Western Hemisphere, and of mixed European African ancestry. As a dark-complected African, Vesey might not have fit in well. Still, his relative social distance from the masses of the enslaved in the 1810s is confirmed in the ending of his marriage with an enslaved woman and his remarriage to a free Black woman. As a result of all this, in 1817–18, when Peter Poyas and others appear to have first discussed rebellion, Vesey may not have been close enough to them to be immediately trusted with such dangerous topics.[18]

It is possible that Peter Poyas recruited Vesey. Vesey necessarily had a lot of social contact with the enslaved in his trade, and Peter was a fellow carpenter. Peter had regular opportunities to bump into Vesey at Bennett's, Duncan's, or Steele's lumber processing establishments on the west side. He and Vesey both lived on the west side. Both were firebrand critics of slavery. And Vesey had a reputation of not being especially quiet about sharing his criticisms of slavery in public. If Peter ever heard Vesey declare that Black people should be equals of white people, or even just heard rumors of his declarations, he would have liked Vesey right away. However, even if Vesey eventually came to imagine he was the sole captain over the whole movement, he could not have been. The other movement leaders might agree with him on a variety of matters, and perhaps they even deferred to his status and knowledge at appropriate times, but their indigenous African political roots would not encourage them to be subservient or to obey commands like the regimented soldiers of a state.[19]

Late in 1821, as the leadership coalition was forming after the *Calypso*'s departure, a curious possible sign of growing rebelliousness occurred. In November, there was a fire at Paul Pritchard's wharf on the Cooper River. Paul Pritchard declared in a city newspaper that the fire was arson, and he asked the public for assistance in finding the perpetrator. Arson was a big deal, because in an era of wood construction and little effective firefighting, once a fire started it was a threat to any part of the city downwind from the blaze. Pritchard was a shipwright, and he and a partner had acquired the wharf when its previous owner moved operations to a new site (see map 1.2).

The fire seems to have started in Pritchard's portion of the wharf, and the damage was contained to his portion (his partner did not have to relocate or even cease operations).[20] Gullah Jack was enslaved to Paul Pritchard. He might have set the fire. Certainly, even if he did not set the blaze, it must have been instructive to him. It gave him a vivid lesson in how a fire in the city might grow, how alarm spreads, and how the city fights fire. And it occurred on a Sunday, which was the day of the week that the rebels would ultimately choose for their uprising. Firing the city would become part of the rebels' plan. By one account, Jack was to lead a raid on the US military and naval stores warehoused at Mey's Wharf (beside Pritchard's). Naval stores likely did not include weapons or ammunition. However, flammable items, such as turpentine, may have been among the items in any cache of naval stores.[21]

Four or five weeks after the *Calypso* departed for the second time, Vesey stopped at Monday Gell's shop to see if he could recruit him to join the small squad of leaders already talking. Monday and he got into a conversation about possibly organizing a rebellion to overcome the whites. Vesey revealed to Monday that he had already been in conversation with several others. Monday asked *who*. Vesey named Peter Poyas, Ned Bennett, Jack Purcell, and Rolla Bennett. He apparently told Monday that they were all committed. Monday and Vesey discussed how many more people they would need. They discussed what a plan might look like. Monday later claimed he did not commit right away but that he did eventually join. How Vesey and Monday had known they could trust each other enough to speak dangerously like this is not certain. However, like Vesey, Monday was literate. They both could read and write (the latter being the rarer skill). These skills gave them a shared distinction. Perhaps their educational attainment had helped establish their acquaintance previously.[22]

Before the end of 1821, Rolla Bennett, Peter Poyas, Denmark Vesey, and a few more had agreed to reach out to others to join them. Around Christmas, Monday's neighbor Gullah Jack probably joined. In their conversations with potential recruits these six or eight early organizers discovered that they would have to work to persuade people, but never because the enslaved defended slavery. Unsurprisingly, nearly all seemed to feel that it was desirable to end their slavery. When recruits hesitated to join, it seemed to be because they were either afraid to risk life and limb or did not believe in the practicality of the idea. So, enhancing confidence, inciting courage, and insisting on the practicality of the plan became common recruitment strategies. The organizers would upbraid people with remonstrations about manly courage. Vesey and Monday read from the Bible. Vesey taught biblical perspectives condemning slavery. He espoused human equality. Gullah Jack worked to assuage anxiety and fear with healing *ngoma* ceremonies and spiritual medicine. Peter Poyas and Gullah Jack invoked Black solidarity and ethnic identity. But none of these approaches reflected a unified, overarching ideology. The movement as a whole was united by the shared goal of overthrowing white power to take freedom. What they envisioned would come after they captured the city has never been clearly settled and may never be. However, a coalition does not have to agree on everything to mobilize together.[23]

It appears that logistical and strategic arrangements dominated the coalition's discussions. This was one of their most savvy decisions. They had started from a weak position, but the leaders and organizers seem to have understood how to use what they had. They used existing social groups. There was an Igbo contingent for Monday to lead and a Gullah contingent with Gullah Jack. There were also work groups expected to act together. For example, the draymen were recruited around the same time and were intended to operate together, since many of them knew each other well and understood the management of horses and wagons. Plantation groups were recruited together. The driver on the Ferguson plantation outside the city may have been tapped to be a local commander. As they moved through the city contacting people, the recruiters often worked in small groups or singly. Many of the more credible stories of recruiting featured just one-on-one or two-on-two conversations. They paid attention to personal, cultural, and social connections. There was little point in Vesey trying to organize Gullahs; Gullah Jack was better for that. Rolla Bennett could hardly organize the many Igbos as effectively as Monday Gell. Peter Poyas would organize craft workers in the city and use his boat to establish contacts out in Christ Church Parish, where his slaver's plantation was. Denmark Vesey was probably most effective with enslaved people born in the Americas and working in Charleston in the crafts. Perhaps Vesey also approached other free Black workers. Being a coalition also meant that if the movement ever came under significant stress, it might fracture into constituent social networks.[24]

Perhaps in January these leaders began widening the circle of people willing to commit. They appear to have agreed on July 14 as the date for the uprising, reportedly at Vesey's suggestion. Such timing would take advantage of the annual departures of some of the white elite during the hottest months of the year. The elite often resided outside the city on nearby islands and plantations, according to an 1820 visitor to Charleston. Some remained in the city, but many moved farther away in June "to the mountains" and even to "springs" out of state. Thus, some significant part of the elite would be leaving the region in June. Some of them would leave their town dwellings or plantations in the hands of unsupervised, enslaved people. Perhaps most important, these departures might weaken command and control of the militia and city guard units if key officers were away.[25]

Unrelated cases of fugitives in the city reveal why the 1822 organizers would want to approach people they knew and why they spoke in coded language. Trusting anyone with a dangerous proposal was tricky, especially strangers. Decisions about when to take their risk had a pattern. One fugitive slave escaped his slaver in rural South Carolina and went to Charleston, a city with which he was familiar. He slept nights beside a familiar tavern where he'd often stopped when he brought "eggs and peaches and other things" to the City Market in Charleston. Pretending to be a hired-out laborer on the Cooper River wharves, he "went down to the stevedore's stand" and "waited there with the rest of the hands to get work." Hired with "a good many others," he loaded "cotton in a vessel." With no money, he pretended to join the work gang heading to buy food but ducked out and returned to the loading dock for safety. Even merely being seen as having no money carried the danger of exposure. Though he hid, the cotton freighter's Black steward noticed him. The two men got acquainted, and afterward "every day he used to give me something to eat." But they did not speak directly about why he had no money or food. The problem was that they were strangers and could not determine whether to trust each other. After some time, they developed enough familiarity and trust and the steward opened a sly conversation about wages and freedom. Soon, the fugitive accepted a carefully worded offer of free passage to Boston by stowing away on the vessel. The case shows how the fugitive ethic made help possible. Such difficulty of establishing confidence is likely why the 1822 uprising organizers generally approached people they already believed they could trust. They approached friends, family, and close coworkers—people with whom they had enduring social connections. Even then they often spoke elliptically.[26]

Everyday life taught the enslaved this fugitive ethics. The phenomenon of fugitives was probably familiar to people in the city. Every newspaper published notices seeking to capture people. Some fugitives were loved ones or neighbors who had been sold away. Others were strangers without friends or family in town. There must have been community gossip. People associated with the Vesey affair may have rubbed shoulders with some of the fugitives occasionally. Robin and January, enslaved brothers with no known connection to the uprising, walked the same Charleston streets as Daniel Payne, Catherine Plumet, and Prudence Bussacre as well as the 1822 uprising movement

Take Freedom 57

members and leaders. The brothers had stolen two horses and some clothing and fled to Charleston to find a ship to take them to their relatives out of state. They needed to stable their commandeered horses before the 10 p.m. curfew on the night they arrived. Would they be able to trust stablers such as the enslaved man Perault Strohecker? Could they trust Monday Gell, whose slaver ran a stable? There were many stables in the city and we do not know where they went, but they would need someone who would not ask too many awkward questions. In doing so, they would have perhaps one degree of separation from enslaved draymen who were participating in the uprising movement. Both brothers were carpenters and could have met some of the woodworkers involved in the movement, such as Vesey, Peter Poyas, and John Enslow. Moreover, a few Black Charlestonians knew that larger fugitive groups lived on their own outside the city. If their uprising launched, they would be betting countryside fugitive communities would join them, perhaps similarly to how their African Church movement in 1817–18 had ballooned from a few people to a few hundred to over 4,000 in a short time.[27]

Other enslaved fugitives also passed through places where the uprising planners were living and working. Mary Woods—the subject of chapter one's epigraph—was a fugitive in Charleston in June 1822. She fled to the Planter's Hotel on Church Street just a couple doors from Monday Gell's master's livery stables. Her husband worked in the hotel.[28] Another fugitive, Hyacinthe, escaped his master, fled to Charleston in early 1822, and was still uncaptured in August. He was very well known on the wharves. He had managed a sloop in the harbor and spoke both French and English. He could have been familiar to the movement planners, who were actively looking for "French negroes" to recruit.[29] In February 1822, a fugitive named Renty left his owner's plantation in Christ Church Parish—an area east of the city on the coast that Peter Poyas was visiting frequently at that time to recruit for the uprising movement. Renty had a wife living in one of the large houses on South Bay Street, which was the street that Peter Poyas's master's shipyard was on and on which Peter himself may have lived. There is no evidence that the two men knew each other or that Renty was looking for Peter, but it is certainly possible they encountered each other on the docks or on the street. Such possibilities probably defined a significant dimension of street culture in the wharf districts of the city.[30]

Even those Black Charlestonians who did not completely leave their slavers without permission were nonetheless like fugitives at times. When they were absent from their slavers or their assigned duties for a few minutes, several hours, or overnight without permission, they were fugitive. In such situations, they needed to rely on individuals who would not reveal their absence. Successfully hiding their absence from their masters meant they could attempt it again. Like the more desperate runaways in their midst in Charleston's streets and wharves, they might deceive people they needed to engage but could not be certain they could trust. Practice evading unwanted attention while finding assistance produced skills. Once the 10 p.m. curfew rang out and the patrol left the Main Guardhouse to capture any Black people still on the streets and imprison them in the Workhouse, the free and enslaved residents of the city were little safer than the escapees hunted by their slavers. People learned to avoid the gaslights on Broad Street by taking the parallel route down St. Michael's Alley instead. They learned which yards to cut through and whether they could approach an enslaved man like Perault Strohecker about hiding out in his master's stable until daylight. People hid in empty boats on the wharves. There were routes that were difficult for the city guard to follow: plank-board walkways across marshy ground at Bennett's Mill Pond or a crossing at Boundary Street to exit the city guard's jurisdiction. Fugitives could find help from individuals—a stevedore, a drayman, or a worker in a hotel serving whites—as long as those people would keep their secrets. The uprising organizers and participants had learned some of these evasive skills, too. They spoke elliptically about *the business*. They chose meeting sites and means for sending messages with secrecy in mind. They sometimes used the Gullah language as a way to code their conversations in the city.[31]

The uprising movement, however, was about insurrection, not just evasion. Talk of killing whites for freedom was far more dangerous than escaping them to get it. The rebels had a reasonable expectation that the fugitive ethics of secrecy would provide them some safety, but there were limits. Discussing armed insurrection would be beyond those limits for some Black Charlestonians. The movement developed two ways to deal with the ways in which the heightened danger of planning increased their risk in trusting each other. First, they administered an oath of secrecy. Second, they accessed each other's social networks. A sibling of a friend is not quite a stranger. They used this method to approach people outside their own immediate social groups.[32]

Despite everything they did, fear remained a common obstacle to persuading recruits. People were very sensibly and rationally afraid of the structure of white domination and its capacity for organized violence. Some recruits therefore were not easily convinced that the uprising had good logistical planning, enough fighters, or adequate weapons. They persistently believed that the movement would therefore fail. Potential recruits often voiced reticence anchored in such understandings. To allay fears and respond to skeptics, the recruiters told people about divisions among the whites regarding slavery. A rebellion could exploit white divisions. The enslaved would be powerful and not simply slaughtered, said recruiters as they sometimes bragged about the weapons they could get or would have. If pressed, they would only allude vaguely to where the weapons were. They sometimes recommended stealing a master's sword or gun. They said they had blacksmiths making pikes and other bladed weapons. Organizers also addressed the fear underlying some of the skepticism with psychological, social, and spiritual encouragements and assurances. They invited recruits to group meetings where they incited each other, taught each other, and raised small amounts of money for practical things the movement needed. These persuasion tactics sometimes worked. Even some persistent skeptics agreed to join, but only if masses of insurrectionists came out for the fight when it commenced.[33]

Exaggeration was a tactic of encouragement. The organizers bragged about thousands of people being ready and waiting. The claims they made that 4,000 (or even 9,000) people had committed to join an army were probably just optimistic estimates of the numbers of people in the regions in and around the city that they had contacted. Asserting that hundreds or even thousands had put their names down on muster lists was likely also overblown for strategic, persuasive purposes. The real number must have been at most a few hundred people, whose commitment was much less formal than the term "army" implies. However, even if there were just a couple hundred who had committed, such a force could be formidable: there had also been only a few hundred slaves at the gathering that launched the insurrection that became the Haitian Revolution. In Haiti, as the news had spread across the northern plains that the slaves had started their own revolution, many thousands of enslaved people who had no knowledge of the plans realized the opportunity for freedom and took it. Enhancing the rhetorical strategy, organizers assured people that allies in other places would help them. Rolla Bennett and others claimed that the British, the Haitians, or even people in Africa would aid them. How that aid might manifest was not entirely clear. It was not clear whether they meant military aid in Charleston. Britain had twice allied with enslaved people during the lifetime of Denmark Vesey himself—first in the American Revolution and then in the War of 1812. However, the aid they expected might not have been military at all. Perhaps all they expected was to be accepted when they arrived on African, British, or Haitian shores.[34]

When Rolla Bennett approached his *bosom friend* Joe La Roche about the insurrection sometime in early February, he probably predicted Joe's reticence. The two were like brothers, according to those who knew them. However, practical needs compelled Rolla to reveal the secret to Joe, despite Joe's likely resistance: Rolla knew that Joe had access to a boat. He also knew that Joe was well connected with many people on Johns Island across the Ashley River. Rolla had been on Johns Island as early as Christmas 1821 but had managed only to get acquainted. He barely knew anyone, and he apparently did not feel safe asking them to join an insurrectionary movement. But Joe could ask them, so Rolla asked Joe.[35]

Amaritta often made meals for Rolla and Joe in the yard she managed on her slaver's property. Joe was her former husband, and Rolla was her current husband. Amaritta had had two children with Joe years earlier, but he was not jealous that she'd chosen Rolla. Joe had been willing to end it amicably and still considered Rolla an intimate friend. Amaritta was assertive and determined. One white person described her as being of a *bloody disposition*. It was a slang way to accuse her of callousness or even a violent temper. It suggests, too, that she would be an ideal participant in an uprising plan. She would serve at least once as a messenger. As Rolla talked to Joe about the movement, it is not hard to imagine Amaritta overhearing or detecting in the body language of the two men that they were having an unusually serious conversation. If she inferred the general topic they discussed, she likely would not object. She was, after all, apparently practical, stony, and loving. She would keep their secret. Rolla asked Joe to come to the movement's meetings. There he would learn the details and be sworn to secrecy, but Joe was skeptical. He asked how they would get weapons and whether they had enough people. Rolla reassured him, but Joe responded it was a sin to kill. Both men were members of a confessional religious study class in the African Church. In class, they often talked with each other, trying to improve their moral practice. Rolla, however, did not seem to see the rebellion movement as a religious matter. For him it was a matter of manliness. So he gently mocked Joe for unmanly cowardice. Eventually, Joe did go to the meeting. Eventually, he promised he would join the rebellion if the attackers came out with enough force when they commenced the fight. And Joe kept the secret.[36]

If Joe's story represents how the rebellion's organizers recruited people born in the Western Hemisphere, Yorick Cross's story reveals a somewhat different process for recruiting Africans. Peter Poyas approached Yorick partly because they both were African born. In fact, Yorick may have had the same or a similar ethnicity as Peter. But as was true of Rolla in approaching Joe, Peter also had a practical motivation: Yorick had a wife living at the intersection of King Street and Boundary Street. This was just a few yards, about a city block, from two or three arms caches the rebels hoped to capture (see map 2.1).

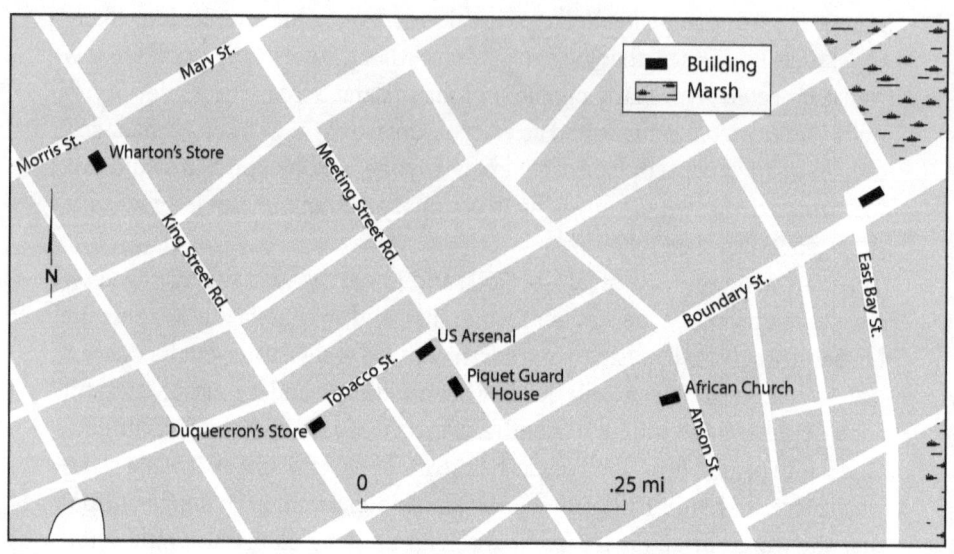

MAP 2.1 Weapons caches. See mappingblackcharleston.org for updates.

Gullah Jack would eventually directly ask Yorick to let twelve men sleep at his wife's house on the night of the attack in order for them to safely get into position before the night patrol could enforce the 10 p.m. curfew—but in these first discussions such operational details were kept from Yorick.[37] Peter simply asked him to join a plan to take the country from the whites to get their freedom. When Yorick asked Peter whether the rebels had enough force to overcome white power, Peter simply claimed they had plenty of men and would be able to get guns and powder. Yorick remained skeptical.[38]

Three of the most active African-born leaders worked Yorick in the days ahead. Gullah Jack, Peter Poyas, and Monday Gell returned to him again and again. Though he remained, perhaps, privately ambivalent, Yorick let them think he might yet join. Yorick learned a lot about the plan, but he did not describe Vesey as the leader. He understood Gullah Jack to be the head man of the uprising. Jack's house was one of the movement's meeting places. Yorick met other people in the movement as well. John Horry and George Vanderhorst at different times each apparently told him that they had joined the uprising and were ready. He learned that Peter went to Christ Church Parish frequently to hold meetings and that he had his own group of recruits both there and in Charleston. But he remained skeptical of the plan throughout.[39]

Africans such as Yorick would have had a pretty good idea what "enough" people and weapons for a war might mean. After all, he had very likely been enslaved either in a violent raid or as a result of a battle—or at least had witnessed skirmishes and battles with raiders in the past. He knew viscerally what having the weaker force might mean. Yorick's hesitation, therefore—like Joe's—was not cowardice. It was perhaps a prudent determination to wait until it seemed possible that the rebellion could succeed. However, according to Yorick, Peter's patience eventually ran out and he threatened to turn all of Yorick's country people (from Africa) against him. This threat spurred Yorick to explicitly join and commit. That such a threat moved Yorick to join underscores how important friends and acquaintances from his homeland were to him. Yorick was quick to add, however, that his cooperation was conditioned on whether the movement demonstrated enough strength when the fight began. Implicitly, it was also a sort of a political counterthreat. He was telling Peter that if the movement were to become dangerously weak, he would not be with them. Peter and Yorick were not as close as Rolla and Joe.[40]

Though Peter's threat got Yorick to join and keep the secret, the organizers could not trump his loyalty to his wife. A map of the city in 1822 reveals why they were interested in her. She lived near the Piquet Guard House just north of Boundary Street, along Meeting Street, at the northern edge of the city limits. Because of the 10 p.m. curfew and the proximity of the Piquet Guard House to her house, being stationed at her place would allow the rebels to capture arms in the neighborhood before whites understood what was happening. The rebels had to get to the weapons first. But when they asked Yorick for permission to have attackers sleep at her place the night of the attack, Yorick refused and that was apparently the end of it. Yorick simply did not have full confidence in the planning. Jack, as he apparently did with many of the recruits, tried healing approaches to bolster Yorick's commitment and attain the goal. He gave Yorick some ritual foods to consume on the morning that the insurrection broke out. He said the foods would help protect him and that he was giving these items to all of his African recruits. To the light meal, Jack added two crab claws he called "cullah." He told Yorick that as the attackers passed, he should put one claw in his mouth so that he could not be wounded. Yorick valued the medicinal cullahs highly. Even when the movement was falling apart and Jack angrily demanded the cullahs back, Yorick refused to hand them over. But it was not enough to persuade him to allow attackers to sleep at his wife's place the night before the insurrection launched.[41]

Trust was sometimes hard to muster even among the committed. One day, Yorick and Monday encountered each other and discussed the rising, elliptically. Yorick, always the skeptic, having heard from Joe Cross that Monday was part of the rising, tried to confirm with Monday by asking a little impertinently if he was in fact the head of a company of Igbo men who would participate in the attack. Monday hedged. Perhaps he did not like the tactless directness of the question and wondered whether he could trust Yorick. Instead of yes or no, he apparently declared ambivalently that *he was sort of a one*. Then, perhaps satisfied with Yorick's nonverbal response, Monday invited him to visit his harness shop if he ever wanted further news about the uprising. Monday would later claim that Yorick had also joined the movement. Yorick would admit as much but hedged the fact by suggesting that he had joined only because Peter threatened to embarrass him by broadcasting his cowardice to all his country people from Africa.[42]

Peter traveled frequently to extend the reach of the movement east and northeast of the city. He traveled into the marshy islands, creeks, and rice-growing areas along the ocean coast. Christ Church Parish was the most clearly identified location mentioned in the documents, but he seems to also have gone, or asked cohorts from Christ Church to go, as far as the Santee River region and to Georgetown (see fig. 2.1). The Poyas plantation was a place where he would know people he trusted. Christ Church Parish was almost a coastal barrier island whose swamps and creeks extended east some forty miles from Charleston's Hibben's Ferry to the Santee River. The ferry was vitally important to Charleston. Its dock was on Gibbs and Harper's Wharf at the end of the Vendue Range opposite the foot of Queen Street, where enslaved people and a wide variety of goods were frequently sold. There was no bridge over the Cooper, so the ferry was the main service link to Mount Pleasant and the mainland beyond. The ferry was also a landmark, and its route to Mount Pleasant was probably the most traveled crossing in the area. Peter and any rebels crossing from Christ Church would be using a very familiar route.[43]

Slow-match fuses and some ammunition were later found under the docks near Hibben's Ferry on Gibbs and Harper's Wharf. There was also the indication of a plan for men to sleep on a nearby wharf the night of the attack. Logistically, it made sense for the rebels to pre-place supplies and people beside the Hibben's Ferry landing in the city. Not only was it a critical crossing point, but many targets were nearby. The banking and insurance district, the most common slave trading sites, and the Main Guardhouse were all a very short walk away. The enslaved from the outlying areas likely conducted most of their city business and activities close to the Hibben's Ferry site. It was close to the City Market, the Circular Church, and the African Church's Cow Alley mission house. These were places that enslaved people knew well. As a result, countryside enslaved people would know the landing and its neighborhood

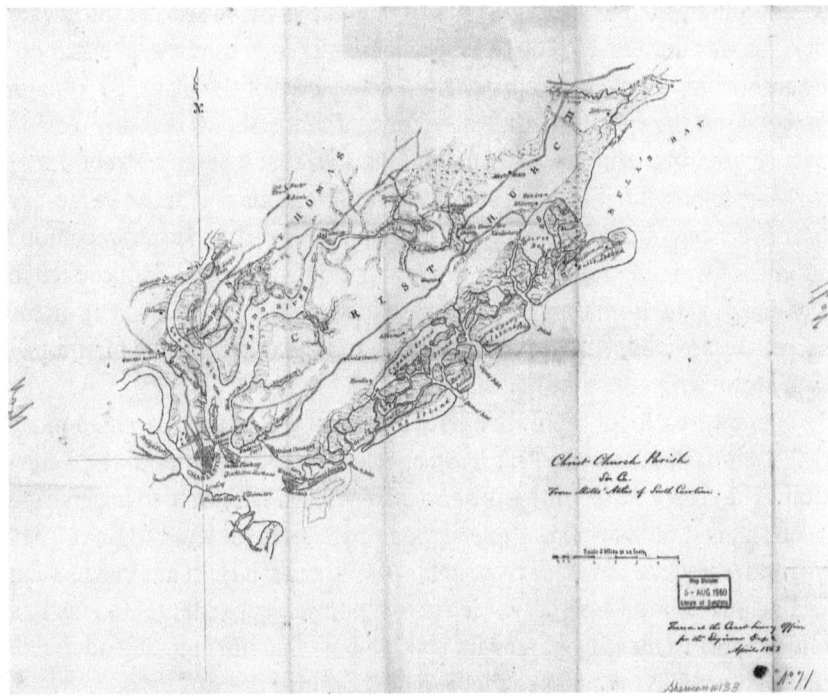

FIGURE 2.1 1825 map of Charleston environs, derived from *Mills Atlas*. Geography and Map Division, Library of Congress, Washington, DC.

better than they likely knew the rest of town. In fact, if country people were crossing from Christ Church, it was probably inevitable that they would land at or near Hibben's Ferry. There was no less conspicuous place for a group of African Americans to enter the city. Sunday services were a great cover for them, both on Saturday evening and Sunday morning.[44]

Perhaps as late as February there was a disagreement at the planners' usual meeting place, though there is no indication where that was or what the disagreement was about. Nonetheless, as a result, some of the meetings began to be held at Denmark Vesey's house. It was at Vesey's that Joe La Roche joined the movement in February. Monday Gell said that he finally joined during a meeting at Vesey's rented Bull Street house. In fact, though Vesey's was a significant meeting site, the movement leaders found safe meeting places in and around the city quite easily. Several slaves said that beyond Vesey's and Gullah Jack's, meetings also took place at Monday Gell's, Thayer's Farm, Bulkley's Farm, and other places in and around Charleston. Some of these were places where women had the opportunity to become familiar with the comings and goings and possibly with the discussions and activities as well. Women such as Prudence Bussacre and Sally Howard became aware of what was underway and understood that the men might get "taken up" by authorities for their activities. They were aware of the planning, though perhaps not the specific plan. No evidence directly shows that any women participated in planning. William Paul insisted that women be kept out of the discussions. But, like Amaritta La Roche, Sarah Paul and Susan Vesey may have overheard enough. During one large indoor meeting, Susan was among a group of women present in the next room doing laundry. Sarah cooked in Denmark's yard. Both women would have had opportunities to pick up on the secret. Susan lived with Denmark. Yet she and the other women mentioned kept secret whatever they may have learned.[45]

There were a lot of highly dangerous secrets. One day in March, Monday Gell, Denmark Vesey, and Perault Strohecker walked together to the waterfront. They carried a letter that Monday had written. They wanted to persuade a cook named William aboard one of the ships to carry the letter to Haiti. They had addressed the envelope to an uncle of William's in Haiti but inside was a second envelope addressing the letter to the Haitian president. Monday had told others in a meeting of movement members that he thought it advisable that they establish contact so they might get refuge there.[46]

Vesey probably carried the letter, because his free status protected him from random searches a little better. Whites sometimes searched enslaved people on the street and took property from them on suspicion of theft—even advertising it in the papers. Vesey also would have had safer access to the ship, because a slave climbing onto a Haiti-bound ship was more likely to get unwanted attention. The wharf, Vanderhorst's, was located at the eastern end of Tradd Street near the southern end of the wharf complex in 1822 (see map 1.2). Any safety Vesey's free status did not give, the wharf complex might have provided. Vanderhorst's was in one of the oldest and busiest parts of the wharf complex. The sight of three Black men walking together through the area would be commonplace, if anyone even had much chance to notice, because the neighborhood was honeycombed with small streets, alleys, and passageways made of cobblestones, wood planks, and even compacted dirt. No part of Charleston was more of a maze. There were small and large buildings, irregularly shaped and made of wood, brick, and stone. These labyrinthine blocks hosted storage, offices, residences, and shops. Livestock, hardware, lumber, and agricultural produce was everywhere in bunches, bales, and stacks. Businesses crowded even the wider lanes with awnings and external platforms to display their wares. People lived on the wharves—probably mostly slaves working for merchants and craftspeople. Attached to the river ends of the wharves were long wooden docks that reached hundreds of feet toward the Cooper River's main shipping channel. Ships waited and cargo was stacked up on the docks. Walking in the wharf districts was so difficult that city administrators of the streets sometimes intervened to maintain throughways. Most sight lines were probably obstructed across any great distance. On this particular day, when the three men reached Vanderhorst's Wharf with their letter for the Haitian president, William the cook agreed to carry it. He, too, kept the secret and departed Charleston within a few days.[47]

Monday risked his life by proposing, writing, and sending that letter, but it was worth it. Haiti was the greatly preferred alternative to the humiliation and social separation that departure to the white-founded colonies of Sierra Leone or Liberia represented. Haiti was more than a symbol, as Ada Ferrer has shown; it was understood correctly as a "free soil" state by the 1820s. The 1816 Haitian Constitution's Article 44 established Haitian nationality and citizenship for any African- or Native American–descended people who merely set foot on Haitian ground. Haiti was a revolutionary, antislavery, and anti-imperial, Black-led state. After 1818, President Jean-Pierre Boyer openly invited African Americans to emigrate, providing funding and free land for émigrés. Enslaved people's escapes to Haiti were reported in the United States as early as 1818. Haiti repeatedly refused to return fugitive slaves, and it was the most important beacon of freedom for Black activists in the United States. It was proof of possibility and a source of confidence for some of the members of Charleston's uprising movement.[48]

The movement also built unity and courage within the diverse coalition through indigenous ceremony. Gullah Jack, Peter Poyas, Tom Russell, Robert Robertson, and other indigenous African practitioners within the uprising movement must have been pressing for ceremony. The movement, according to Gullah Jack, certainly, needed technologies to address anxieties and fears among the participants. On the night of April 27, a large group of men held a gathering at 8 p.m. at Bulkley's Farm outside the city. There were probably significant numbers of Gullah people present—part of the Gullah band within the movement. It was about an hour past sunset, by which time the sky was completely dark. The farm encompassed sixteen acres in a rural area more than a mile north of the Lines and east of Meeting Street Road. It was secluded enough that, with the plantation owner out of town on business, the place was safe for gathering. Gullah Jack headed the affair. According to Billy Bulkley, the group included Peter Poyas and others, all of whom sang and prayed until dawn. The event functioned a little like a South Carolina version of the Bois Caïman ceremony that launched the enslaved masses' entrance into the Haitian Revolution in 1791: it stoked confidence, unity, and secrecy. But it also had distinctive features that possibly had not been part of the Haitian ceremony. At Bulkley's Farm, Gullah Jack seems to have led the men in a version of a *ngoma* ceremony. Such a ceremony had apparently become a regular event at Bulkley's Farm for Peter Poyas and Gullah Jack. Shared singing and praying probably continued all night, because in *ngoma* each person—men and women—might take a central position one at a time, announce their fears, and receive the response of the group gathered around. We do not know for certain that women were part of the ceremony, but we can assume they were at least aware of the goings-on; the farm was only sixteen acres, leaving little doubt that the sounds of the event would be heard in the Bulkley slave quarters. The community's responses to confessions represented guidance from ancestors, sung by the participants to assuage anxieties and strengthen the determination of the afflicted.[49]

Billy seems to have learned most of what he knew about the uprising during these gatherings, which were biweekly for a time and often ran late into the night. Denmark Vesey does not appear to have personally attended these gatherings, perhaps because of his own ardent Christianity. However, Vesey apparently was in the habit of going to the farm and was quite close to Billy Bulkley. At one meeting Gullah Jack and Robert Robertson half cooked a fowl and ate it together as a bonding ritual—a demonstration of their commitment. At another meeting, a gun the men had with them served a symbolic function. Each person tried to fire it but only one of them could, according to Billy. The majority, those who could not fire it, were considered *safe*. The specific meaning seems to have been poorly understood by the white person who recorded the story, but it was obviously partly about friendship and bonding as well as increased familiarity with a firearm. Such bonding was central to the organizing. The movement's *Gullah Society* probably included people from both the countryside and the city. Presumably with Gullah Jack's direct facilitation this society seems to have met monthly for these ceremonies, which on one occasion apparently attracted sixty people. These meetings were the greatest demonstration of Gullah Jack's influence in the movement. Some of the movement members described themselves as feeling almost compelled to commit to the uprising because of Jack's knowledge and charisma.[50]

Monday Gell's saddle-making shop and quarters near the northeast corner of Meeting and Market Streets also became an indigenous gathering place. People shared and learned news of the movement at Monday's. His shop became important both because of where it was located and the Igbo politics that influenced its movement function. Because it was adjacent to the City

Market, the shop allowed the curious, the movement participants, and the leaders to meet inside and outside as well as behind the building and in a cabinetmaker's lot next door. They met at Monday's shop during business hours and after. Gatherings also happened randomly on the way to or from the shop when men accidentally met in the streets. This fluid environment allowed information from random conversations in the street to circulate safely. Monday personally encouraged this information sharing. Coming from one of the Igbos' decentralized and nonstate societies, he facilitated and was quite comfortable in a decentralized information and decision-making arrangement. Meetings at Monday's were free flowing, unscheduled, and open to all comers, while at Denmark Vesey's the proceedings were more scheduled, choreographed, and closed to invitees. Bulkley's Farm, Vesey's house, and Monday's shop exemplified some of the best resources the movement had to support its organizing and planning. There were more meeting sites than these—Gullah Jack's place and Thayer's Farm, for example—but these three were the sites we can know best. There was no specific rule or formula. Instead, these sites operated around cultural scripts that were available and that worked. Vesey's place was like a church, with books and Bible readings, but Monday's was more equal and unscheduled. In all cases, the meeting sites appropriated space within the slavers' city for dangerous, rebellious talk. Discarding the white supremacists' slave law in these locations was an expression of the rebels' growing liberation. The movement was beginning to upend relations of power in the city. In a sense, all this talk was the uprising in progress. It was how they began living the new order they hoped their rebellion would bring.[51]

Monday told men with whom he spoke to come to his shop if they wanted news about the uprising planning. Though whites often passed close by and sometimes came into his shop, Monday rarely showed fear. He knew that gatherings of enslaved and free Black men and women were unremarkable near the market. And the market distracted the whites, anyway. They descended into it preoccupied, like the buzzards on top of the kiosks, strolling into the crowds of people. Confident in their safety because the city protected them, they moved with their eyes on bits of discarded meat—fixated on spotting and taking what they wanted. Here, whites' own wants discouraged attention to the voices of anyone who was not calling out products and prices. Weaving between the shoppers, they were insensate to the revolutionary planning going on nearby.[52]

At the margins of the market, movement participants learned a lot about who was doing what for the *rising* at Monday's. Pharo Thompson told Monday one day about wishing to run away. William Colcock came to his shop to discuss how many men he had recruited. There was tell that Frank Ferguson recruited people in the countryside for the rebellion. Saby Gaillard—a freeman—shared news about Haiti. Edward Johnson, another freeman, boasted that he would join in if the insurrection began. Through his shop and his own organizing and coordinating, Monday learned that Tom Russell, a blacksmith, made pikes for the uprising. Scipio Sims had gone to Middleton plantation to recruit for the uprising. Many people came through Monday's shop or shared information with him elsewhere about their commitment to the uprising movement or what they planned to do when the attack commenced: Paris Ball, Luis Remoussin, Jack Glen, Smart Anderson, Perault Strohecker, Bacchus Hammett, Billy Palmer, Denmark Vesey, John Enslow, William Garner, Sandy Vesey, Mingo Harth, Joe Jore, Denbow Martin, John Vincent, and Stephen Smith were among these people. There were roughly a dozen unnamed draymen as well that Monday learned were planning to support the insurrection with horses. Monday's shop and the yard beside it seems to have bustled with news-sharing activities.[53]

By the middle of spring, perhaps sometime in April, movement members and leaders were moving about town on behalf of the uprising quite easily and speaking about it with each other quite freely. What had been unspeakable was becoming authorized in the revolution they were creating. In one example, Yorick Cross was headed to the City Market. Charles Drayton was walking near the market with another enslaved man, named Joe, who had once been enslaved in the same household with Yorick. Seeing Yorick crossing the street, Charles called out to him. Yorick stopped to greet the two men. With Joe there, Charles talked to Yorick about the insurrection plan. Among other things, Joe told Yorick about a specific aspect of the organizing about which he had learned.[54] In a second example, Frank Ferguson reportedly rode into the countryside and recruited four plantations to join the rebellion—probably all in the vicinity of the Ferguson plantation, where his people lived. He returned and shared that report with men in town.[55] And in a third, Perault Strohecker, according to Monday, made a habit of visiting an old man outside of town in a small house by a shipyard, probably in the vicinity of Gadsden's Wharf. There, Perault and others he had invited along discussed the plans with this old man as freely as if they'd come on a work-related errand.[56]

This network labored to locate, make, and secure war materials. Despite months of preparation, it appears that this riskiest and most difficult task may never have been fully complete, probably because of the danger and difficulty of getting and hiding weapons. During May and June, rebels completed and stored a half dozen pikes for the initial assault. They also made and hid pike poles. They acquired and hid fuses. Several men stole swords or guns from their masters or made daggers and swords for themselves. One night, Perault Strohecker and Bacchus Hammett brought a keg of powder to Monday's shop, and Monday agreed to let them store it until Gullah Jack, who lived just six steps away from Monday's back door, came to take it away. They had apparently stolen it from Bacchus's master Benjamin Hammett, who was an officer in the militia.[57] Bacchus seems to have bragged that he would also facilitate capturing 500 muskets from Benjamin Hammett.[58] Beyond acquiring these limited weapons, all the movement had done was identify where they could immediately capture hundreds of guns and all the shot and powder they would need on the night of the initial surprise assault.

Capture and Keep the Initiative

Emerging from an "interminable forest," a carriage carrying a visitor to South Carolina came "upon an open swampy district." Beyond the marshes along the Ashley River, the visitor noted, "Charleston extended before us" in the distance. The pleasant-looking little city was still a mile away across the water. Water separated and connected everything in Charleston. Charlestonians were always negotiating water. A convenient causeway "constructed of fascines" crossed the wetlands, and a rare and fashionable "eight horse team boat" crossed the river. Approaching the city via Bridge Street and turning right onto Pinckney Street, the visitor and fellow passengers enjoyed the "entirely novel spectacle" that the larger houses of the Charleston Neck suburb presented. "Most" were "surrounded by gardens" with "splendid" oranges and other fruit. There were "monthly roses" blooming and a variety of other "flourishing plants." On the lightly and genteelly populated Pinckney Street, the visitor saw "piazzas and spacious balconies" and "walls and columns" covered in "creeping vines." There were profusions of passionflowers, and he "felt delighted with this Southern climate."[59]

When the carriage finally crossed over the "log causeway" of Cannon's Bridge at Boundary Street, the visitor got a closer view of Bennett's Mills across part of the pond before entering the city proper at Boundary Street. Unbeknownst to him, he'd toured one of the most vulnerable approaches to the city. The rebels' planned night crossing of the Ashley River would land them at or near the same banks. As the passengers obliviously enjoyed the whites' command of water and labor for pleasure and industry, the carriage wheeled close by several rebel targets. If the rebellion went as planned, men on foot or horseback might come down the same dirt streets lined with mansions, fruit trees, and flowering plants. They would raid some of these wealthy slavers' genteel homes. A detachment would capture the lonely powder magazine located a short distance from Pinckney Street. Another detachment hoped to capture and hold Cannon's Bridge. All the while, the rebels would be recruiting new adherents in the neighborhood from among the Black people's housing clusters that the white visitor did not mention. If they succeeded, Lucas's and Bennett's picturesque mills might be under their control or burning before dawn.[60]

The rebels first chose July 14 at midnight for their surprise attack; then they moved it up to June 16. Why they chose these two nights has always been a little unclear. Scholars have focused on the fact that both days were Sunday. Because Sunday was a day of rest for some, a day of revelry for others, and a day of prayer for the religious, many people would be distracted or sleeping off a party by midnight. The enslaved could move around greater Charleston a little more easily. But why these particular Sundays? Why not choose Sunday, June 2, 9, 23, or 30? Why not July 7? It has been speculated that they might have chosen July 14 because it was Bastille Day, important in the tradition of commemorating the French Revolution. But June 16 has no such political logic. It turns out that June 16 and July 14 were very similar Sundays in terms of the moon phase. Both nights were only a couple days from a new moon, and therefore moonrise occurred a few hours after midnight. There would be no moonlight as the rebels moved into position and started their attack around midnight. Further, new moons, like full moons, create especially high and low tides. On both June 16 and July 14, the tide at Charleston was still coming in at midnight and would continue rising until near dawn. An incoming tide slowed the river currents and made crossing into Charleston safer. A full tide made the marshes navigable by small boats and canoes. High tide meant that the millponds were full and created obstacles for white, land-bound defenders. Somebody—perhaps Denmark Vesey—had consulted an almanac and had brilliantly suggested these Sundays as the most tactically advantageous.[61]

In addition to crossing the Ashley River, rebels planned for reinforcements from outside the city to cross the Cooper River or to come down the peninsula from the north. Like the Ashley crossing, the first strategic goal of these two additional attacks was to help city-based rebels capture any (or all) of several buildings where they knew guns or powder were located. The guns were mostly located along the spine of the peninsula as defined by King Street and Meeting Street. At the intersection of Meeting Street and Broad Street was the Main Guardhouse, where the city's core arsenal was stored and protected

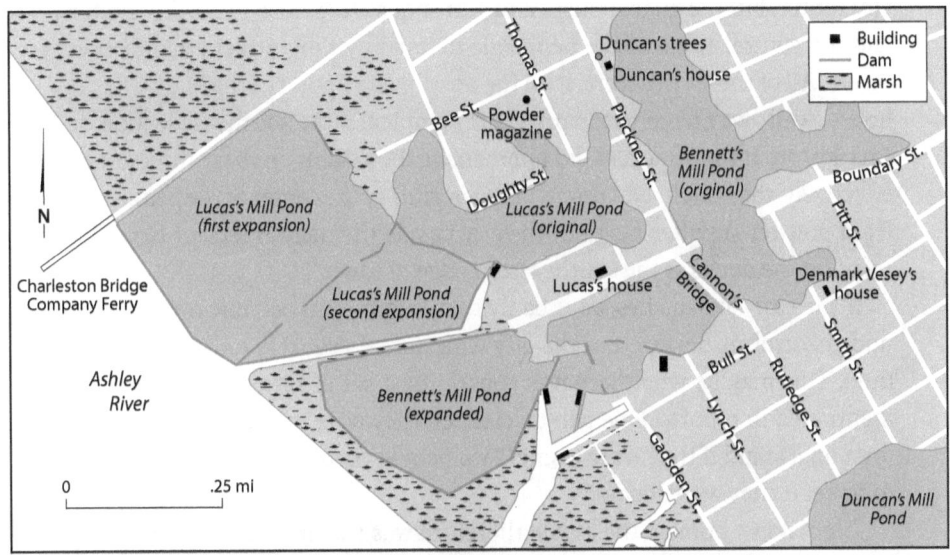

MAP 2.2 Mill complexes. See mappingblackcharleston.org for updates.

with scant security—a lone guardsman. Along Meeting Street, on the north side of Boundary Street, there was the smaller, so-called Piquet Guard House as well as the US Arsenal, which would have stored caches of guns, powder, and shot for ready use (see map 2.2). It is unclear how well guarded these sites were at night. A few yards away was Duquercron's Store at the corner of Tobacco and King Streets, where hundreds of guns and bayonets had been advertised for sale repeatedly in the fall. Lastly, a store farther north, at Mary Street and King Street Road, held the arms and some of the powder of the Charleston Neck Rangers—a state militia unit. Though the private store had changed hands frequently in the years before 1822, the planners appear to have known how to gain access easily and quietly. One of the recent proprietors had been Benjamin Hammett, an officer of the Rangers who appears to have continued to use a room in the store for the militia. His slave Bacchus had access to the key—something the planners reached out to confirm with Bacchus as they recruited him.[62] The more of these supplies and weapons the rebels could capture by surprise at midnight, the more likely it was that they would capture the initiative, and the early odds would tilt in their favor.

Mapping the targets to the geography, however, reveals that there were strategic problems to resolve. The primary targets were awkwardly distributed in three different areas. The gunpowder magazines were on opposite sides of the peninsula on the Ashley and Cooper Rivers and were well outside the

Take Freedom 73

city center, but the guardhouses and gun shops were close to the city center and the central spine of the peninsula defined by King Street and Meeting Street. All of these sites were, with the possible exception of the Main Guardhouse, well away from the main wharf complex in the southeast section of Charleston. If the attackers did not manage the assault on these three zones effectively, they might end up cut off from guns in the center of the peninsula, from powder supplies north of the city beside the main rivers, or from the ships on the docks at the southeastern edge of town.[63]

If the early skirmishes went badly they might even become trapped and find themselves besieged in the city with defeat probably only a matter of time. This may be why there was apparently a set of retreat contingencies mentioned in reports. One person claimed they were to retreat to the Lines for a final stand if they were losing. Two people claimed that fires were only to be set if they were losing.[64]

The riskiest hour of the attack therefore was the first hour, and nothing was as likely to prematurely alert the city than the plan to capture the Main Guardhouse. The city center around the Main Guardhouse was lit at night with gaslights, and the rebels apparently planned to solve this problem with a disguise and luck. Vesey reportedly acknowledged a plan to have an attacker wear a wig and white powder to try and appear white. They hoped the ruse confused the guardsman in the dimly lit night just long enough to keep him from sounding the alarm. Peter Poyas reportedly daydreamed optimistically that he just needed to get close enough to the guardsman so he could grab him by the throat and dispatch him with his sword. If this surprise ruse did not work and they failed to capture the guardhouse, the rebels would lose their advantage of surprise as alarms rang out across the city. In that case, the first hour of their assault would become very difficult and the entire insurrection might fail.[65]

This plan required tactics that were an enormous challenge for untrained attackers unless the whites remained unaware until after the attacks had begun. The rebels were able to form only the most rudimentary attack units. They would be loosely organized and have uncertain command and coordination. The draymen, for example, were expected to act as cavalry, but they had no opportunity to drill on maneuvers as a unit. Their cohesion derived entirely from the fact that they knew each other from worksites and they were expert horsemen. If they named a commander they recognized, they probably could have maneuvered together and been effective much of the time. But they might just as well have dissolved into chaotic movements and scattered when challenged by better-trained and equipped opposition. The attack groups coming from plantations, on the other hand, had experience working together as an organized and disciplined task gang under an enslaved driver. Such drivers could become commanders of task gangs that became informal militia. In fact, on at least the Ferguson plantation, the driver was apparently the linchpin to forming a military unit out of the work gang on the farm. Historians have also observed this transformation of drivers into martial commanders in the Haitian Revolution. The enslaved sugar workers in Haiti were accustomed to taking commands from enslaved drivers; they knew the voice and the person and perhaps trusted them. In South Carolina, a few years after the 1822 uprising, a driver-commander would lead a *marronage* of "Eighteen Slaves" who "went off under the driver" and sustained themselves as a unit for some time. If the 1822 rebels planned to do this, it would have resolved much of their command problem, but we do not know how many plantation drivers planned to take on such a role.[66]

Mapping reveals that the plan might have compensated for deficiencies in equipment and training by placing groups of rebels near their targets the night of the attack. For example, one man claimed that a group was planning to sleep at the cooper shop of James Mitchel on Smith's Wharf on East Bay Street the night the rebellion was to begin. Smith's Wharf was less than a block from Charleston's banking and insurance institutions near the Broad Street and East Bay intersection (see map 1.2). The rebels wanted cash from these sites to assist with resettlement. Smith's Wharf was also only about three blocks from the Main Guardhouse. From Smith's Wharf, the attackers could make a straight line down the alleys to the guardhouse, avoiding the gaslights on Broad Street. Reports also show that Gullah Jack asked Yorick Cross to arrange for twelve men to stay in his wife's yard the night of the attack, which would have placed a unit within a block of the Piquet Guard House, the US Arsenal, and Duquercron's Store.[67]

One report claimed that a group of plantation slaves was slated to cross the Ashley and land somewhere along South Bay Street at the tip of the peninsula. An especially good place for a surreptitious landing in 1822 was in the remnant marshes on the southwestern corner of the peninsula. This was ground Peter Poyas knew well as a ship carpenter at the Poyas Wharf immediately adjacent to these marshes (see map 1.1). Landing there with small boats or canoes, a contingent could enter the city unobserved, flank any mobilizing guardsmen, and assist in the capture of the Main Guardhouse. Once rebels within the city captured the Main Guardhouse's weapons, countryside reinforcements moving up from South Bay Street and west from East Bay Street would improve their ability to oppose a white counterattack.[68]

How might the organizers have come to such strategic conclusions about a multidirectional assault on tactically significant sites? One answer has always been that Denmark Vesey was a reader who was aware of the Haitian Revolution and some of the battles fought in Haiti. That certainly was true, and it must have contributed to decisions about the attack. However, some of the core planners had been adults in Africa when they were captured. They had witnessed or participated in maneuvers. Perault Strohecker had been captured in battle and enslaved as a result. As a son of a king, he had likely been in a command role. Moreover, Perault was not the only 1822 rebel who understood diversion and flanking maneuvers. Gullah Jack, Monday Gell, and several others of the core planners had likely been enslaved by raiders. They and their kin had possibly tried to fight off the attackers in some organized way—perhaps many times over years. Some communities were regular targets and therefore developed concerted defense plans to fend off slave raiders. To defeat raiders, even small villages sometimes built defensive works. They practiced maneuvers to divide attackers, kill them, or evade them. Thus, the slave-trafficking system itself gave a portion of the uprising movement familiarity with combat tactics.[69]

Strategic experience helps explain how the attackers came up with what appear to have been their most insightful choices. At least two groups may have been designed to commence the attack from a camp at Bulkley's Farm. For months, Gullah Jack had been holding all-night ceremonies at the farm. On the night of the attack, the familiarity with the farm that scores, possibly hundreds, of enslaved people had gained would become useful in a new way. The farm was near the fork of Meeting Street Road and King Street Road and had great access to both of these routes into the city. It also had excellent access to Pinckney Street, which was the least trafficked of the routes through the Lines into the city (see map 1.1). The north and south sides of the Lines on Pinckney were sparsely populated. The neighborhood was flood prone, which was good for the tidal mills and a slew of slaughterhouses that notoriously dumped offal into Bennett's Mill Pond. Groups of attackers camping at Bulkley's Farm could have entered the city by crossing from Meeting Street Road to Pinckney and heading south (see map 1.1). This move flanked the more densely occupied King Street Road and Meeting Street Road corridors, which in 1822 had numerous small shops and houses along them.

Bulkley's Farm was also a remarkably good staging point for capturing two powder magazines. The first was located about one and a half miles north of the Lines, east of Meeting Street Road. The site was surrounded by farms on three sides and marshes to the east. On the night of the attack, the draymen intended to rendezvous at Payne's Farm, a little distance south on the road. The farm was on high ground beside the road and was quite visible from the south. It was also probably well known to the enslaved, and Charleston-area draymen may have done quite a lot of carting to and from the farm. William Payne, together with his sons John Payne and William Jr., was the namesake of the Charleston company William Payne and Sons. Payne's company was one of the most active slave trading firms in Charleston at the time. It sometimes advertised dozens of people for sale. One ad was for an auction of 100 people, including whole families. Given how crowded their Broad Street storefront must have been on the eastern end near the wharves, they may well have frequently imprisoned enslaved people at their farm.[70]

Payne's Farm was a good rendezvous point because it was familiar, but Bulkley's Farm was where the rebels planned to store their horses before the attack. Both the location and the layout of Bulkley's Farm must have been high on the list of reasons the organizers contacted Billy Bulkley in late winter. Bulkley's Farm was closer to the powder magazine than Payne's. From Bulkley's farm, the powder magazine was less than half a mile across fields of dry ground undivided by creeks or roads. Bulkley's Farm had several structures, including livestock shelters. The draymen who would make up an irregular light cavalry using horses appropriated from their slavers wanted to store the horses there before the attack, and Billy agreed to let them. The Bulkley farm seems to have been under the care of its enslaved laborers for months at a time when the Bulkleys were in New York on business.[71]

A second powder magazine was located near the city boundary line. Lightly populated, this area was ideal for gunpowder storage. A magazine had been located there, "fronting Doughty Street" and just to the west of Thomas Street, in the first decade of the century. The city and some private persons stored the bulk of their most readily available powder in it. Mapping suggests that the uprising planners were aware of the facility and were specifically planning to take it.[72]

One night sometime during the spring of 1822, Monday Gell, Gullah Jack, Denmark Vesey, and Frank Ferguson reportedly held a meeting outside in Cannonsborough, at or near the intersection of Pinckney Street and Doughty Street just north of Boundary Street. In the court records the site is identified as being under "Mr. Duncan's Trees." Probably, this indicated the prodigious arbor Patrick Duncan had planted at his mansion on Pinckney—a landmark in the town at the time (see map 2.1). Frank Ferguson told the court that they met at this landmark to discuss the uprising plan, but he did not say why and the tribunal did not offer an explanation. Why meet here on the edge of the

FIGURE 2.2 Lucas's house (built in 1809) on Boundary Street. Photo by the author, 2021.

city far from the prime targets? The answer is that it gave them the chance to examine and discuss (1) Cannon's Bridge as a tactical choke point and (2) the powder magazine as a target.[73]

Duncan's large house and grounds were on the eastern side of Pinckney Street, a couple blocks north of Boundary. The site was outside the city guard's jurisdiction because it was outside the city boundary. In addition to being at a higher elevation and serving as a vantage point over the ground subject to flooding, the area became a small peninsula in Charleston Neck at high tide. Whenever the millpond was filled, the ground around Duncan's house remained a peninsula until the millpond was drained to power Bennett's Mills. When flooded, the area's only connection to the city to the south and east was via Cannon's Bridge (see map 2.2). On the night of the planned attack, the tide would be nearly full and still rising at midnight, filling the millpond like a moat. The powder magazine would be isolated from the city, with only Cannon's Bridge offering a quick connection to town.[74]

The uprising planners wanted to capture Cannon's Bridge, and they tried to recruit Bram Lucas and Richard Lucas to lead the attack. In 1809, their slaver Jonathan Lucas had built a significant house beside Cannon's Bridge—one of the few large houses on the far west end. Formidable and built of brick and stone, it still stands today (see fig. 2.2). In 1822 it was within the tidal mill complex, which included Lucas's own mills. Bram and Richard probably lived in or near the house or property somewhere, which meant they could reach the bridge within a minute or two. Capturing the bridge at high tide when the millpond was full would put a rebel force between the white militia's largest, most accessible weapons cache at the Main Guardhouse and its closest substantial powder supply on the Cannonsborough tidal peninsula. The rebels' smart strategic thinking about the geography and the powder magazines is impressive evidence of the plausibility of their plan.[75]

The initial attack stood a good chance of presenting Charleston with a fight for its survival. After this initial attack succeeded, one report claimed that the rebels would keep fighting until help came from abroad. Another report stated that at least some of the revolutionaries would escape the United States. In either case the wharves and docks that were mostly concentrated on the east end would become critical. Detailed reconstructive mapping reveals that several of the planners worked at and sometimes may have slept at sites near targets, such as Pritchard's Wharf, Vanderhorst's Wharf, Smith's (old) Wharf, and Crafts Wharf. The east side wharves were a space for storage, hiding, and escape by fugitive slaves. Such fugitives' knowledge could have informed the rebellion planners about how to use these sites as staging points, a defensive honeycomb, and pathways to escape.[76]

We know from testimony that some of the rebels planned to set at least one fire as a distraction, but other reports suggest that some planned to use fire only as a last resort if they were losing. The targets were Bennett's Mills on the west side and possibly some of the docks on the east side, such as Gadsden's Wharf or perhaps Mey's Wharf, where there were flammable naval stores that the rebels reportedly planned to commandeer. Such an attack would set fire bells ringing and send a large portion of white men of fighting age to the western and eastern edges of the peninsula. With fewer forces then at the center of the peninsula, the rebels would possibly find it easier to flee to the Lines for a final stand or to escape into the countryside, as one rebel reportedly claimed. If they got really lucky, lighting fires because they were losing might send enough whites to the edges of the peninsula to open a route to South Bay Street to commandeer ships at Saltus's Wharf and Poyas's shipyard.[77]

This plan was tactically logical but ran a significant risk of a fatal disaster if there were even small operational setbacks in the first hours. The rebels planned to gather people from the countryside into the city in such numbers that they could hold the city against white counterattacks. But Charleston is a peninsula. Concentrating all their movement's force in town would essentially trap them in a prolonged siege that they would lose when food and ammunition ran low. Staying and holding the city, as Peter Poyas apparently once suggested, was probably suicidal. They needed to capture Charleston's weapons supplies and break out of the city almost immediately by land or sea or both. Escaping the city northward by land would be a way to spread the rebellion and attempt the monumental task of taking the country from the white population.[78]

An escape by sea to Haiti was the most explicitly and specifically named geographic destination that the uprising movement planners articulated, according to reports. Denmark Vesey and others talked of fleeing the city for Haiti once the initial capture had been effected. They may have known that Northern activists who had lived in Haiti described the island nation as the best place for, in the words of one writer, "people of colour... active and brave men, determined to live free, or die gloriously in the defence of freedom." Haiti was the only place that the 1822 planners seem to have attempted to contact, and they appear to have monitored Haitian news. With the white militia at least temporarily disarmed by the rebels' seizure of their weapons and powder, unless the countryside exploded in supportive insurrections for a general abolitionist revolution, it was likely that escaping to Haiti on a flotilla of commandeered ships was the rebels' only chance of liberating themselves and their families, friends, and acquaintances.[79]

Black Skin, White Power

On a clear day beside the water near the end of May, William Paul stood on a wharf just below the fish market at the end of Market Street. The wharves jutted out into the Cooper River, receiving cargo and preparing ships for departure all day. Looking out at the water and the traffic, William noticed another enslaved man beside him. This was Peter Prioleau, though William did not yet know his name. Peter did not know William's name either, though he knew that William belonged to the Paul family. In front of them, ships and boats maneuvered the docks in the main shipping channel a few yards away. The two looked on in silence.[80]

In slave narratives, watersides are sometimes settings for forlorn or outraged reflection on slavery and freedom—sites for wondering about their treatment in a Christian nation (as in Harriet Jacobs's narrative) or for contemplating desperate feelings of abandonment (like Solomon Northrup). Frederick Douglass tells a story in his narrative of standing on the banks of the Chesapeake Bay, watching ships go by, pleading with God to know why he is a slave and discovering a resolve not to remain one. Perhaps William Paul had similar thoughts and feelings as he noticed a ship flying a flag he could not recognize. Peter and William were discussing the scene casually, when William decided to risk the serious topic on his mind. Did Peter know that the slaves in Charleston were going to throw off their bondage soon? Shocked, Peter turned to leave. But because they were in a crowded public place with people nearby who he feared might have noticed them together, Peter quickly retorted that he was entirely satisfied with his status and grateful to his master.[81]

William should not have said anything to Peter. He was a stranger, not a friend and not part of the movement networks. The movement now depended on what Peter might choose to do next with his own fear. A careful ethical discernment about power and danger presented itself to Peter as a dilemma—a problem without a good solution. Should he tell the whites and expose another enslaved person to the possibility of death? That would be condemned by large parts of the Black community, which generally expected people not to make such reports about unauthorized activities. Telling tales endangered people. It betrayed them to their exploiters. It should not be done. But Peter had not been told about a small-scale plan for a family or a couple of friends to escape. He had not been asked for help by a fugitive needing food or passage out of the city. Should he remain silent and risk the conflagration of the city that William seemed to intimate? Who would be hurt? He and family and friends alongside slave owners? If he did not tell, was there a chance someone else heard him and William talking and would report them, exposing him to punishment or even the risk of death by execution? He hesitated, but Peter decided to tell. Shortly after, William was arrested. Within a few days William had said enough to get Peter Poyas and a couple of others detained and interrogated. Feigning ignorance and surprise, Peter Poyas outwitted James Hamilton (the intendant of Charleston) and the city wardens and was released. William Paul, however, was not released. He just languished in "the black hole" where the guard had left him, though he said nothing more—for a while.[82]

Denmark Vesey apparently proposed to the other organizers to move the attack's date up from Sunday, July 14, to Sunday, June 16. This was a challenge, because they were not ready. They had been exaggerating their readiness to prospective recruits and had expected another month to make the exorbitant promises more realistic. Then, on the day before the new June 16 date, as the planners were working almost frantically to get everything together in time, the entire city guard suddenly came out into the streets fully armed. Not only had the element of surprise been lost, but the weapons and powder the attackers had hoped to capture for themselves and deny to the whites were now being carried around by white militiamen and cavalry. Two enslaved friends of Rolla Bennett's had revealed some of the details of the plan to white authorities. Their primary reason for telling—when the expectation would be to keep quiet—was apparently fear. It is incredible to think about, because their betrayal of their friend would cost him his life, but they probably told out of a Christian love for Rolla's immortal soul. Afraid of a war, they may also have feared the consequences of the mortal sin of murder. White authorities found and detained Rolla. Soon, others disappeared from the streets. Governor Thomas Bennett mobilized state militia units outside the city. Movement leaders went underground and members feigned noninvolvement and hoped not to be identified.[83]

When the waning sliver of the moon rose before dawn on June 16, its dim light shone only on armed white patrols. As dawn broke around 6 a.m., hundreds of enslaved people entered Charleston on the water for religious services. No battles and no general insurrection accompanied or greeted them. Men, women, and children arrived peacefully, perhaps mostly along the City Market wharf and public landing. Their arrival was a common sight on Sundays. The worshippers may have been surprised to learn that this time the city guard had been mobilized all night. They might have wondered what was happening. Perhaps a few already knew and wondered only whether their friends and relatives had been arrested. Intendant Hamilton ordered such Sunday arrivals counted and soon concluded that at least 500 enslaved and free Black people entered the city weekly. He speculated that the number was normally much higher under ideal circumstances.

As the epigraphs to this chapter suggest, the rebels had planned an uprising to take their freedom from whites, because whites *kicked and cuffed and abused* them while exploiting them and loved ones for profit regardless of their affections for each other or their status as free or enslaved. Further, whites had closed off all legal pathways to freedom, leaving organized rebellion as the only remaining option for emancipation of oneself and one's loved ones. In the weeks to come, the white reaction to the foiled uprising would demonstrate the truth of the rebels' protest: slavery was *dreadful* and its denial of Black people's humanity *abominable*.[84]

CHAPTER THREE

The Workhouse Fight

> These fellows behaved with so much composure . . . that the Wardens . . . were completely deceived.
>
> —A description of how two Charleston rebels outwitted interrogators

At the Workhouse, the movement became a fight for survival as one person after another was detained. The interrogators demanded to know the plan: Who had known? Who had committed to the movement? Who was the leader? The imprisoned rebels and others who testified seem to have used a different set of questions to guide how they answered. They seem to have wondered how to evade their captors. They tested to see how little they might say and how they might protect the movement, themselves, and others: Can I avoid naming people? Can I admit to writing? Do they already know about the gunpowder? Can I steer them away from Sarah Paul, from the women more generally, or from family, friends, and loved ones? Under interrogation, speaking deceptively or keeping silent were their best weapons, and they deployed them with the tact and fugitive ethics they had needed on the outside. Not every silence meant ignorance, nor did every speech signal mean compliance.[1]

Rounded up and incarcerated, the movement members' unity would soon begin to fragment. Their coalition had always existed without a unifying and shared goal beyond taking freedom. There had been no single unifying ideology about life after white supremacy. Denmark Vesey was virtually alone in making "rights of man" assertions. There were not many assertions of Christian justification besides Denmark's, either. The movement was influenced by Gullah Jack's medicine, Monday Gell's Igbo politics, Gullah culture, and other African indigenous knowledge as much as it was by Denmark. The rebels had come together and mobilized because slavery was *dreadful* and whites had been aggressively making it even more awful. There was even a rumor among the enslaved in early 1822 that whites planned to cull their numbers by slaughtering Black Charlestonians like surplus livestock. Trusting each other was sometimes challenging because of fear of surveillance and traitors, but the community value of not telling tales against other enslaved people facilitated cautious trust. The movement came together on this trust and the oath of secrecy until death. As the movement flowed into the Workhouse, the whites managed it like water impounded in a tidal millpond: they would let people out of confinement only once they had fueled the tribunal's investigation. Or to use another metaphor—one possibly close to perspectives of the enslaved—the whites planned to evaluate the detainees like livestock and cull those they perceived as guilty. The threat of death or banishment became a danger that each detainee had to face.[2]

Shortly after William Paul and a few others were detained at the end of May, Robert Harth affirmed his resolve to uphold the ethic against revealing secrets to the whites when, in the street, he rapped his knuckles on a tree box and declared to Peter Poyas and Ned Bennett that he will *never say one word* against them. Enslaved women such as Prudence Bussacre and Sally Howard made similar choices when they learned details of the movement from the men and did not reveal them. Of course, in the end, all three of these people gave evidence to the tribunal and that is how we know them by name and get a sense of what they said. However, their betrayals revealed, too, that they had followed the ethic of silence by holding their tongues for weeks, possibly even months.[3]

Most people with knowledge of the movement and who had been part of it never reported to the white authorities at all—ever. Susan Vesey and a group of women were reportedly ironing clothes in Denmark Vesey's house one night during a meeting about the rebellion planning. Neither she nor the other women present appear ever to have told what they saw or overheard, and Susan may have heard a lot over the series of meetings that happened in the house. An enslaved woman belonging to Mr. Cross reportedly had picked up bits of information that she passed on to other enslaved people, but she never came forward to inform the whites either. Sarah Paul, one of Denmark's children, cooked in Denmark's yard often and had multiple opportunities to overhear. She must have known things, yet she did not inform. Groups of draymen that Monday Gell said had joined the movement chose not to come forward with what they knew. When the tribunal itself eventually declared that parts of the story remained unknown because of people who kept silent, scores of people in the Black community did not need to be told. They already knew. They had deliberately stayed silent.[4]

The community's denial of information about the movement to white authorities was aided by the fact that many whites could not believe that their enslaved workers were unhappy in slavery. Whites allowed the comforts that enslaved workers provided them to stunt their understanding of how unequal power changed communication. In the luxurious Planter's Hotel, down the street from where Monday Gell's owner had his livery stables, one visitor journaled about the pleasures of "a warm bath" and a sumptuous dinner with local gentlemen. All the "grand ease" he experienced was prepared by enslaved people, who "impressed" him with how "respectable, happy, and healthy" they seemed. Sometimes he had "six or seven males, and as many females," attending to his needs. One or two were present "at all meals" merely to "fan away hungry flies" with peacock feathers. To him, there was "no want of happiness amongst" them.[5] But like masters more generally, he mistook a compelled performance of happiness for actually felt happiness. Such performances were no more about contentment than the birds in the City Market eating butchers' offal was about a preference for rotten and trodden meat waste. Willingness indicated compliance with a situation, not desire. They were safer from the worst harms when they complied. What the guests in the Planter's Hotel saw and misrecognized were people making choices to perform and avoid greater suffering. The ethical nuances of their consciousness, and how they deceived that visitor as part of the task, completely evaded him.[6]

Peter Poyas used this white delusion to outwit authorities when they arrested him the first time at the end of May. He helped James Hamilton and the wardens continue believing that he was merely the contented slave of a respected white shipbuilder on South Bay Street. Within weeks, however, he was no longer able to evade suspicion. When George Wilson and Joe La Roche came forward, they unwittingly confirmed what the still-imprisoned William Paul had said about Peter Poyas and the planned rebellion. The independent confirmation dispelled white delusion with a bolt of fear. Peter was arrested again. From then on, the whites' suspicions were alert and focused, though not quite at the level of paranoia and panic. With the new revelations, the movement's chances of success began a precipitous decline. The remaining leaders appear to have continued trying to coordinate an attack for a couple weeks after the arrests. There was reportedly talk of rescuing prisoners. But whites flexed their power, and interrogations led to more arrests. An agonizing rhetorical battle in the Workhouse ensued, like a fighting retreat over the truth of the movement. The records of the investigatory proceedings, executions, and banishments resulted from this fight.[7]

The Literature of the Tribunal

When the tribunal admitted that the silence of many of the enslaved prevented it from finding everyone involved, it conceded a kind of defeat that it tried to minimize. The tribunal insisted it had captured and killed enough rebels to intimidate others. However, Black resistance denied the tribunal even more than it may have realized. The community did more than withhold information. They shaped what the tribunal learned, too. They distracted and diverted the magistrates' attention, sending them down relatively safer lines of inquiry. Read this way, the 1822 archive becomes one of the most agonized, intimate, and detailed portrayals of Black struggle for survival during the era of chattel slavery. Its representation of Black agency complements what can be read in countless slave narratives. Texts such as Mary Prince's *History of Mary Prince* (1831), Frederick Douglass's *Narrative of the Life of Frederick Douglass* (1845), Solomon Northrup's *Twelve Years a Slave* (1853), or Harriet Jacobs's *Incidents in the Life of a Slave Girl* (1861) also offer portrayals of the struggle to take freedom and defend loved ones. Reading the love and loyalties of Black Charlestonians into the 1822 investigatory records, as this chapter does, reveals the wrenching but tactful choices of people treading in the pool of white power and struggling to keep up their stamina. A few people make awful decisions to betray others and save themselves. Others float, sodden or seething, resisting in a way that distorts the official story. Several very conspicuously choose to die rather than drag in family and friends, and their resolve helps an untold number escape the trap entirely.[8]

In June, Charleston employed a 1740 law for regulating enslaved and free Black people to form a tribunal. Consisting of two magistrates and three freeholders, the tribunal was given the task of investigating the insurrection movement, but unofficially it was always also an investigation of the Black community in general. It could authorize arrests and interrogate the detainees. It could conduct "trials" and decide guilt or innocence. But nothing about the proceedings or its recordkeeping was normative. There was no jury. There was no defense attorney unless the slavers of the accused wished to have someone there to represent their property interest. The tribunal had the ability to mete out punishment, including whipping, banishment, and death. There was no appeal of convictions. Armed with this rare and grave power over life and death, the tribunal quickly focused on the institutional and social life of the free and enslaved Black community. Almost without regard to contradictory evidence, they connected the organizing they learned about to (1) Black autonomy in the African Church, (2) unsupervised hiring out of the enslaved, and (3) the leadership of the freeman Denmark Vesey. They ignored or downplayed testimony that pointed to multiple enslaved leaders, to other churches, and to unrest over slavery and its racism. Over seven weeks of investigation they detained approximately 100 people, executed thirty-five, and banished thirty-one.[9]

Governor Thomas Bennett's enslaved men Rolla, Ned, Mathias, and Batteau would all be ensnared. Because of the potential loss of property, damage to his mill operations, and harm to his reputation arising from the accusations, Bennett himself became discomfited. Eventually he would move from discomfort to criticism of the proceedings, though he never doubted that the insurrection movement was real. In official correspondence and a circular, he questioned whether the tribunal was legally constituted, whether the tribunal properly used its authority, and whether all of its findings were fully proved against his enslaved people. He was skeptical of the proceedings and he directed his questions to the tribunal on at least two occasions discreetly. He also wrote to the attorney general of South Carolina. The attorney general affirmed the legality of the tribunal. However, Thomas Bennett nonetheless concluded that the "tribunal" had been "illegally constituted." He probably worried about the loss of property, knowing that the owners of enslaved people could expect only a fraction of the value of the enslaved who were executed, unless the legislature acted.[10]

Ironically, we have this critic, Governor Bennett, to thank for the only copies of the tribunal's own manuscripts, a fact that has never previously been documented. Bennett hired the clerk who made what have become the only known copies of the June and July investigatory manuscripts. It was a simple matter for Bennett to anticipate that the 1822 movement would be a major issue in the fall/winter 1822–23 legislative session. He had been a member of the South Carolina House of Representatives when an 1816 insurrectionary movement in Camden had become a legislative agenda item. To facilitate legislative discussion of the 1822 uprising, he could have simply distributed the tribunal's already published *Official Report*, which was mostly a volume of transcribed investigatory documents. He could have purchased two copies on the state's budget and given them to the House and the Senate. Instead, he chose to spend public money on the more difficult enterprise of having the original handwritten manuscripts copied in duplicate and distributed those copies to each chamber. Bennett also wrote his own narrative of the events, copied it, and gave each legislative branch his interpretation as a kind of introduction or cover letter. He had presumably read the *Official Report* as soon as it came out in October. His decision to present the full manuscript to the legislature appears to have been a political strategy, perhaps especially focused on the errors and oversights of his main rival, intendent James Hamilton.[11]

On November 20, Bennett paid Christopher Jeannerett thirty-five dollars for "copying" unidentified "documents." It was just a few days before the fall legislative session convened. To establish that the copies Jeannerett made were

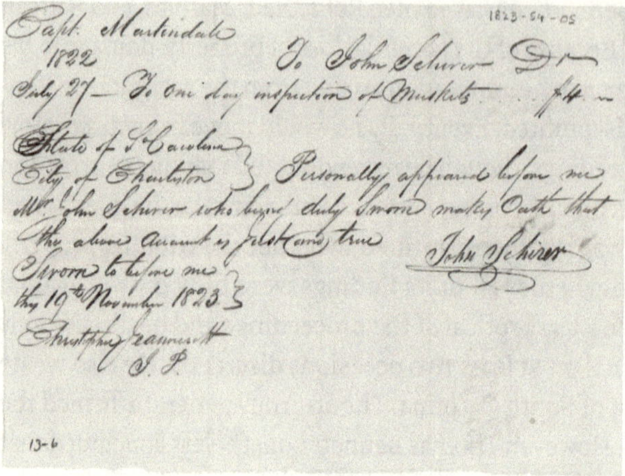

1823-54-05

Capt. Martindale
1822 To John Schirer Dr
July 27 — To one day inspection of Muskets ... $4.—
State of S. Carolina }
City of Charleston } Personally appeared before me
Mr. John Schirer who being duly Sworn makes Oath that
the above Account is Just and true
John Schirer
Sworn to before me
this 19th November 1823
Christopher Jeannerett
J. P.

13-6

FIGURE 3.1 A receipt from July 1822, copied and signed by Christopher Jeannerett in 1823. Item 54, series S165015, Petitions to the General Assembly, South Carolina Department of Archives and History, Columbia.

these investigatory records is tricky. The copies are unsigned. Our alternative is to determine whether Jeannerett's handwriting—and only his—matches the investigatory records. Fortunately, a previously unknown and uncatalogued document in the South Carolina Department of Archives and History offers a known handwriting sample for Jeannerett (see fig. 3.1). It is a very close match to the tribunal's records for June and July presented to the legislature. However, to be certain, we need to get writing samples for others who could have made the documents and eliminate them from contention, if possible. Bennett's handwriting does not match. Lionel Kennedy's and Thomas Parker's handwriting does not match. Handwriting identification in fact eliminates approximately forty other handwriting samples collected.[12]

Christopher Jeannerett's handwriting and the handwriting of the person who made the tribunal's investigatory records share a set of distinctive features that no other writing samples shared. Combined, these characteristics strongly support the idea that Jeannerett made the copies and eliminate all other possibilities (see afterword). Taken together with the fact that Bennett named Jeannerett as the person he paid for "copying certain [unidentified] documents" just before he presented copies of the investigatory records to the legislature, for the first time we can reliably ascribe authorship of the existing manuscripts: Christopher Jeannerett was the clerk who made the existing collection of tribunal records for June and July that have been preserved by the State of South Carolina since 1822. The originals—if they exist—are still lost.[13]

As soon as he commenced copying the tribunal's records, Jeannerett realized the papers were a jumble, but he had been hired merely to "copy" and not to "arrange" the papers. Arranging some of the government's papers was a different job, for which the governor hired a different person that year. And anyway, Jeannerett had never been a member of the investigatory tribunal. He had no special need to defend the proceedings. So he loyally reproduced the mess. His copies lack coherent pagination, are chronologically inconsistent, do not necessarily group papers from individual tribunal proceedings together, and do not always offer complete records of the proceedings against specific people. Some entire proceedings appear to be missing. The original trials and manuscript records were not faked. However, there was some manipulation of the evidence by tribunal magistrates Lionel H. Kennedy and Thomas Parker in their published report, which included some trial record transcriptions.[14]

Love, Loyalty, and Deception

Although the interrogations and trials appear to have been held almost exclusively in the Workhouse, captured people whom whites suspected of participating in the movement were detained in the Workhouse as well as the adjacent poorhouse and city jail. These detention sites all stood near the old arsenal on a single block on the northeast bank of Duncan's Mill Pond and defined by Magazine, Mazyck, Short, and Back Streets (see map 1.1). On the warm summer days of 1822, the detainees could smell the marshy pond. Back in 1819, a visitor had seen 100 people being held in the Workhouse. More than 80 percent were men, with the small minority of women being housed in a separate department. Because visitors were allowed throughout the facility, he was able to give a valuable description. It had "large and airy" rooms that could hold as many as twenty people each. And "the terror of the lash constantly brandishing" enforced the orders of the keeper.[15] He saw "black ministers . . . earnestly engaged in prayer with the black prisoners," one of whom was in jail for "the murder of his master." The Workhouse tried to separate prisoners according to the severity of the charges against them. Antislavery revolutionaries would certainly have been separated from the rest of the Black prisoners as much as possible. And during the uprising investigations, visitation was restricted to slaveholders, their representatives, and certain other officials.[16]

On June 19, Rolla Bennett—enslaved to the governor—became the first man to be led from his cell in the Workhouse and put on trial for his life. Nothing animated the ambitions of politicians in a slaving society better than slave insurrection, and this event implicated the sitting governor's reputation. Both Governor Bennett and his rivals knew the white public expected leaders to protect them from slave insurrection as much as from foreign invasion.

But for Thomas Bennett, Rolla was also valuable property. He wanted his property preserved if possible. This potential conflict of interest between what white Charleston wanted of him and what he might want for himself would soon lead him into trouble. Bennett made enemies because of how he responded to the tribunal.[17]

Magistrates Lionel Kennedy and Thomas Parker were well-established middling professionals in the city but with considerably less stature than the governor. In 1822 Kennedy was thirty-five years old. He was a state legislator, a sometime orator, and a lawyer. One prominent jurist described him as respectable but of somewhat lesser talents than some others. Kennedy had married into an interracial family—a connection that neither he nor any of his white relatives wished to admit publicly. Still, if he had any sensitivities to this fact, sternly regulating the Black population would help him exhibit sufficient seriousness about protecting slaving interests and the white citizenry.[18] Thomas Parker was younger than Kennedy, just twenty-nine years old in 1822. That year, he finished a five-year stint as treasurer of the St. Cecilia Society. Until 1820, the society had put on concerts. Parker owned a flute, engraved with his name and stamped to identify Charleston as the place of manufacture. Such an instrument was an indicator of his formal education. It also represented his aspiration for a reputation as polite and genteel. He would eventually partner with a group of men to buy and share a tract of land in the countryside for a summer retreat north of the city. In sum, both men were young, aspiring middle-class public figures when they became the lead magistrates on the tribunal.[19]

George Wilson and Joe La Roche were very credible. Both men came forward voluntarily; neither was ever detained or in any danger of imprisonment, nor were they forced to give their statements. These choices potentially went against their own interests, because they could have remained anonymous and silent. They could have pretended not to have known about the insurrection. Yet, instead, at the tribunal's proceedings against Rolla Bennett, Joe La Roche confessed something that was dangerous to say to men such as Kennedy, Parker, Hamilton, and the tribunal's white freeholders: he admitted that he had known about the uprising plan for months and had not warned white authorities. He even offered that he had promised to join the uprising if it ever launched and showed strength. Though he feared an uprising might be futile and thought killing was potentially murder and a sin, he revealed that he had been unwilling to betray Rolla, whom he considered a close friend. He had stayed silent because of contradictory fears and affections, but he ultimately informed against Rolla because of similarly contradictory feelings.

His affections for Rolla and his love for other friends, relatives, and the two children he had with Amaritta were in conflict. He had never been among the most committed to the movement, anyway. He had joined reluctantly. Now he feared the plan was weak and that he would lose everyone he loved. Joe's betrayal of Rolla was tragic. It was not a cold calculation for a personal reward.[20]

Rolla and Joe were both members of a religious study class, possibly within the African Church, though Rolla was a member of the Circular Church. These class meetings were confessional, and participants learned to understand and correct their own and each other's feelings and yearnings. Their trust and mutual affection was based in family connections and on this deeply religious and personal bond. George Wilson was almost as close to the two men because he was the leader of Rolla and Joe's religious study class. He had endeavored to teach them and grow with them religiously and morally through mutual confessional practice. On hearing about the plan on June 14, George persuaded Joe to report the uprising movement to the whites. George and Joe do not appear to have discussed fear of punishment by whites as a reason to confess, though that must have been a factor. Rather, their fears were mainly about each other as living friends and as immortal souls. George wept as Rolla declared he could not disavow a plan that was days away from execution. George's tears were tears of loss. The dilemma, a problem without a good solution, poked like a blade tip at George's consciousness. He was either going to let Rolla lose his soul through the mortal sin of murder, or he was going to report him and hope for leniency. And who else would be hurt if he stayed silent? His own friends might be killed in a futile and sinful attempt.[21]

Joe and George faced Governor Bennett's lawyer, who called four witnesses to try and impugn their credibility. But Sambo La Roche, who ostensibly was there to help Rolla, mostly hurt his defense, according to the manuscript records. He was the brother of Rolla's wife Amaritta, and he lived on the La Roche plantation. He told the tribunal that he sent word through Amaritta to Rolla that he would be in town on Saturday night last, which was the fifteenth of June, the night before the insurrection was planned to launch. Sambo implicitly admitted that he was part of the plan to pre-position rebels in and near the city and that Rolla's wife Amaritta carried messages for them. He asked witnesses if there was any enmity in Joe toward Rolla as a consequence of Rolla *taking* Joe's wife Amaritta from him. All four stated that as far as they knew Joe had no personal vendetta to settle with Rolla. All testified to the two men being *intimate, bosom friends*, and even *living like brothers*. At the close of the presentation of the evidence, Rolla himself reportedly confessed. He denied some charges, but he admitted the most important, made references to the biblical exodus, and named Peter Poyas as a fellow organizer. Then the court unanimously convicted him. Finally, Rolla gave a second confession to the Reverend Daniel Hall, a Methodist minister.[22]

The tribunal considered Joe and George highly credible, but they completely missed the significance of Amaritta La Roche. She was at the center of the relational network between Rolla Bennett, Joe La Roche, and Sambo La Roche. All the men were related through her. For these people, the insurrection story was a family story. They presumably had a desire to spare each other alongside a desire to spare themselves. Such affectionate ties were undoubtedly a powerful disincentive to invent a false story that would get Rolla punished. Moreover, the official blindness to the obvious logistical role of Amaritta is a key to reading the rest of the literature of the tribunal. She was a messenger, meal provider, and proprietor of the yard in which Joe and Rolla planned. Her brother Sambo lived on the La Roche plantation in the countryside, her ex-husband Joe visited in order to recruit people, and Amaritta was the messenger at other times. Yet the tribunal did not even want to interrogate her? Perhaps they considered her and her relatives on the plantation as outside the city's jurisdiction. But the tribunal's lack of interest in her should also be understood through their patriarchal assumption that men mattered as soldiers and women did not. Instead, slavers valued enslaved women as mothers—as breeders—of future property for owners. The tribunal's approach here indicates a predisposition to dismiss all indications of women's involvement in the movement. They were encouraged in this prejudice by rebel William Paul's testimony in May, and it shaped the evidence the tribunal gathered and the story the *Official Report* could tell.[23]

Joe credibly testified to a great deal that shaped the tribunal's decision to kill Rolla. He also shaped their early impression of the movement as a whole. Joe said he was told there were many slaves in the country already lined up to participate in the rebellion. Though nothing in the records proves a direct connection, there were active rebels in the surrounding parishes and there was some awareness of them among some of the rebels. In the most significant example, a slave named Joe killed a planter near Georgetown and then eluded capture in the Santee River region. He escaped even when organized militia units attempted to locate him when the General Assembly and Governor Thomas Bennett established bounties. Enslaved people "flew to his Camp" and Joe "soon became their head." The maroons lived safely in the midst of the Santee plantation country, well hidden, until an enslaved man gave information to white militias that made the destruction of the maroons possible. Even so, the rebels fought using "well charged musquets." A separate incident also in 1822 produced a small maroon community in Christ Church that included whole families and eventually even children who were born in the woods. In the *Official Report*, the court claimed that the Charleston uprising planners had traveled as far as Georgetown, Santee, Combahee, and the Euhaws. One enslaved person testified that they went as far as Hell Hole Swamp, a large swamp fifteen miles from Charleston, in the heart of Santee country. None of this proved coordination between the countryside and Charleston, but it demonstrates that a significant possibility of a wider uprising existed if an insurrection had commenced. Nonetheless, the tribunal was unwilling to believe slaves could organize effectively across so wide a territory, and the men within the movement who did the most for countryside recruitment—Peter Poyas and Gullah Jack—kept silent, thereby deliberately hamstringing what the tribunal could record, the people it could capture and punish, and the story it could tell.[24]

The proceedings against Rolla Bennett confirmed most of the tribunal's general story outline. From Rolla and a handful of other credible people they learned about the goals, the organizing methods, some of the leadership, the regional ambitions, and the idea of a multipronged attack on the city focused first on capturing weapons. Irregularities in Rolla's proceedings, as compiled in Jeannerett's copies of the tribunal's manuscript records, raise questions about the official story the Intendant and the tribunal later published. In Hamilton's *Negro Plot* and Kennedy and Parker's *Official Report*, the proceedings against Rolla and a few others appear much less formal than the published accounts claimed. Though the proceedings definitely happened, the manuscript reveals that some of the witnesses may not have been physically present in the Workhouse, as the published reports suggested. Instead, those witnesses' confessions or interrogation notes were perhaps simply read aloud for Rolla and counsel at the proceedings. And Rolla's own version of the story came out slowly and not entirely during the proceedings. He slow-walked his revelations, trying to tell as little as possible. Before the verdict and his sentence of death came down, Rolla claimed not to be able to remember anyone he saw at a meeting at Vesey's when he partially confessed. Though he named Denmark Vesey, he did not assert that Vesey was the overall head of the movement. Even after he was sentenced, he only named people—Ned Bennett and Peter Poyas—whose names the tribunal already had.[25]

The fact that Rolla eventually spilled his story was a betrayal of his oath to keep silent, but the slow and incomplete way in which he did so indicated maneuvers to deny the tribunal useful knowledge. He wanted their mercy. He wanted to survive. But he did not want to give people up if he did not have to. This was a pattern that continued throughout the investigations. Detainees engaged in a rhetorical fighting retreat for the duration of the proceedings. In response to the tribunal's questions, intimidations, and increasingly specific knowledge, other prisoners also chose secrecy, deception, partial confession, and deflection as tactics. Peter Poyas chose to keep completely silent and did not even attempt to defend himself. He admonished others *to die silent*, as he planned to do. Gullah Jack and Denmark Vesey did the same. They denied the charges and kept quiet, giving no revelatory statements. Other prisoners, like Rolla, dribbled out mostly true statements—or at least plausibly true statements—that omitted facts or deflected attention to others. Bacchus Hammett's and William Paul's testimonies were great examples of withholding, deception, and deflection. Even the men and women who named names seem to have practiced some deceptions and deflections on the magistrates, perhaps in an effort to protect people who had not yet been named. It was improvised, haphazard, and chaotic. It formed the official story in ways the tribunal did not fully realize.[26]

Peter Poyas was hauled out of his cell to be evaluated on June 19, according to James Hamilton's *Negro Plot*, but the tribunal's *Official Report* does not offer a date. Although the *Official Report* says that Peter's enslaver and his enslaver's lawyer were both present, the manuscript reports no formal trial and reveals that some of the statements against Peter were given on the twenty-first, two days after Hamilton says the trial occurred. Perhaps the tribunal magistrates had these accusatory statements read to Mr. Poyas and his lawyer on both dates and the published accounts are wrong. Perhaps the tribunal merely convicted Peter on the twenty-first. Either way, the confusion reveals that the *Official Report*'s representation of the tribunal as uniformly officious, punctilious, and accurate is not correct.[27]

Nonetheless, difficulties in the tribunal's timeline do not undermine otherwise credible statements. The enslaved man Robert Harth gave a highly credible statement about Peter on June 21. Robert spoke early in the proceedings—before many rumors may have gotten around. He was never detained, and he was given immunity by the tribunal for his testimony. He did not come forward on his own, but the tribunal claimed he agreed willingly and unhesitatingly when asked. The tribunal also claimed not to have received any evidence of any kind that Robert was part of the movement. Robert spoke mainly about Peter Poyas and barely mentioned Vesey. He did not identify leadership and he did not name many people, probably because he was not really part of the movement and didn't know much. But he reported that Peter worked hard to convince him to join. Trying to persuade him, Robert said that Peter told him the movement started back when the African Church was first attacked and harassed by whites in 1817 and 1818. All this time, Peter apparently told Robert, they had been meeting to discuss rebellion and had not been betrayed yet. Robert claimed to have learned many of the details of the attack plan, too. But he was not as compliant as he seemed. He followed the fugitive ethic of keeping secrets until the arrests began and he was approached for information. People enslaved by the Harth family, such as Mingo, were being named by detainees such as William Paul. Robert must have wanted to survive, but he probably did not want to put friends in danger. Perhaps this is why he only named people the tribunal already knew of, singling out Peter. The tribunal condemned Peter to death. However, the proceedings so far had demonstrated that the magistrates assumed there was an overall leader. They wanted a name.[28]

When Denmark Vesey was tried in the Workhouse a week later, on June 26–27, it was clear the court had already formed an opinion. The lead magistrates believed a free Black man such as Vesey was "absolutely necessary in the Chief of a conspiracy." At trial, several people gave statements against Vesey. On the twenty-sixth, three of the original witnesses who had named Vesey were "examined again," according to the Jeannerett manuscript copies. They were cross-examined by William Cross, Esq., as Vesey's counsel. Those witnesses were William Paul, Joe La Roche, and Rolla Bennett. William apparently testified that Vesey was always working toward persuading the enslaved to engage in an insurrection against white Charleston. He claimed to know Vesey fairly well, and he said Mingo Harth had told him that Vesey was the leader. Though the tribunal would conclude that Vesey was *the* leader, other witnesses testified either that Vesey was merely one of the leaders or that other men, such as Gullah Jack or Peter Poyas, were *the* leader. And William's statement was hearsay: he claimed to know only what Mingo Harth told him about Vesey's leadership. After William, Joe La Roche and Rolla Bennett gave statements that represented Vesey as interested and active in the planning and recruiting. Rolla appears to have told the proceedings that Vesey told him directly that he was the leader. However, Vesey may have meant that he was the leader of the band Rolla would be part of, in the same way that Monday Gell was the leader of the Igbos or Gullah Jack was the leader of the Gullahs. Though each man was cross-examined by Vesey's counsel, the tribunal's manuscripts only offer general notes that must be read alongside other statements.[29]

The last witness against Vesey on the twenty-sixth was Benjamin Ford, "a white Lad about 15 or 16 years of age." Ford's testimony is revealing because he does not seem to have anything material to say about Vesey committing a crime of any kind. Ford did not accuse Vesey of trying to incite insurrection, or getting weapons, or even offering a dangerously controversial opinion such as that slaves ought to rebel. Instead, according to the tribunal, he said that Vesey was bitter about hardships and rigid regulations and laws placed on "the blacks," by which he seemed to mean free and enslaved Black people in Charleston. Ford declared that Vesey felt "the blacks had not their rights." Other than that, Vesey had mostly talked with Ford about religion and applied it to slavery, apparently suggesting that slavery was immoral and contrary to God's will. It was a highly credible description of Vesey's character but not evidence of what the law would consider a crime. Its admission is meaningful to historians as a description of Vesey's critical intellect, but as a matter at trial it was perhaps prejudicial. It suggested that Vesey must be guilty of leading the insurrection movement because he had an educated, critical opinion against slavery.[30]

When Vesey's trial continued the next day, Frank Ferguson claimed that Vesey told a meeting that there was a "little man" with a "charm" (Gullah Jack) who could not be killed and that this man "would lead them" in the fight. This was the second time the court had been told that Gullah Jack may have been the overall general or leader. Frank said he knew Vesey but did not describe him as a friend. He had been to Vesey's house, but he also claimed that Vesey threatened him because he refused to join the uprising. According to the tribunal, Frank told Vesey that he felt he lived well. Vesey, annoyed, told Frank he was part of the problem. Reportedly, Vesey even threatened that he would remember Frank's unwillingness to help if they succeeded in taking their freedom. When Adam Ferguson spoke next he also added nothing that established Vesey as the sole leader and instigator. In fact, Adam described Vesey doing things very much like what Monday Gell, Gullah Jack, and Peter Poyas were doing: recruiting people, gathering resources, and identifying targets. Vesey was a courageous and critical recruiter and partner in leadership, but he was not the imperious, overbearing captain the tribunal wanted him to be.[31]

During his appearance at the proceedings against Vesey, Adam Ferguson pointed to Jesse Blackwood in the courtroom and identified him as one of the men tasked with going into the country to recruit support. Called out so directly, Jesse apparently asked to speak and told those present about aspects of the planning that included Vesey. He expanded on the descriptions of Vesey's efforts to get word out to some of the outlying plantations. But Jesse said that as far as he knew, both Monday and Vesey were the leaders. This was at least the third time since June 19 that the court had heard of people other than Vesey being a leader, or even *the* leader. Yet despite the mounting evidence of multiple leaders of diverse origins, at the end of the proceedings against Vesey, the tribunal concluded that Vesey was the overall leader and sole originator.[32]

Vesey reportedly shed a single tear when the tribunal condemned him to death. He knew that he was morally not guilty. According to Reverend Hall, Vesey said he had only helped advance *a great cause*. Vesey understood that slavery was the crime, and he believed he had been planning a just war against that crime. The manuscript records do not contain a text of the tribunal's sentence, but the tribunal's published *Official Report* offers a version—possibly strictly accurate, possibly heavily edited after the fact, we might never know. In sentencing Vesey, magistrate Kennedy heaped morally stigmatizing language onto him. He ascribed to Vesey the sole responsibility for instigating the movement, despite the contrary evidence he had just heard. He scorned Vesey's assertions that the doctrine of natural rights applied equally to Black people. Kennedy then made one of the first public rebuttals to the substance of Vesey's biblical arguments that God wanted all enslaved people to be free. Instead, he quoted sections of the Bible telling servants to obey their masters. He explicitly identified Vesey with his race. In this and other sentences Kennedy handed down, he invoked the era's anti-Black stereotypes by referring to Vesey and the movement's members as "diabolical." It was all just an irrational "infatuation" of a barbaric people possessed of a desire to "riot" and indulge in "rapine."[33]

These racist tropes demonstrate why the magistrates and freeholders were so ready to condemn and kill a free person such as Vesey in a proceeding they would have found unacceptable as a felony trial for any white person. Vesey's proceeding was possible because the law allowed free Black people accused of insurrection to be tried by the slave law. Free white people such as the magistrates and freeholders of the tribunal would expect a jury of peers if they were on trial for their lives, but it was good enough for a free Black person to get a jury of prosecutors and judges. Enslaved people could not testify against free white people, but they testified against Vesey. The slaves who testified against him were not sworn in, because the slave code did not allow it—only the white youth Benjamin Ford was sworn in. Vesey had no right to appeal. Less than a week after his trial began, he was hanged and in his grave. The proceedings against Vesey and several other free Black people, such as Edward Johnson, Saby Gaillard, Prince Graham, Quash Harleston, and Robert Hadden, demonstrated the same racist dynamics even though the punishments were less severe. The Reverend Morris Brown was not formally accused by the tribunal, but he was forced to leave the city and his church was destroyed. That he had to leave Charleston permanently only underscores the precarity of free Black people's rights in South Carolina. Slavery's racism smothered Black freedom.[34]

But the enslaved were not quite ready to give up, according to reports. Yorick Cross met Charles Drayton in the street on July 1. They discussed the fact that Denmark Vesey, Peter Poyas, Rolla Bennett, and three others were scheduled to be hanged the next morning. Charles apparently urged him to be ready to attack at any time in order to free the prisoners and start the revolt. Inside the Workhouse, the men were anticipating death. Peter Poyas reportedly told his cellmates to die silently, as they would see him die. There were rumors of a possible rescue. Early the next morning, before six, Yorick Cross, Harry Haig, Charles Drayton, and others waited for Gullah Jack to order them to launch the attack. But no order came.[35]

After sunrise on July 2, Denmark Vesey, Peter Poyas, and Rolla Bennett, as well as Jesse Blackwood, Ned Bennett, and Batteau Bennett, were led to the scaffold. It was a long walk from the Workhouse on Magazine Street to the gallows east of Meeting Street Road, north of the Lines. Situated on "Blake's Lands" near the former New Market racecourse, the gallows may have been in sight of Payne's Farm, where the draymen had hoped to rendezvous the night of the attack on June 16. That morning, those six men became the first movement participants to die for the cause. No order as to how to bury their bodies seems to have been given, but existing city ordinances would have mandated that they be brought back to Charleston and interred at the city's public burial ground. The death of these movement leaders and members, and the failure to even attempt to rescue them, was ominous for those still out of the tribunal's reach. After their friends had been hanged and they had done nothing to stop it, Yorick Cross and Charles Drayton bumped into each other again in the street. They discussed regrets and hoped they would continue to escape the whites' grasp.[36]

White authorities displayed their power on the Fourth of July. At 6 a.m., the militia mustered outside the Main Guardhouse at Broad and Meeting Streets for a parade. Their assembly had been promoted in the city newspapers for days. Governor Bennett ordered live ammunition, and the armed parade marched east down Broad Street and then south on East Bay Street to the Battery. They fired live ammunition in artillery and small arms salutes. The rebels were in custody, on the run, or in the grave.[37]

It was ironic to celebrate liberty while possessing slaves and repressing their desire for liberty. Highlighting that liberty-and-slavery paradox in this period has been an important theme for historians. However, another perspective emphasizes how this contradiction formed a racializing and colonizing republican culture for the United States and for South Carolina. Creating policy that structured society around the subordination and exploitation of Black bodies was a part of how whites produced the wealth and the political institutions to support the liberty they wanted. Governor Thomas Bennett ran his mill with skilled Black slaves and marginalized free Black laborers alongside white workers. The racist structure of his society was highly profitable to him, and it benefited white workers over both free and enslaved Black workers. Political citizenship and its social benefits were restricted to white people. The needs of slavers and the protection of slaving from the enslaved were central priorities in South Carolina and the United States more generally. This was a shaping, productive, and long-standing reality of South Carolina: racialization was a part of its modernization and democratization. The Fourth of July was an opportunity for this "rational liberty" of racial hierarchy, a white republic, and profitable slavery-based commerce to celebrate itself. According to Governor Bennett, that order must dominate the parade's display as well as the life of the city. Calling for precision and punctuality from the parading white militia, Bennett observed that only such discipline would properly express unequivocal gratitude for the happiness the republic created. Bennett mourned the loss of his property in Rolla, Ned, and Batteau. He had pled for the tribunal to ease their sentences. But he accepted the outcome nonetheless. He had not used his pardon power to save their lives.[38]

The growing confidence of the white community aside, the community ethic of silence and the movement oath of secrecy had continued to hold: Vesey and Peter had died without naming names, and the tribunal remained unable to identify most of the movement's participants. Monday Gell watched the example set by Peter and Vesey and did not speak. Gullah Jack was jailed, but he also stayed quiet. Charles Drayton was arrested and kept quiet. The women closest to the participants had also stayed silent and evaded interrogation, but like the men there were some who had divulged information. Sally Howard was possibly the first woman to speak to the tribunal when she spoke against Jesse Blackwood in late June. She knew Jesse Blackwood well and he benefited from Sally's silence for some time. Jesse came to Sally's master's yard to see his brother, but Sally did not like what he had to say. For weeks—maybe months—across several visits she heard him speak about the uprising movement and did not reveal the plan to authorities. She only threatened to inform when the mid-June wave of arrests following George's and Joe's revelations got underway. She told Jesse she would inform if he kept talking about killing all the white people in her master's yard. Why had she kept quiet about it until then? She knew that such talk could get them all into difficulties, but she had not revealed anything to the whites. The sharpening racial hostility toward Black Charleston since the late 1810s might have informed both her silence and her decision to talk. Perhaps she both supported and feared rebellion, like so many of the men. Her commitment to confidentiality was perhaps strengthened by the fact that she was related to Jesse. Her mother was Jesse's brother's wife. While the danger of keeping Jesse's secret was less than the danger of revealing it, she would probably want to protect him. Her family would likely expect it. But as the story got out, the danger increased and the family's ability to protect not only him but her and others diminished. Her continued silence might become untenable. Her case is a model of how some people decided to end their silence as June became July.[39]

Her decision to inform against Jesse was a betrayal but it was not sneaky. She had warned him she might talk. Her betrayal was driven by how the Workhouse investigations changed relations of power and the impossible dilemmas this forced. Eventually, betrayal looked like survival for her and others. Her decision was not craven interest in personal reward, and there must have been many men and women with information much like hers who did not speak to the tribunal. Jesse placed her and the rest of their loved ones in some danger through his organizing. However, the day that seemed to set her on the path to making disclosures was June 16. This was the day the rebellion was expected. Jesse had been up all night. He arrived at Sally's yard so early in the morning that his brother hadn't even arrived yet. Jesse waited and when his brother arrived, Sally overheard Jesse say that he had a horse with which to go into the country. She heard him describe the plan to bring enslaved people down to take the city from the whites. All Saturday night long into Sunday morning he'd been attempting to get out of the city to meet them. Though two patrol parties allowed him to pass, a third party brought him back. Incredibly, they had not imprisoned him in the Workhouse for violating the curfew. Sally listened to Jesse narrate his difficulty. The city guard had been out in force throughout Charleston all night for the second or third night in a row. Several men had been arrested, but Jesse was not intimidated. He only wished that there were more intrepid men like himself. And he swore that the rebellion would still happen. By 3 a.m. Monday morning, all the white people would be killed. She had never had arguments with Jesse, but he might get them all into trouble now. When whites started

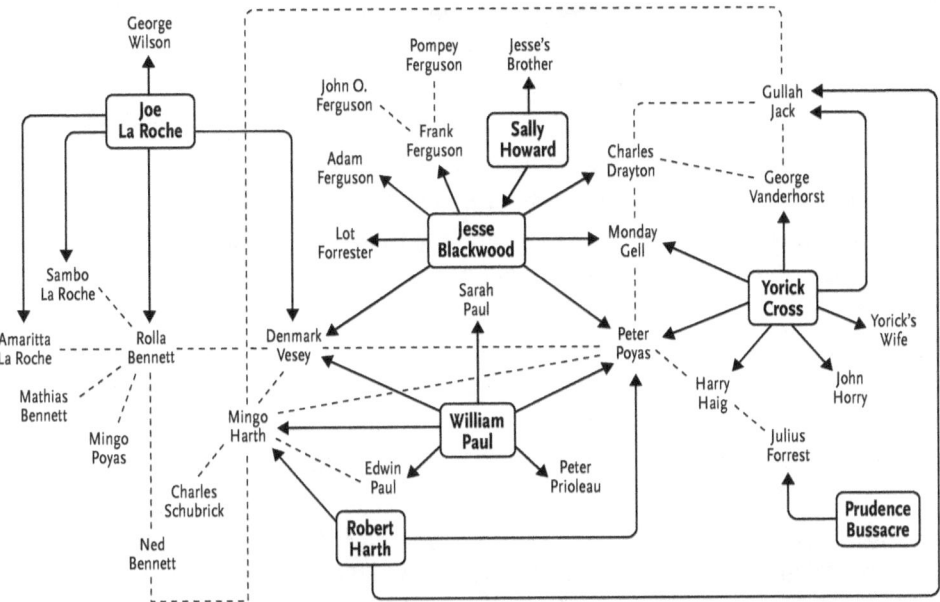

FIGURE 3.2 Social network flowchart for certain testimony in the 1822 investigation of the uprising movement in Charleston. The flowchart shows speakers' names in boxes. Solid lines with arrows connect each speaker to the people they mentioned. Dotted lines indicate someone that the speaker heard about through an intermediary.

asking about Jesse sometime around June 23, she answered their questions. The social bonds and the value of mutual protection that had kept her silent now urged her to betray the story to limit the harm.[40]

We can visualize how information flowed confidentially through personal relationships and see how these relationships then structured the Workhouse fight by using a social network flowchart (fig. 3.2). More than the published accounts of the proceedings, the manuscript records reveal how family relationships and friendships formed what the tribunal learned. When Rolla Bennett faced the tribunal, almost everyone who spoke for or against him were siblings, spouses, bosom friends, or close confidants. The relationships among Joe La Roche, George Wilson, Sambo La Roche, Amaritta La Roche, and Rolla Bennett were the context of their organizing and their testimony. We should look to that context for causes, and we should not accept the assertion that people such as Joe La Roche would premeditatively, cynically, or tremblingly turn on beloved friends and relatives without direct evidence of such a motive. Everyone was aware of the danger white power represented to beloved friends and relatives as well as to themselves. George and Joe appear

The Workhouse Fight 101

to have believed they were rescuing a friend and their people from a futile, calamitous rebellion, and they mistakenly—even foolishly—overestimated the likelihood that whites would be merciful toward Rolla.[41]

Amaritta only appears briefly in the investigatory archive, and she never spoke to the tribunal. She never broke her silence, and she was not detained. This was true even though she became part of the organizing when she carried messages between Charleston and the La Roche plantation, where her brother Sambo La Roche lived, about twelve miles away on St. John's Island near Stono. Sambo had certainly chosen his sister for a messenger because he already knew she was familiar with what her former husband (Joe) and her current husband (Rolla) were planning. He knew she would reliably relay his message and easily get by the patrollers while traveling with or for her slaver, her mistress, who kept a house in the city.[42] Amaritta probably made the trip often, and maybe on her own sometimes. She was one of many women making similar trips. The city markets drew enslaved women from the countryside into the city on a regular basis to sell and buy food. She had prepared meals for Joe and Rolla while they discussed the uprising plan. She ended that service by carrying Sambo's message that he would be in town the Saturday night before the uprising launched. The feelings in this social group were so strong that George wept and Joe, having betrayed Rolla, became distracted with remorseful feelings about the awful betrayal he had visited upon his friend. Yet Amaritta, despite clear evidence of her opportunity to learn details and assist the movement, had not been arrested, had not been asked to give a statement, and had not even been brought by the La Roche family to court to try to defend her husband Rolla. Perhaps her mistress was afraid she would be arrested and more of her property would be at risk. Perhaps Amaritta was kept on the plantation outside the tribunal's jurisdiction.[43]

The court generally downplayed or ignored such social connections in the *Official Report*. However, these relationships were pivotal. Like Rolla Bennett, other movement members and participants were also organizing with friends and relatives. Denmark Vesey's son Sandy was married to a sister of Jesse Blackwood's wife. Sally Howard's mother was married to Jesse Blackwood's brother. William Paul's slaver also owned Sarah Paul, who was Denmark Vesey's previous wife's daughter. These are just some of the family, friendship, household, and coworker connections among the free and enslaved people ensnared by the tribunal in 1822. We can layer and correlate these relationships to the communications among the most credible, early statements to the tribunal. Visualizing this evidence in figure 3.2, we see how the flow of information to and from Prudence Bussacre, Yorick Cross, Robert Harth,

Sally Howard, Jesse Blackwood, Joe La Roche, and William Paul both overlaps and diverges in complimentary ways. The flowchart shows speakers' names in boxes. Solid lines with arrows connect each speaker to the people they mentioned. Dotted lines indicate someone that the speaker heard about through an intermediary. For example, Prudence Bussacre spoke directly with Julius Forrest and learned from him that he was speaking with Harry, but she did not speak with Harry directly. The flowchart shows that at least one woman was close to each of these groups. Women seemed to know about the movement—though almost no evidence suggests a high likelihood of their active participation in it, with the possible exception of Amaritta La Roche.[44]

Read without reference to his relationships and to other testimony, William Paul's statements about the movement to white investigators seem questionable because he had been arrested and might have feared severe punishment or death. At first, William denied having said anything to anyone about an uprising. When he started confessing, he gave up only a little information. His more extensive revelations came after suffering several days' imprisonment in "the hole," presumably alone. The court itself observed that, over time, he probably came to fear the "scaffold" and "summary execution." However, as horrible as the hole certainly was, we should not assume a simple mechanism from fear to false confession. Fear makes experienced people tactful in the face of interrogators. It does not necessarily make them fabricate information. Likely, William had experienced or witnessed white interrogations, humiliations, and beatings multiple times. He probably knew that lies could help him only if he did not get caught. When he did start talking, he held back information. He gave just Mingo Harth to the investigators. Later he added that he had also spoken directly with Edwin Paul about the rising. He added details to the overall reporting. However, he continued to profess an inability to recall the specific names of some people and places. Eventually, he said that he spoke directly with Denmark Vesey. In the end, in total, he named Mingo Harth, Peter Poyas, Ned Bennett, Edwin Paul, Sarah Paul, Denmark Vesey, and Gullah Jack. People he was not personally close to were among the first people he named (Mingo and Peter), and those he was closest to were commonly among the last he named.[45]

That William named people he was closely associated with only later suggests that he tried to protect them from the tribunal at first. Within his slaver's household of co-sufferers, William had friends, especially Edwin Paul (a fellow slave in his household), Sarah Paul (who probably cooked for William), and Denmark Vesey himself (who visited the yard sometimes). Because he named them only after extended confinement in the hole, judging his betrayal of them as a capricious, cynical act would misunderstand what happened. He lost a harrowing struggle with white authorities who were fully empowered to abandon him in the hole virtually forever if they chose. Cornered after weeks of rhetorical retreat, William was revealed as unwilling or unable to resolve to die silently. Dejected, he begged the tribunal to leave the women alone, reportedly claiming they knew nothing about the movement. Much of William's story was soon independently confirmed by Joe La Roche and Robert Harth (see fig.3.2), both of whom were never accused or imprisoned with William Paul or anyone else.[46]

In figure 3.2, the set of lines radiating out from the name Yorick Cross further confirm names others had volunteered already. Like Joe La Roche and Robert Harth, Yorick Cross was not arrested. Further, Yorick was even promised protection from prosecution before he made any statements to the tribunal. He did not need to fear punishment very much, to the extent that the promise of immunity could be believed. Yorick named Gullah Jack as a major ringleader, but Jack had already been executed. He named several other men who became very important to the proceedings, most especially Monday Gell and Charles Drayton. In addition, importantly, Yorick independently confirmed details that William Paul had offered in prison. Yorick confirmed William's identification of Gullah Jack and Peter Poyas as part of the uprising. Lastly, Prudence Bussacre had also come forward voluntarily without being imprisoned. Her testimony was about Julius Forrest, a man she had raised practically as her own child. Julius told Prudence that he hoped Harry had not mentioned him to the court. Prudence's testimony, therefore, independently confirms Yorick Cross's information about Harry Haig.

Prudence Bussacre and Sally Howard (see fig. 3.2) seemed to know almost no one involved—unless they were keeping information from the tribunal. Prudence came to know of Julius Forrest's participation only because of her close relationship with him. In her testimony, she described the admonitions she had previously given to Julius to stay away from Harry Haig. She spoke in a way that suggested she had understood Harry was a source of danger or trouble. Sally Howard claimed to have heard several conversations about the planning but could name only Jesse Blackwood. She had been present for the conversations because "his brother" was enslaved in the same household with her and married to her mother. And even though these relatively marginal people—Sally, Prudence, and Robert—named people whom others were also naming, neither they nor any of the other speakers named one another (see fig. 3.2). They might not have even known one another. Furthermore, their general fact patterns about when and how the plans were supposed to work complement each other. They had known these details for weeks or months and had kept quiet because the people from whom they had learned the information firsthand were friends and relatives they wanted to protect. They loved one another, not slavers.[47]

Because Black Charlestonians kept each other's dangerous secrets, if Gullah Jack wondered whether he should flee to avoid capture, he might have reassured himself. He believed with certainty that his healing powers could protect him from the whites, according to Yorick's statement to the tribunal. Experience had taught Jack that whites could not capture him on their own. From the beginning of his enslavement to North Americans in 1805, none had been able to take his medicine bag from him, prevent him from practicing, or shave his distinctive facial hair. In 1822, Jack still had his medicine bag and his whiskers. On June 30, he tricked two investigators who came to Pritchard's Wharf looking for him. Investigators were actively seeking him based on his distinctive appearance. Anticipating that he would be sought out this way, Jack had shaved his face. When the investigators arrived at Pritchard's they walked right up to Jack and failed to recognize him. When they asked him if he knew Gullah Jack, he said he did not, and they departed. Prophetically, Jack believed whites would capture him if they were helped by Black people.[48]

Yorick Cross and Gullah Jack were both Africans, and they had become close associates in Charleston. Yorick told the tribunal that he had known Gullah Jack for a considerable time. Their work brought them together. And he narrated numerous specific visits and encounters with Jack during spring and early summer. He admitted that he had joined the movement. Even after the arrests had started, he had kept silent for weeks. After Jack was detained on July 5, Yorick said he had participated in discussions to launch a rescue attempt on July 6 and free the prisoners (including Gullah Jack). But now he was betraying all that history and breaking his vow of secrecy. Why? He had not been arrested and he valued Jack's skills so much that he refused to return Jack's "cullah" (crab claw) when Jack demanded it. If he gave evidence, there had to be a powerful motivator.[49]

Gullah Jack was already imprisoned in the Workhouse when Yorick spoke up. Peter Poyas was already dead. It was proof that Jack's protective medicine was not working, and Yorick may have feared he would be named. He knew he could argue Peter Poyas had cajoled him into the movement. Peter had threatened to turn all of Yorick's country people from Africa against him, but Yorick might wonder whether the white tribunal would care. He had feared from the beginning that the movement would prove too weak. When he had agreed to join, he conditioned his willingness on the movement coming out with enough strength to beat the whites. It was over. Hopefully, the white tribunal would believe that he was a cajoled skeptic and not a truly ardent believer if he were named before he came forward. Yorick had less to fear from the movement's power to enforce secrecy, too. The executions on July 2 proved that the movement was brittle, and in fact it was crumbling. Jack's reported plan for a July 6 uprising was more desperate than the July 2 rescue. Defeated and regretful of the danger he was in, Yorick nonetheless only told the whites his tale when they came asking. In answering their questions he betrayed his friend and manifested Jack's prophesy that Black people would be his undoing—that whites could not defeat him on their own. But neither Yorick nor anyone else had signed up merely to die. They had agreed to take freedom for themselves and their closest beloved people. They were not looking for martyrdom. With the prospect of taking freedom fading, the movement was ending.[50]

When Gullah Jack was arrested toward the end of the first week of July, Monday Gell had not been condemned to death yet. On July 1, Monday had declared himself innocent in his proceeding before the tribunal, but the magistrates and freeholders pronounced him guilty. When Jack entered the Workhouse days later, he joined Monday in refusing to name people, perhaps heartened to see his old neighbor and friend Monday still keeping silent while awaiting the tribunal's decision. If he had the chance and the inclination, Monday might have told Jack how he had witnessed powerful examples of silent resolve from Denmark Vesey and Peter Poyas when they were awaiting their execution with Rolla Bennett, Jesse Blackwood, and others. Jack knew they were dead, but did he know how they had behaved in the Workhouse? James Hamilton wanted to jail the detainees separately, but there were still too few free rooms in the Workhouse at this stage. So Monday would have heard Peter Poyas's speech reminding them all to die refusing to talk. Monday would have heard—or heard about—Vesey scornfully declaring to a group of white ministers who visited to question him that he was to die for a righteous cause and that he would tell them nothing. He would have watched these partners and friends being led out to their execution in the morning. He might have told Jack all this. And when Charles Drayton and John Horry were also arrested, he might have told them, too. After they were all tried and convicted "there appeared to be a pause" in the investigation. No new revelations emerged.[51]

During the day on the ninth, the court sentenced Monday Gell, Charles Drayton, Gullah Jack, and John Horry to death. The *Official Report* claims that Kennedy sentenced Gullah Jack in particular with a formal statement. Kennedy denounced Jack in derisive and pejorative terms, such as "wicked," "mummery," and "superstitious," and asserted that his indigenous medicine was only able to influence people who were governed by ignorance. To him, Jack was a barbarian practicing the dark arts of the devil.[52] With this, Hamilton believed there was "some prospect of the investigation closing" after the killing of these four detainees was carried out on July 12.[53]

The Workhouse briefly jailed these possibly last condemned men together after their sentencing while guards arranged separate cells. Charles Drayton was understandably agitated and upset about being condemned to die in a couple days. In the street just a few days earlier he had told Yorick that he was ready to rise up on the night of July 6 and rescue their imprisoned friends, such as Monday. Now on the ninth, Charles was himself suddenly awaiting death. The specter of death drove away his sense of unity with his fellows. He walked up to Monday and denounced him for having gotten him into this situation. Monday was indifferent. He stoically replied that death was all they had a right to expect because they had failed. Then Monday softened a little, perhaps because of his friend's pathos. He and Charles began to discuss the organizing and people who were still on the outside. Charles had not been one of the leaders, and there were probably many things he did not know. Monday may have inadvertently filled in some gaps because a short time later that night Charles summoned the wardens and Hamilton and made a confession, naming a few new people he had learned about from Monday. The white authorities had seen that Monday was not "disposed to make any confessions." They had tried to get him to confess "to others," but Monday had kept his oath of silence with people—white or Black—who did not deserve to know the movement leadership's secrets. The tribunal now saw that "he might be inclined" to confess "to his friend Charles." Charles agreed to help the whites. The tribunal concocted an excuse to put Charles in a cell alone with Monday for twenty-four hours. His task was to gather more information for the investigations without arousing Monday's suspicions.[54]

Charles deliberately betrayed Monday. He did it face-to-face. He saved himself by tricking Monday into giving him more information for the tribunal. After the twenty-four hours with Charles were up, Monday was isolated in his cell again by the end of July 10. A wave of new raids and detentions occurred July 10–12. Of the thirty new detainees, only three were people Charles had named on the ninth after his short confrontation with Monday. The other twenty-seven may well have come from Charles's deeper, more cynical abandonment of Monday during the night of the ninth and the day of the tenth when he served as a confidential informant for the tribunal.[55] All told, by the twelfth, the new detainees included key people such as Tom Russell, Bacchus

Hammett, Perault Strohecker, Billy Bulkley, John Enslow, Smart Anderson, and Saby Gaillard (a free Black man). Not all of the names necessarily came from Charles. Sometime during the July 10–12 interval, as new prisoners appeared in both the poorhouse and the Workhouse, Monday Gell may have become aware of the new arrests and concluded that Charles was passing along his information. Monday completely and radically changed his strategy. He decided to name names. Like Charles, he was given a temporary respite from his death sentence in exchange. He would have been hanged on the twelfth with Gullah Jack and John Horry if he had not turned informant.[56]

In the weeks that followed, Charles and Monday became central witnesses in a string of new proceedings. Only Perault Strohecker and Harry Haig would rival them for testimony condemning others. Twenty-two men were hanged on July 26, and it was mostly because of Monday Gell. Harry Haig confessed about the same time as Charles, but like Charles he had few names that were news to the tribunal. The decision to put Monday and Charles in a cell together did not produce collusion on false accusations. Rather, Charles's decision to heinously and personally betray his friend put him in an adversarial relationship with Monday. Monday found himself about to die while Charles survived using information he had stolen from him. The movement was over for Monday. Everyone was going to hang. He was going to try to survive.[57]

As it sentenced Gullah Jack to death the tribunal urged him to make "a full disclosure of the truth," but Jack was unwilling. On July 12 at the gallows, this white power physically had its hands on him but he struggled to try to get free. He had believed in his power to evade the whites. His success in keeping his medicine bag and his whiskers throughout his enslavement in Tanzania and America had demonstrated that he was invulnerable to the whites on their own. But he had, after all, been betrayed by other Black people, as he had predicted might happen. Unable to take his freedom alone at the scaffold, and with no rescue from his defeated friends in the community materializing, he nonetheless kept his oath and died without naming others.[58]

When the magistrates and freeholders returned to their investigatory chambers in the Workhouse on July 13, they were ready to hear Monday's confession. This would be momentous for them. Of the known leaders, Monday was the only one to betray the movement's oath of secrecy. The confessions and statements he would make in the coming weeks decimated the band of rebels he had gathered around himself. Though he was only one of six witnesses whom Hamilton and the tribunal came to regard as especially useful, all the others except Harry Haig had been betrayed either by Monday or by Charles using Monday's information. In the end, Monday Gell,

Charles Drayton, and Harry Haig were "very efficaciously" used and had their sentences reduced to transportation; Perault Strohecker, John Enslow, and Billy Bulkley also became "witnesses for the state," were "tried on their own confessions," and sentenced to transportation.[59]

Monday opened his first confession dramatically when, according to records, he declared *I come out as a man who knows he is about to die*. This dramatic opening was performative. Yes, he had been sentenced to death and he knew it, but he was acting the role of the prostrate slave willing to become the transparent servant of the slavers' will. Intelligent, astute, and tactical, he knew how to maneuver in the teeth of white power. He had a statement to make. As he would admit when caught in a lie later, he knew he had to shift the blame to Denmark Vesey for at least some things that he feared whites would not be willing to forgive. Vesey was already deceased. Blaming him falsely would not hurt him any further. He also knew he had to reveal a lot of truths about himself, about Vesey, and about Charles, Harry, and Perault. His stories needed to be true, or true enough that others could not contradict him persuasively. If he failed, he might die while a faithless friend like Charles Drayton survived.[60]

The confession Monday gave was just the kind of thing the tribunal had wished Vesey, Peter Poyas, and Gullah Jack had given them. Monday named dozens of people on the thirteenth. Only nine of these people had been arrested based on Charles's disclosures of his conversations with Monday in the Workhouse. Most of the thirty people who had been detained between the ninth and the twelfth after Charles named them were either acquitted or released for lack of evidence. Most of the people Monday named would be declared guilty in the eyes of the tribunal. On July 23, Monday gave a second confession, in which he elaborated and added some facts and a couple new names. The new details did not change the general story much. He claimed to have made a list of about forty rebels, only to destroy it out of fear he would be caught with it. However, in his two postconviction confessions, he rebuilt all or nearly all of that list. From memory, he named a total of thirty-seven people.[61]

Monday lied sometimes. On the twenty-third he admitted to a lie and revised the timeline of how early he had joined the movement. He had said he had not joined until days before June 16, but his revised confession was that he joined sometime in April. Monday in fact lied in both his confessions about other things, too. Face-to-face, Perault Strohecker accused Monday of writing the movement's correspondence to Haiti and accused him of lying when he said that Vesey had written the letters. Perault asserted that he had been there with him, too, during the walk to Vanderhorst's Wharf with the letter. Monday "confessed that the fact was so," in James Hamilton's words. However, he pleaded with the tribunal by saying that he had only chosen to lie because he was afraid that *if it were known* he had committed *such an act, all chance of mercy would be denied him*. So he piled guilt onto Vesey to enhance his own chances of survival. Doing so could not increase the sorrows of the deceased.[62]

Monday's statements suggest that he might also have slow-walked his disclosures, offering information only as necessitated by the proceedings. In other words, he tried to have it both ways: loyally protect secrets and also reveal enough to enhance his value alive. Reportedly, both Monday and William Paul had kept lists of people committed to the uprising. Monday said he never saw William's list and that he had destroyed his own list. Then he claimed he could not remember all of even his own list. Though he named a lot of people in his confessions, he did not quite fully reconstruct the list he had described. At least three and possibly up to a dozen people who might have been on his list never got named. He omitted details about the actions of the people he did name. For example, he claims that William Garner told him that he was recruiting draymen and had procured about a dozen horses, but he does not say who any of the draymen were by name or description. Monday says that Jack Purcell told him that Scipio Sims had traveled as far as Bacon's Bridge to recruit for the movement. This is very specific and logistically crucial information. Bacon's Bridge, twenty miles away, was the Ashley River bridge crossing closest to Charleston. It controlled land routes through the region and water routes to Charleston. Yet previously Monday had not mentioned it. Monday said that Denbow Martin belonged to the uprising and had told him about other people that he thought were in it, but he did not share the names of those other people. Such omissions suggest that he might have been trying to protect people until, perhaps, the tribunal gained further information and questioned him, in which case he might suddenly have seemed to remember so as to save himself.[63]

In both of Monday's postconviction confessions, there were also people Monday insisted were not involved, even though falsely implicating them could have enhanced his value to the tribunal. He pointedly cleared Morris Brown, the pastor of the African Church. This was arguably not what the tribunal wanted to hear. Kennedy and Parker and many others in the city blamed Brown's church, describing it as the seedbed for the insurrection. Yet Monday insisted that Brown and the other top leaders in the congregation had known nothing. Further, in clearing Brown, Monday directly contradicted other testimony, risking his credibility if the magistrates and freeholders chose to believe others over him. Monday's credibility with the court—as the only core leader of the movement who confessed and named names in detail—certainly helped spare Brown and the other church officers. According to the investigatory records, Monday said he and the planners believed the church leaders would betray them.[64]

If Monday was not willing to lie to incriminate all the people the court seemed to blame, why did he choose to incriminate Vesey but clear Morris Brown? He certainly had understood the white hostility toward Brown and his church. The reason for these choices may be held in something he reportedly told Charles Drayton: that the rebels had accepted the possibility of death when they commenced organizing a revolution. The risk of being killed was *what they could expect*, whether in battle or on the scaffold. Vesey had agreed to such a risk, but Brown and the other church officers had not. Vesey was an organizer of the uprising movement, and Brown was not a member. Monday's choices are a clear indication that the general fugitive ethic of not currying favor with whites' cruelty still mattered to Monday, despite his dreadful betrayal of his friends' and acquaintances' trust that he would keep the movement's oath of secrecy even if he lost his life in doing so.[65]

Monday also could not know with complete certainty whom Charles had named. Still, he often named people the tribunal had already executed or already had in custody. Three people he named had already been executed. A fourth (Jack Purcell) may have been someone Charles had betrayed after his covert conversations with Monday. Jack was detained on July 12. By naming him on the thirteenth, Monday put himself in greater danger. Monday even testified against Jack during the tribunal's proceedings against him. Jack had been a minor figure in the movement and not even effective in what he had attempted. But, called to testify against him, Monday needed to show his usefulness to the court if he was going to survive. In his betrayal of Jack, Monday fully inhabited a snitch's amorality. Perhaps Monday absolved himself of this guilt with the fact that Jack had joined the movement and therefore death was all he could expect in failure. But it seems a weak absolution, since he himself had committed to the revolution and was determined to survive. Jack Purcell was just the first of many minor movement members Monday was willing to identify for the court. Just a few weeks earlier, these were people that Monday and the other key organizers had been trying to reassure as they recruited them. Jack was declared guilty and then hanged on the twenty-sixth as part of a twenty-two-person mass hanging that might never have happened but for Monday's self-interested reaction to Charles's embittering betrayal.[66]

During the middle weeks of July, disclosures came quickly and the tribunal resolved statements' contradictions to fit its preferred narrative. For example, in the proceedings against Tom Russell on July 15, Perault Strohecker gave the most extensive and damning descriptions of Tom's activities. Perault said Tom made weapons, attended meetings, and agreed to join the movement. However, having declared that he had met Tom at Vesey's well before June 16 at a meeting that determined the new date for the insurrection, on cross-examination Perault admitted he had not met him at Vesey's until June 16. He said he was with Charles at Tom's shop and discussed the insurrection, but Charles contradicted him and said he met Tom at Monday's shop and that he, Perault, and Tom had never been in each other's presence at the same time anyway. Despite the conflicting statements, the tribunal sentenced Tom to death. The tribunal also continued using both Perault and Charles for statements against others. In mid-July, the tribunal reached its apotheosis: it was little different from a drumhead expediency practicing summary show trials on the way to convictions and executions.[67]

When the tribunal slowed down, it battled with individuals they believed were still withholding information. Bacchus Hammett was one of those. In the second week of July, he was still at large and still keeping the oath of secrecy. Monday Gell or Charles Drayton had almost certainly named him sometime on July 9 or 10 and Benjamin Hammett, an officer of the Charleston Neck Rangers state militia unit, committed Bacchus to the Workhouse on the 11th. He was briefly confined in a cell with his friend Perault, who reminded him of the oath of secrecy and told him not to speak about the movement to anyone at the Workhouse. Bacchus dutifully tried to keep his promise, refusing to talk when Benjamin Hammett first sought his statement on the morning of the twelfth. But this resolve may have lasted only hours. Bacchus suddenly had a change of mind. Perhaps the interrogators told him what they knew about his actions and he got scared that he would be executed. He confessed to Hammett and two other white men, who signed his statement as witnesses on July 12 in the Workhouse. When Bacchus appeared at the tribunal's proceedings, his slaver let him plead innocent to try to save his life, but he was eager for the court to know that he was not entirely opposed to Bacchus being punished, either.[68]

The core contradiction of slaving and slave law—that the enslaved were both property and people—had always presented Black Charleston with a dilemma, a problem without a solution. How do you protect yourself from people for whom you are property? People who conceive of your love, will, and desire almost exclusively in terms of profits and their own wants and needs?

That problem haunted Black community life. It had gotten more sorrowful and oppressive in recent years, as seen in attacks on the African Church, the closing of self-purchase and manumission as pathways to greater security, and the emigration of parts of families to white colonies in West Africa. The same problem threatened the lives of the detainees and their families and friends inside and outside the Workhouse. How does one keep loved ones and friends out of the hands of this irregular and outraged tribunal while also surviving its wrath? Attempt to at least appear to give it the information it demanded? Slavers did not care much, if at all, about Bacchus as a person even though they had to contend with him; they cared primarily about Bacchus as property, and they would cull him from the gang of enslaved laborers like livestock from the herd if they felt it would preserve their investments.

Bacchus made at least three confessions, but even as he made revelations he concealed and distorted information to protect himself and others. His general purpose in his statement on the twelfth seems to have been to minimize his own participation, avoid exposing friends, and perform compliance. In that first confession, Bacchus named only people who had already been executed or were in custody. He declared that he had refused to join the movement. He assigned responsibility for the most affirmative acts in support of the movement to others when he could. For example, he blamed the deceased Vesey for his decision to join the movement and he blamed the newly executed Gullah Jack for getting him to take gunpowder from Mr. Hammett's storage room. But he made several confessions. With each new confession, he provided more detail. On the thirteenth he gave the name of a living person who wasn't already in custody when he gave up Ceasar Smith, reportedly saying that Ceasar had taken a sword from Bacchus that Bacchus had stolen from Hammett. Ceasar was captured, tried, and then hanged on July 26. However, Bacchus gave this name seemingly reluctantly. He named Ceasar when answering questions about what had become of a pistol and sword that he had already admitted to stealing. With that admission he had cornered himself into needing to say what happened to the sword. Beleaguered, by the time Bacchus gave his third statement on the seventeenth, the tribunal records show him pleading with the magistrates and freeholders, saying that he would have informed earlier if not for Perault always telling him to keep the oath of secrecy.[69]

Bacchus cooperated as little as possible, and the tribunal noticed. With the exception of Ceasar Smith, he named only people they already knew about. Bacchus seemed credible to the tribunal, apparently. He seemed to have been present for meetings, and he seemed to have been critical to the plan to capture weapons. Nobody contradicted him, and despite the tribunal's pressure on him, only minor details changed in his several statements. For example, in the July 12 version of his confession, Bacchus apparently confessed that Denmark Vesey and Perault Strohecker had both revealed the planned uprising to him. But an undated private set of notes claims that Bacchus said that only Perault told him about it, as Vesey looked on silently. Although in his July 12 statement he claimed that Vesey had threatened him to make him join, the undated private version tells a story in which Vesey persuaded him with talk of how God planned for him to be equal to whites like his slaver Benjamin Hammett. Because the magistrates and freeholders found Bacchus credible, they believed he was part of the movement and they may have expected more names from him. Because he seemed to them to be reticent, they thought he was unrepentant. Bacchus may have been trying to seem cooperative while protecting almost everyone he knew in the movement who was still unknown to the tribunal. At the end of his proceedings on July 18, the tribunal ordered him to be hanged on the twenty-sixth.[70]

On the day of his execution, Bacchus became defiantly buoyant, according to a report. He laughed and waved on his way to the gallows, bidding farewell to friends and acquaintances watching the procession. Among the witnesses to the procession, there may even have been people he had deliberately avoided naming at the cost of his own life. He had protected them. Displaying no remorse for his revolutionary desires and actions, he reportedly laughed just before the hood was put over his head.[71]

After his death, however, the tribunal got the last word and perhaps played a trick on their less-than-fully-cooperative informant. The *Official Report* published a distorted version of Bacchus's confession. Their edits of Bacchus's statements seem to be calculated to make him look more eager to comply than he was. The report includes what it describes as his complete confession, submitted before Bacchus submitted a plea denying guilt, but in reality they published a deceptively edited and incomplete version of what he had told them. First, they combined Bacchus's July 12 confession with his "further confession" given the next day. Second, the court pretended that this combined version had all been offered on July 12 before he entered his plea of not guilty. In reality, the July 13 statement was given after he was convicted. Third, Bacchus had made a third confessional statement on July 17, but the tribunal included none of its text in the *Official Report*. Fourth, the magistrates changed the text from third person (referring to Bacchus as "he") to first person (Bacchus speaking as "I"). These changes played up Bacchus's compliance by suppressing evidence of the interventions by his slaver and the repeated pressure from the tribunal for him to confess and confess again because they were unhappy with his apparently limited disclosures. Representing the text in the first person amplifies the unmediated feeling, as if Bacchus is speaking directly to the reader when he is quoted as saying "I took the keg of powder out of the back store of my master, and carried it in a bag to Denmark."[72]

The magistrates' edits of Bacchus's statements also strengthened the tribunal's theory that Denmark Vesey, his religious and secular antislavery, and the independent Bible classes of free and enslaved Black people at the African Church were the primary causes of the rebellion. In fact, by excluding Bacchus's July 17 third confession from the *Official Report*, they excluded evidence of leadership by Monday Gell and Perault that undermined their theory that Vesey alone had conceived of and led the movement. On the seventeenth, Bacchus told the tribunal that Monday said the movement began in 1817 when the African Church was first attacked. In that year, Vesey finished the long and difficult process of becoming a member in full Communion at the white-dominated Second Presbyterian Church. It is possible that he left the Presbyterians to join the African Church, but there is no direct evidence in church records of his departure from them or of his joining the African Church in 1817. If discussions had begun that early, Vesey was not likely party to them yet. By suppressing that information from the third confession in their *Official Report*, the tribunal denied the public an independent assessment of the evidence and offered a portrait of Vesey's role more friendly to their conclusions.[73]

Perault Strohecker's truthfulness must be doubted, because it is relevant to understanding how the detainees' and Black Charleston's agency played a role in constructing the magistrates and freeholders' official story. While Bacchus's proceedings and confessions were playing out, Perault twice revealed himself as possibly an unreliable witness. During Tom Russell's proceedings on July 15, Perault was made to contradict himself and the tribunal did not allow it to impugn his credibility. In fact, they continued to seek his testimony for weeks. Perault also spoke at their hearings against Nero Haig on or about July 23. However, James Haig raised doubts about contradictory statements Perault was making. James Haig said he had been present at Perault's initial interrogation when he was first arrested on July 10 (Haig was the Workhouse operator). He declared that notes "taken at the examination" were "destroyed" shortly thereafter. Haig reconstructed the notes a day or two later and gave them to Mitchell King, a lawyer representing some of the owners of the enslaved people under investigation. James Haig appears to have been prompted to speak up when Perault told the court that Nero had agreed to forcibly break

Gullah Jack, Denmark Vesey, Peter Poyas, and the other prisoners out of jail before they could be hanged (they were executed July 2). With his notes in hand, James Haig declared that Perault had said the opposite on July 10. At that time, Perault had reportedly said that Nero refused to participate in the breakout because *it was too late*. James Haig admitted that his notes were made from memory after the fact, but the tribunal recorded his objection in its manuscript record. Haig's intervention may have saved Nero's life: though the tribunal declared him guilty, it banished him from the United States instead of killing him. The tribunal, however, continued to consider Perault truthful and reliable. In their *Official Report*, the magistrates singled Perault out for praise and did not report Nero's case or Haig's objection.[74]

On a late spring morning, Agrippa Perry and Scipio Sims rode out of the city on horseback. Their ride would eventually come to the attention of the tribunal, and this offers a uniquely detailed example of how the fugitive ethics of mutual protection outside the Workhouse became relevant to the fight for survival within it. Enslaved, they had been told by their slavers to look for work in the city or the country. The two men had found a job together, and they needed tools that Agrippa had back at the plantation. Everyone agrees that Agrippa and Scipio started near the Second Presbyterian Church and rode through the Lines on Meeting Street Road to the Perry family's plantation in the more rural districts north of Charleston. They arrived sometime before dinner, or maybe an hour or two after dinner. In the morning, they collected Agrippa's tools and left after breakfast to return to town. From July 18 to July 24, both men would fight for their lives in hearings before the tribunal over the truth of this ride's purpose. Their community would have to come to their assistance with testimony.

Scipio and Agrippa's ride can be understood in at least three ways. Seen in the way the tribunal concluded, the ride was a nefarious errand to recruit people for a barbaric, criminal conspiracy motivated by a desire for murder and rape. Seeing the ride from the uprising movement's perspective would mean seeing that they were helping organize people to free themselves as well as friends and loved ones from an exploitative, violent, and racist white power. But both men said they were innocent of the tribunal's charge. They declared that they had nothing to do with the movement. So there is a third way to view their ride: they were simply two coworkers who needed to retrieve some tools for a job.[75]

In the proceedings against Scipio on July 18–19, Perault Strohecker again played a central role. Although his accusations were specific, they were not all that impressive. He told the tribunal that Scipio said he was part of the movement and that he hired a horse from him June 8 to go into the country to get more people to come down for the uprising. Perault said that he saw Scipio a second time and they talked about the uprising then, too. On a third occasion (June 30) he said he encountered Scipio on King Street and they agreed that the movement was over because of the arrests and the cowardice of their friends and allies. Monday Gell and Charles Drayton corroborated Perault's claim that Scipio was part of the uprising movement, and he was convicted and sentenced to transportation out of the United States on pain of death if he returned. One loose end remained, however. Perault had said there was a second man in the transaction regarding the horse, but he did not know the man or even his name. Perault did say that he would recognize the man if he saw him again. Fortunately for Perault, that man had bravely come to the proceedings and given a statement in defense of Scipio, which allowed Perault to identify him. The tribunal gave Agrippa's slavers a few days to collect witnesses, and Agrippa then stood trial for his life on July 23–24.[76]

The only evidence against Agrippa was Perault's statement that Agrippa had told him he hired the horse and went into the country to recruit men for the uprising. Agrippa denied it, but Perault claimed that Agrippa told him he had succeeded in recruiting *some* men, according to the tribunal's manuscripts. Three women and one man belonging to the Perry plantation stepped up to describe details of Agrippa's and Scipio's movements at the Perry plantation that they must have thought would exonerate Agrippa. Their statements reveal the love and loyalties in their life on the Perrys' land, and they help us understand the power struggles with the tribunal over the truth regarding the movement.

After Scipio and Agrippa hired the horse from Perault on June 8 and left him, they met Robin Perry, who joined them on the ride out of Charleston. According to Robin, they left the city about 10 a.m., made no detours or stops, and talked with no one on the way up the road. They arrived between 3 and 4 p.m. Though Robin did not stay with the two men, he saw their horses in the pasture together at 4 or 5 p.m. All the horses were stabled for the night by 8 p.m. Agrippa and Scipio went to bed by about 8 p.m. Robin said he came looking for them after 8 p.m. and they answered when he called them. Doll Perry said that Agrippa and Scipio arrived an hour before sunset and that Agrippa went to his mother's place while Robin came into the house. She said she saw their horses in the pasture at sunset and added that they sent someone at dusk for clabber (soured milk). She next saw them all again after breakfast, and Robin said he saw them at breakfast. Lidy, Agrippa's mother, told the tribunal that Agrippa and Scipio arrived not long before sundown, came to her house, and slept there all night. She said she did not think it possible they could have left in the night without her knowing. And, anyway, they told the tribunal that there were no able-bodied adult men left on the plantation because they had all been told to find work in the city. Robin and Doll saw them around breakfast time. The two got Agrippa's tools and then Agrippa, Robin, and Scipio returned to Charleston together.[77]

Incredibly, given this testimony, the court allowed a one-line statement from the proceedings against Scipio a week earlier to corroborate Perault's statement against Agrippa. Perault had said that Scipio told him he had recruited some men. On that basis, the tribunal disregarded all these exonerating statements about Agrippa and convicted him. He, like Scipio several days earlier, was sentenced to banishment from the United States on pain of death if he returned. Banishment meant that Agrippa lost his mother and anyone else he cared about. He lost the geography of what was probably his native country, too. And he lost the reputation he had created despite living under slavery's racism.[78]

Why did the court allow Perault's irrelevant statement against Scipio to outweigh four other people's exculpatory statements? One explanation might be that there were some inconsistencies in the timelines Agrippa's family offered. First, Robin said that he, Scipio, and Agrippa arrived about 3 p.m. However, the three women (Lidy, Kit, and Doll Perry) offered an arrival time possibly five or six hours later, close to sundown. Perhaps after nearly two months the various witnesses simply had somewhat different memories of the otherwise unremarkable day, or perhaps there were several unaccounted-for hours in which Agrippa and Scipio could have been recruiting for the uprising. Second, Robin said he called for Scipio and Agrippa in the night and that they answered, saying they had gone to bed. However, Agrippa's mother Lidy said Robin got no reply, despite calling three times. This could mean Robin was lying when he said they replied or that Lidy simply did not hear the men reply. Third, the white Perrys claimed other plantations were much closer than Agrippa's friends and relatives had asserted. Even Doll admitted that Agrippa and Scipio could have gone to a nearby plantation without anyone seeing them if they went across the field. In short, everyone agreed that they had arrived, turned in for bed, and had breakfast before leaving the following morning, but nobody could fully alibi them. Their statements could be interpreted as inconsistent, perhaps contradictory. It was possible that Agrippa and Scipio were recruiting before coming to the Perry place or during the night.[79]

Is anyone lying? If so, who? Perault? Or Robin? Or maybe Lidy, Kit, and Doll? We cannot tell. However, there was no reason the tribunal had to believe Perault over the others. They were choosing to believe Perault, who had made himself a weapon against the community and the ethic of mutual defense the tribunal held in contempt. It was absurd that the magistrates and freeholders pretended a statement against Scipio was a statement against Agrippa. But if they believed the four who testified to Agrippa's noninvolvement, then not only was Agrippa innocent but they had wrongly convicted Scipio. And they might have to start doubting Perault's credibility. Faced with this incommensurable contradiction, the tribunal decided to protect its power and reputation by downplaying their potentially enormous error.[80]

Agrippa's family and friends on the plantation had courageously showed up for him. Showing up was dangerous. Agrippa had showed up and testified to clear Scipio, and he ended up on trial for his life. His mother (Lidy) as well as Doll, Kit, and Robin all could have reasonably been concerned about the danger in appearing before the court because of what had happened to Agrippa. The tribunal was very enthusiastic about executions at this moment. A couple days after declaring Agrippa guilty on this flimsy evidence, twenty-two other men would be hanged in a grisly mass execution on the Lines near Meeting Street Road. Perault had testified against a bunch of them, too.[81]

Power and Discretion

All that the enslaved in the Workhouse had for a weapon was discourse: when to speak, when to stay silent, whom to name, whom to keep secret, and how to express themselves. The detainees used this weapon to fight with the whites for personal survival and the survival of others. They were not entirely alone. Outside the gates, their friends, family, and acquaintances in the community, men and women, fought the tribunal with their strategic silence—never volunteering information against the detainees—and with their testimony in defense of friends and relatives. The 1822 investigatory archive leaves a trace of their movements on that field of combat. Reading the statements and silences of the archive is like using the torn-up ground to understand the battle. As literature, it shows how the rhetoric of struggle between pursuers and fugitives gradually shifted from Black insurgency back to white power from late May into early July. In the Workhouse, the confidence of some of the rebels gradually waned. Outside, confidence had been a sign of rising expectations and anticipation resulting from their self-mobilization. But inside it succumbed under the pressure of isolation, interrogation, and the execution of friends and acquaintances.[82]

Nonetheless, how the detainees and their friends, relatives, and acquaintances outside the Workhouse grappled with the proceedings shaped the literature of the tribunal. They shaped what the tribunal could learn about the movement and the community. Some of the 1822 rebel defendants showed sacrificial, revolutionary commitment and by refusing to testify, denied the tribunal the full story. And they incited their friends to resist informing. Peter Poyas pledged to die silently, charged cellmates to do the same, and followed through. Denmark Vesey silenced the reverends who came to encourage him to disclose people and plans. He kept his vow of secrecy to the end, against his own interests. Gullah Jack behaved similarly. The role of relationships in galvanizing such resolve to take risks and to sacrifice are common themes in the narratives of Frederick Douglass, Solomon Northrup, and Harriet Jacobs. Harriet Tubman returned to Maryland to rescue family and community members from enslavement despite the danger to her life.[83]

However, fugitive ethics permitted the sacrifice of others, too. Tubman occasionally had to threaten people she was helping if they endangered the group. In one extreme case, she confronted a man whose resolve was weakened by hunger, thirst, and setbacks. He wanted to abandon the escape and return to the plantation on his own. Pointing her gun at him, she told him that he could either continue with the escape or he could die right where he was. If he gave up, she knew, he endangered their escape, their friends left behind, and any future escapes. She would see him die instead. He persisted in the journey and attained freedom. A fugitive ethics is an agonized ethics of power. Sally Howard made a similar threat to Jesse Blackwood in 1822. After he frequently visited her yard to plan and organize for the uprising movement, she told him after one particularly insurrectionary statement that she would report him if he did not stop talking in a way that could *get us all in trouble*. She had allowed the earlier visits and the coordination, but people were already getting arrested and the city guard was out in force. He was going too far, so she followed through on her threat. Doing so meant that the threat of his actions was contained just to her and other mutual relations. Prudence Bussacre warned Julius Forrest and then informed against him, trying to separate him from what she saw as the greater danger (the uprising). George Wilson warned Rolla Bennett and then reported him. Unlike Tubman's threat, these were warnings to remain enslaved. Sally Howard was not proposing escape instead of war. But Tubman and these Charleston men and women had in common a concern for keeping the larger social network safe from the reckless actions of one person.[84]

The fugitive ethics of power and discretion among enslaved and free Black Charlestonians prioritized both helping others survive and ensuring personal survival. But even the least faithful detainees, such as Charles Drayton, Monday Gell, and Perault Strohecker, were not willing to get just anyone hanged, regardless of the truth. They exonerated people, too. William Colcock heard a rumor that the US Congress or the state legislature might be about to free the slaves, so he visited Monday Gell's shop. He went there often because he knew he would learn the news. His hope for freedom and curiosity about the news of the uprising got him hauled in before the magistrates and freeholders in July. When he appeared for his proceedings in front of the tribunal, he gave an incorrect date for the uprising and got other details incorrect, apparently. It was clear he had not wanted to join a revolution, especially when he told an acquaintance that he would rather go quietly to his bed. Monday, Charles, and Perault each confirmed that they had seen him at Monday's shop several times, but they all also said he never joined. Monday even said he had never told William anything about the uprising planning. William was declared not guilty by the tribunal; there were other cases like this in which the star snitches showed themselves unwilling or unable to coordinate false stories about people to get them punished. Even at the worst depths of their betrayals in mid-July, the ethic of community care still had an effect on the tribunal's proceedings.[85]

The white tribunal deployed its formidable legal power of discretionary judgment to dissect the movement and intimidate the community to protect slavery. The feeling among white authorities of a state of emergency may have lasted only into early July. After the tribunal executed Denmark Vesey, Peter Poyas, Rolla Bennett, Jesse Blackwood, and two others on July 2, enslavers felt their power returning. What little life was left in the movement probably died with Gullah Jack on July 12. Not long after the July 26 mass hanging, the tribunal members resigned their positions. Their work was complete. White Charlestonians, restored to their high perches in the market, received magistrates Lionel Kennedy and Thomas Parker's *Official Report* and Intendant James Hamilton's *Negro Plot* in the late summer and fall. With large portions of the archival materials printed in their pages, these works carefully told a story of the just-in-time discovery and destruction of the movement by assiduous and responsible city officials, including themselves. As politicians, they were concerned with advancing their reputations. Domination of the free and enslaved Black community was part of any such politics. The tribunal portrayed itself as investigating a conspiracy. But it also revealed itself investigating Black life generally. The tribunal had assessed the free and enslaved population as a whole, as well as the institutions and quasi freedoms of Black people in the city. To them the African Church was a rot on religion, and Black autonomy was a rot on Charleston. They had cut these from the social body, discarding them as awful, as the barbarous heart and vitals of resistance to racialized enslavement.[86]

Intimidation was an announced function of the tribunal's discretion. The magistrates wrote that they wanted to scare and dominate Black Charleston in general, not just judge the movement. Discovering every movement participant was not necessary. They could treat the people they caught hold of in such a way as to intimidate the rest of the community. They knew they did not get everyone. The "companies" that had been organized by "Vesey, Peter, Ned, Rolla and Gullah Jack" had all "escaped detection and punishment," they wrote. Nonetheless, the court believed by the end of July that "enough had been done to serve as an example." Death, banishment, and humiliation would cow the Black community, they argued. Further, even discretionary mercy could be imagined as an intimidation technique. When the court sought to spare Monday Gell, Charles Drayton, and Harry Haig from the gallows and instead banish them from the United States, it justified the decision partly as a way to divide the Black community. They reasoned that giving favorable treatment to unfaithful leaders would spur distrust of similar organizers in the future.[87]

The mercy of these slaving authorities may have been quite frightening. Governor Bennett pardoned a very old and infirm man because the evidence used to declare him guilty suggested the man had only a very casual connection to the rebels. Bennett made a side arrangement with the old man's slaver to sell him out of state. The market became the mechanism of punishment, and while the slaver protected his financial interest, the old man lost his entire support network of family and friends. Although almost none of this is recorded in the manuscript or published records of the proceedings, the old man and his community certainly would remember. Second, the story of an old blind man named Philip, whom officials interviewed but whom the tribunal seems not to have subjected to proceedings, has no recorded outcome. Nonetheless, the interview itself may have been intimidating to old blind Philip and his family and friends. Third, proceedings against Benjamin Cammer were postponed immediately after they began. James Hamilton declared that Benjamin was to be released for lack of evidence, but the tribunal recorded nothing. Here, too, despite the inaction in the end, merely being hauled in would have had a frightful and intimidating impact, given all the executions and banishments. The fact that these incidents are so poorly recorded in the manuscripts further reflects the extraordinary discretion that the laws allowed officials. The law established no recordkeeping requirements and specifically placed the adjudication of cases into inexperienced hands chosen by political leaders—not the courts. Kennedy and Parker (magistrates) and the three freeholders with them were inexperienced and subject to political oversight, but they were nonetheless empowered to declare guilt, kill, and banish people with little independent review and no possibility for the accused to appeal.[88]

Discretion also facilitated intimidation every time weak or not credible evidence stood in for truth and irregular process sufficed as fair. In other words, something close to a lynching spirit pervaded the investigations and outcomes. Hamilton may have saved Morris Brown's life by prevailing on him to leave Charleston permanently, but it was still intimidation rather than a just legal process. Even the critic Governor Bennett made capricious determinations when he ordered militia commanders to arrest *anyone* who merely appeared to have been possibly engaged in insurrection. The militia could "capture or destroy all such persons as the emergency may warrant." While such an order was in force, being an enslaved or free Black person on the road without an unambiguously valid pass or freedom papers could get you assaulted or summarily executed. W. E. B. Du Bois fully appreciated this relationship between slavery and lynching. He wrote that "slavery was the arch-crime" of America. Slavery made "lynching and lawlessness" the twinned siblings of racialized injustice.[89]

The intimidating power of discretion also showed itself in how free people (even a few poor white people) were treated by the city, the tribunal, and the courts. At its discretion, the tribunal tried the freeman Denmark Vesey in a summary slave trial and condemned him to die even though no insurrection had occurred. Not one person had been attacked and no property had been lost. However, the law gave the tribunal this discretion. By contrast, the law required a formal trial in a courtroom for four white men accused of aiding and abetting slave insurrection (the uprising movement). A white sailor named William Allen was the most radical. Allen was saved from the death penalty only because of language in the insurrection laws that required an actual insurrection to be underway for a white person to be convicted of a felony. Allen could be convicted only of a misdemeanor. If the free Black man Vesey had been allowed the rights of this free white man, he would never have been hanged. But the judge did find and use discretion in the interest of extreme punishment in Allen's case. He conditioned the defendant's release from prison on the payment of a fine and security he knew would be too high for Allen to ever be able to pay. Allen would never get out of prison. As the judge observed, it was as good as a life sentence.[90]

Much of this discretionary power and the tribunal's denunciations of Black rebels as barbaric lustful monsters had flowed from a racist presumption about manhood: white men were appropriately free and worthy of basic legal rights in the Anglo-American tradition and Black men were not. Further evidence for this general racism comes in a passage in the *Official Report* that describes with derision the modest freedoms of the African Church, free Black people, and hired-out urban workers. Because Black men bought their freedom, built churches, and worked independently, the magistrates reasoned that it should not be "wondered at" that "an attempt to create an insurrection [was] ... contemplated!" In their minds, when Black people were freed from strict white control, their savage natures would soon turn to rapine.[91]

Their discretion allowed them to try to tell the story of the uprising movement the way they wanted, but they still failed. All summer, the tribunal had heard testimony about the protests and agitation of enslaved people. They had heard that there had been several motivating incidents, many meeting places, and multiple leaders. They repeatedly wrote down evidence of a diverse coalition of the enslaved and the free in their manuscript papers. Regardless, the tribunal's *Official Report* concluded that the freeman Vesey had conceived, instigated, and led the movement himself. The report concluded that the African Church was the seedbed, and that the cause was the inherent barbarity of Black people. But even though they told the story this way despite contradictory evidence, they could not identify and punish people without a description, a name, and an accusation. Their prejudice about Black cultures and Black freedom being well known by the free and enslaved Black community, it became a mortal weakness for their story. Their investigatory reach was limited. The rebel defendants and the Black community at large told them some of what they wanted to hear but resisted telling all—maybe even most—of what they needed to know if they were to catch everyone and know the truth about the movement. People survived because of that rhetorical, fighting retreat.

CHAPTER FOUR

Burials and Aftershocks

> Like the civil war that was black reconstruction's aftershock . . . it
> turns out the war of "national liberation" has always been going on.
> — FRED MOTEN, 2008

The City of Charleston had custody of them when they were alive, so it had to bury them after it killed them. At least some of the men the city killed would have been interred in a public burial ground colloquially called the potter's field. One free Black man in Charleston who had known Susan and Denmark Vesey said that's where the bodies were taken after the executions. In 1822, the potter's field was located in the millpond district on land bounded by Bee, President, Doughty, and Thomas Streets, between Lucas's and Bennett's Mill Ponds (see map 1.1). By city ordinance, any of the rebels' bodies that were not released to family, friends, owners, or a church would have been buried in the field within four hours. The city would not have allowed dumping of the bodies, which was viewed as a health hazard. The 1822 rebels whose final resting place was in the potter's field would be buried inches apart in unmarked graves alongside a few hundred other people buried there that year. Most names were not even recorded by the keeper of the yard. A burial in the potter's field was about as anonymous as a mass, unmarked grave. Without headstones, traditional phrases, or conventional records, burying the rebels in the potter's field was almost like hiding the bodies.[1]

Into this field of white forgetting went the first eight people the city executed for the planned rebellion (six on July 2 and two on July 12). Among these eight were several of the best-known leaders of the movement: Gullah Jack, Peter Poyas, and Denmark Vesey. Vesey had become so controversial that there may have been nowhere else to bury him. Susan Vesey presumably wanted to take custody of Denmark's body, but in one final demonstration of the limited meaning of Black freedom under racial slavery, he was probably consigned to the potter's field. It's hard to see how the city would allow any other site for these rebels, regardless of their last wishes or the wishes of anyone who loved them.

For the mass execution on July 26, the tribunal callously offered the bodies to surgeons for dissection if requested. The offer was published in the newspapers. The tribunal also ordered that any bodies not claimed by surgeons must be buried beside the site where they were executed on the Lines. Among other things, this would avoid burial fees for the public burial ground. By late August, however, neighbors complained about the health hazard created by apparently incompetent interments. The city council immediately ordered reburial of the bodies. The Lines were on private property that had been temporarily appropriated by the military emergency of the War of 1812. Shortly after the Denmark Vesey affair, the property reverted to private owners and the Lines were demolished for development. It is possible that the men executed in late July are still buried along the north side of Line Street in the vicinity of Nassau on the east side. Alternately, they might have been moved to the potter's field.[2]

A plat of the potter's field made a few years after the 1822 executions marks two areas with the word "Burials."[3] These sites were grassy fields gently sloping downward from a stand of trees in the west to a finger-shaped marsh in the southeast (see fig. 4.1). Any of the executed people buried there would have been interred a minimum of five and a half feet underground, not more than one foot away from neighboring graves. The bodies of Denmark Vesey, Peter Poyas, and Gullah Jack joined the hundreds of others buried there in 1822. It was one of the busiest years for the cemetery, which received the enslaved, free Black people, and paupers, as well as orphans, sailors, and visitors who died in Charleston. The grounds were segregated by race. It was closed to burials about 1840 and afterward was built over by the US Arsenal, then the Porter Military Academy, and finally the Medical University of South Carolina.[4]

In the 1960s, the construction of new medical school buildings disinterred about 100 coffins. More graves may yet be found under open spaces, gardens, and paths in various areas of the block. The current medical school had, until recently, an exercise park and community garden that may have stood over graves. Maps and documents portraying the building history of the area since 1822 suggest that some parts of the campus grounds have never been deeply disturbed. Under the gardens, some of the parking lots and paths, and a grassy area beside the drug research building there may still be some graves. Since it is already a public park and garden, it could become a site for a memorial project.[5]

At the end of the Civil War, over forty years after the 1822 uprising movement, without any grave markers or other ways to publicly remember the executed uprising members, Black Charlestonians nevertheless remembered. In May 1865, Martin Delany stood before an audience of 4,000, largely made up of Charleston's newly freed Black community, and invoked the Vesey affair.

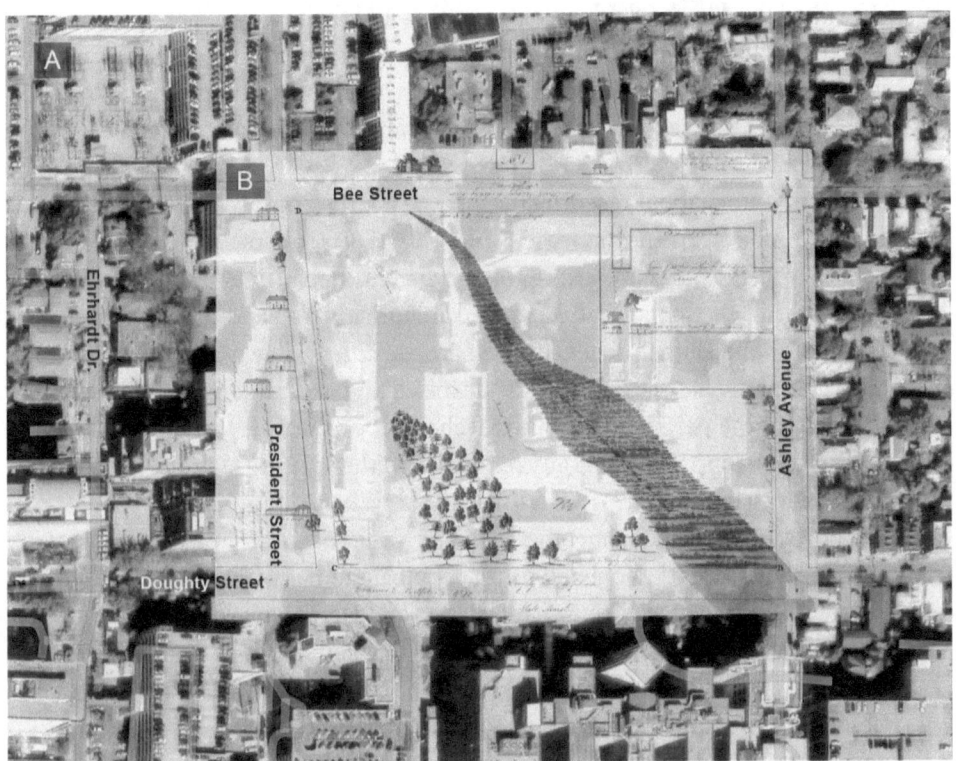

FIGURE 4.1 1837 potter's field (public burial ground) plat overlaid on 2024 ArcGIS map of Charleston's Medical University of South Carolina. Records Related to Charleston Arsenal, South Carolina, Series Plans of Military Posts in the United States, 1840–1947, Records of the Office of the Chief of Engineers, 1789–1999, RG 77, National Archives and Records Administration, Washington, DC; ArcGIS.

He was there as part of ceremonies for the rebuilding of the African Church, which white Charleston had taken apart piece by piece in 1822, selling off the lumber. But he noted that locals still remembered with bitterness how some people had betrayed others in 1822. In so large a crowd, there probably were relatives and friends of some of the scores of people who had been interrogated, accused, banished, or hanged in the proceedings of 1822. We may never know how many Black Charlestonians in their fifties, sixties, and seventies remembered what had happened. But sixty-five-year-old Hannah Vesey must have. She still lived in the city and may well have been present to hear Delany. She had always been free, had married a son of Denmark Vesey's, and before the war had become a well-known "market woman" in the City Market, beside which so much of the organizing had happened. Hannah

Vesey had lived in the shadows of those sites and their story of betrayal and defeat and had thrived as much as possible under slavery's racism. She had lived to see a version of the movement vision accomplished: the city sacked and burned because it was the only way, apparently, that slavery would ever be abolished.[6]

Delany's story about resentments and the memory of the Vesey affair recalls Solomon Northrup's story in *Twelve Years a Slave* of how slaves remembered another insurrection effort. Northrup claimed that, in 1837, an enslaved man named Lew Cheney had instigated an uprising plan and then betrayed those who joined him to benefit himself. Northrup had known Cheney during his own enslavement. Cheney was "despised and execrated by all his race throughout the parishes" for this treachery, according to Northrup. As in Black Charleston, the community remembered the uprising plan and reviled the man who betrayed it.[7]

Cheney's community remembered him as a traitor because he had revealed a dangerous secret that opened other people up to harm and ruin. He had violated the ethic of silence. What Delany's and Northrup's stories of Black remembrance of uprising planning reveal is that communities continued to condemn tale-telling betrayal years later. The condemnation was a political lesson for the living drawn from historical experience. It taught the value of unity in the face of white supremacy. A memorial to the 1822 movement at the site of the former potter's field, now the Medical University of South Carolina, could include a marker that notes that value of unity in the struggle against slavery's racism. It could acknowledge the multiracial, multiethnic pauper burials that were, nonetheless, probably mostly of enslaved and free Black people. And it could specifically notice that at least some of the 1822 rebels were buried there—probably including Denmark Vesey himself.

The piles of dirt and paper under which white Charleston tried to bury the revolutionary Black freedom movement of 1822 constitute a white memorial. Gravediggers excavated and returned the grave dirt, and clerks recording the proceedings mixed ink to complete an archive proclaiming the vindication of public safety and muffling Black voices of liberation. Christopher Jeannerett's ink originated from deposits that gall wasps made on trees. Processing the galls, workers discarded the most of the acids that would have eventually destroyed the paper on which the uprising archive is written. Then they would have baked it until it became iron gall ink powder. Jeannerett's supply of this ink powder was probably purchased from a local printer or importer. To make the powder into ink, he added a liquid, perhaps water from a Charleston well. Depending on its remaining acidity, the ink and the paper could last for centuries. This archival durability contrasts with the unmarked graves to shape a partial or biased memory of 1822. Grave dirt consumes bodies, but acid-free ink and paper last.[8]

The whites' ink memorial preserved the orders, information, interpretations, and policies that made up the white perspective. Governor Bennett wrote letters ordering state militia to mobilize and "destroy" any Black person on the roads who seemed like a possible rebel against slavery. The newspapers wrote stories about investigations, confessions, and heroic public officers serving public safety. Residents wrote letters to acquaintances out of state about the fear that they'd felt on the night of June 16, which was supposed to be a night of battle, but which passed quietly because of the city guards. Such stories spread to periodicals all around the Atlantic world. In the summer, publications including *Reflections Occasioned by the Late Disturbances in Charleston* and *A Refutation of Calumnies* appeared to explain the events and defend slavery. In the fall, the *Official Report* and Governor Bennett's commentaries on Jeannerett's copies of the investigatory records for the state legislature made similar contributions. Unsurprisingly, slavers and their allies attributed the causes of rebellion in general and the 1822 uprising in particular to Black freedoms and privileges rather than to slavery and racism. They concurred that the Vesey affair was an offense against public order led by the freeman Denmark Vesey, seeded in the African Church, and requiring new and heavier regulatory chains on free and enslaved people.[9]

An 1822 publication titled *Memorial of the Citizens of Charleston to the Senate and House of Representatives of the State of South Carolina* made policy recommendations to the legislature that targeted free Black people for expulsion from Carolina—or gradual elimination through policy that encouraged their emigration. The free Black population enjoyed economic and social rights and privileges, if not voting or due process rights, according to the memorial, such as "the power of moving unrestrained ... acquiring property, amassing wealth to an unlimited extent ... procuring information on every subject, and of uniting themselves in associations or societies." This freedom was the problem, these white authors argued. Slavery was not the problem. Rather, free Black people and free people of color, if not restrained, "will expect and claim all the privileges, rights and immunities of citizens." Since such equality was not possible and must be denied, free Black people will try to take "by force what cannot be effected in any other way." The state legislature immediately passed new legislation to regulate the free and enslaved population. In a gesture to their seriousness about inhibiting Black freedom, the legislature also changed the law to allow death sentences against white people without benefit of clergy if they were convicted of merely coordinating with Black people to incite or support insurrection, regardless of whether an insurrection occurred.[10]

Other changes to the law targeted the meager autonomy and freedoms of the Black population that might remain in the city regardless. Masters were forbidden to hire out enslaved people. Hiring out, it was alleged, had inspired men such as Monday Gell and Gullah Jack to rebel and allowed them to move about the city without direct supervision. If masters persisted in allowing hiring out, the relevant slaves could be seized and auctioned. New legislation also required *free* Black persons fifteen years old and older to have a white guardian. The guardian had to personally certify, whenever required, that their Black ward was of good character and habits. The law also required all adult free Black men between fifteen and fifty years of age to pay a tax of $50 per year (approximately $1,380 in 2024). Previously, free Black people had sometimes quietly refused to pay the special taxes placed on them (Denmark Vesey included). After 1822, the state reserved the right to enslave free Black people who failed to pay the new tax.[11]

One act of the general assembly called for temporary confinement of all free Black sailors working on ships doing business in the harbor. Not even an accusation of crime was necessary. Their Blackness was enough. Within weeks, enforcement began. On February 13, 1823, the British ambassador in Washington, DC, relayed concerns about the new law. From the consul in Charleston, he had learned about the difficulties that the new law had already created for British interests. South Carolina had begun to require that all arriving ships—including British—commit any free Black crew to the city jail until the ship departed. Adding further insults to such a racist policy, the law required ships to pay the jailer's costs. It further required a bond from the captains that they would depart with their jailed crew after having paid expenses. The British ambassador objected that these measures compounded unfair trade practices. He had been protesting tariffs and shipping fees for years. Now he asked Secretary of State John Quincy Adams to intercede and "prevent the recurrence of any such outrage in future" in South Carolina. The federal government attempted to intervene, but South Carolina continued enforcing the act on grounds of states' rights. In August, a federal judge in South Carolina deemed the act unconstitutional and void. He called it a threat to the union, but he could not enforce his order. In December, the state legislature modified the law to allow Black sailors abandoned by their captains in the jail to voluntarily leave the state rather than face enslavement. They also exempted US naval ships. However, the state continued to enforce the law.[12]

In 1825, the social effects of this white, inked memorial were inadvertently recorded by a visitor to Charleston. He recorded local elites' defense of the "Negro Sailor" law. White Charlestonians recounted that "the negroes of the country" had recently conspired to overthrow the city. They told the visitor that an investigation revealed that the plot originated with "free negroes" who had traveled to "the northern section of the union" to become "Methodist preachers." They'd returned to Charleston and "preached freedom to the slave population." As a precaution, the state adopted "severe" prohibitions "against free negroes" ever returning to the state if they'd left. He was told that, under the law, if he had showed up in Charleston with a free Black servant, the whites would have incarcerated the man or woman unless the visitor could pay a "considerable" security deposit. As this short local history of the causes and consequences of the 1822 uprising movement reveals, prominent whites thought the cause of rebellion was Black freedom. They thought the solution was Black subordination. It was impossible for slaves to organize a rebellion, they believed, and therefore it was "absolutely necessary"—to use the tribunal's terms—that free Black people had conceived and led it. The enslaved, they believed, could never participate equally in such intrepid and intelligent planning. This had been the core argument of the tribunal's *Official Report* in 1822. Whites only further convinced themselves of this after 1822.[13]

This slaving racism presaged the Jim Crow segregationist racism that emerged after the Civil War. Like the segregationists, slavery's racism had constructed a cordon around Black freedom, too. Black freedom had always been fugitive. Black Charleston had always been running. Slavery's racism had had its own "color line" or lines. These color lines expanded rights and privileges for middling and poorer whites while reducing rights and privileges for all free and enslaved Black people. It kept free Black children out of the state's free schools. It incarcerated white and Black prisoners separately. Churches and even the public burial ground had separate sections. Free Black Charlestonians such as Thomas C. Brown, Catherine Plumet, Saby Gaillard, and Hannah Vesey experienced a society that often separated people according to race in physical space and in law. Their political and social citizenship rights and privileges were curtailed.

W. E. B. Du Bois identified this distinct form of slaving racism in 1903, when he assessed the causes of slave rebellion. He argued that the racism of slave society as much as its exploitation of enslaved people caused antislavery rebellion. In *The Souls of Black Folk*, Du Bois observed that rebellions were part of a "movement" against slavery that drew on aspects of Black life not strictly about the treatment or legal status of slaves. Rebellions were a path to taking control of their whole social being as people—as African and African-descended people, as Black people. Resistance movements therefore might include such things as Black church formation, according to Du Bois. Some of the uprising planners, such as Vesey, might have agreed with Du Bois that Charleston's Black church movement in the years before 1822 was part of a struggle with slavery. The Black community's memory of white attacks on their churches came up in the tribunal's investigatory records as a cause for the rebellion planning. Whites—even the poorest—had certain social citizenship rights that were denied to even free Black people. High on the list of such racialized rights was religious autonomy.[14]

Thus, "the color line" was not entirely new in Du Bois's era of segregation. Slavery was a structure of the racism that preceded and contributed to Jim Crow. Slaving racism is part of the explanation of the 1822 uprising movement. Slavery associated a tyrannical and absolutist ideology of permanent ownership of people and all their descendants forever with another ideology of the collective, inherent, and permanent inferiority of Blackness and of African-descended bodies. The two ideologies arose together out of even older practices of exploitation and domination. Slavery's racism targeted the whole Black community, both free and enslaved, and the 1822 Charleston uprising movement archive offers particularly good evidence of this: Whites physically dismantled the African Church, a symbol of community institutional aspiration, board by board. Denmark Vesey would have likely hated the special taxes and regulations that targeted the entire free Black population. He likely suffered even more, emotionally, from the suffering of those of his children who were legally out of the reach of his care and protection by virtue of being someone else's property. If he visited with them and found they had been beaten by their slavers, he could do nothing about it legally. Buying their freedom, if possible, was once a partial solution. But once the legislature all but banned that option in 1820–22, only ending slavery could solve the problem of protecting enslaved loved ones—family or friends—from terrible abuses at the sole discretion of slavers. So while Vesey was free, he was not free in the way white workers were free. He was still subject to slaving racism. As Du Bois was aware, it was partly an impatience with this situation that produced leaders like Peter Poyas, Gullah Jack, or Denmark Vesey.[15]

Both the enslaved and free Black people of Charleston in 1822 wore a mask, something like "the veil" Du Bois later described in *The Souls of Black Folk*. For Du Bois, the veil was a symbol of a split in African American consciousness as constructed in an anti-Black society: a racially subjugated social consciousness of belonging and alienation for those who were at once Americans and African

Americans. It obscured feelings and expressions—especially in the presence of dangerous whites. In Charleston in 1822, the veil mediated a consciousness of being at once a permanent outsider and an essential part of the city. The terms of belonging defined by Charleston's whites were always already alienating. But the veil was also asymmetrical in other ways. The accused behind the veil could see through the veil better than outside interrogators could see into it. From behind this veil, Black Charlestonians clearly observed whites' behaviors, attitudes, and beliefs toward them, while whites' views of Black consciousness remained obscure. This asymmetric knowledge was power, and it manifested in the Workhouse fight. Tacticians such as Monday Gell, Perault Strohecker, and Charles Drayton—who knew much of the truth about the movement—knew at least the types of information that white investigators wanted to learn and could estimate what was safest to reveal, alter, or hide entirely. They knew the kinds of things the whites could do with such information, regardless of what they promised. Whites, however, failed to detect the full membership, leadership, and plan of the social movement because they could not see behind the veil they forced the accused to wear as if it were natural. Du Bois writes of surpassing the skills and efforts of the white children in his school and watching them get all the "dazzling opportunities" anyway. As an adult, despite his brilliance and accomplishment as a scholar, Du Bois was denied memberships, employment, and respect by the white historical profession. Similarly, how much better a carpenter must Vesey have been than the great majority of white carpenters in order to have achieved the modest property he apparently had when he died? All his adult working life he had either been a slave or a freeman who'd seen his livelihood reduced by taxes and fees that white workers did not pay. Slavery's racism was not the same as the Jim Crow racism that Du Bois lived with and wrote about, but it was the lineal ancestor and Du Bois rightly noticed the family resemblance.[16]

When Du Bois mentions the Vesey affair in *The Souls of Black Folk*, he globalizes the controversy over slavery by comparing it to "serfdom." The 1822 movement and other rebellion efforts "voiced . . . the disappointment and impatience" of Black people "at the persistence of slavery" and the "serfdom" of free Black people. Calling it serfdom associated American chattel slavery and its racism with global unfree labor systems and located its origins in European systems of exploitation. Identifying Black Charlestonians' impatience with slavery as a feeling that both free and enslaved "Negroes" in general shared was an argument at the most advanced edge of scholarship about the African diaspora, imperialism, and colonialism in Du Bois's time. His observations were a bit like the thinking reflected in the Haitian Republic's

Burials and Aftershocks 133

1816 constitution, which promised freedom to Black and indigenous people from anywhere in the world: just get to our island Black republic and you will be free.[17]

Confirmation of Du Bois's reading of enslavement and its racism in the incomplete record of 1822 emerges from our expanded archive of the Vesey affair. We cannot know the 1822 rebels' ideologies from the white archive with any specificity, but we can see their global outlook on the exploitation of Blackness in the coalitional structure they chose for their movement. We can see that they targeted both slavery and its general exploitation of Black people in the city. The movement acted as if it understood the lie in Susan Vesey's and Denmark Vesey's supposed freedom. Only overthrowing slavery and its racism would make the Veseys free as fully dignified social beings whose kin, friends, labor, talents, institutions, and citizenship whites would be compelled to treat justly. The lives of the 1822 rebels upend the notion that the Declaration of Independence and the US Constitution had even identified, much less promised, universal human freedom. Vesey, Gullah Jack, Monday Gell, and many others in Charleston had known forms and sources of freedom in Africa that white Americans did not comprehend in 1822, let alone 1776. Movement participants did not need the American Revolution to appreciate the Haitian promise. It was self-evident.

The 1822 uprising was not about resolving the United States' contradiction of slavery and freedom; it was about realizing an African and African American freedom, a Black liberation. The Vesey affair became a way station on the road to the Civil War and to emancipation for many commentators and historians after 1822. However, seen through the origins, actions, and targets of the whole coalition, 1822 was about something more capaciously encompassing. It was something partly new. The coalition spurred collaborative, cross-cultural resistance to capitalism's tendency to forcibly produce castes fit only for sharp exploitation. When the 1822 rebels threatened Charleston's mills, weapons caches, vaults of cash near Broad and East Bay Streets on the east side, and the ships along the wharves, they threatened this racial capitalist order. Capitalism was not consciously their target, but its facilities would have been downrange in their gunsight. By devising these plans, affirming to each other their capacity to take freedom, and convincing each other of the rightness of doing so, they showed us what they understood to be the power in their way. Their actions revealed again the inhuman contradiction at the heart of a racial capitalism: the outrage that Charleston's plantation, merchant, and industrial capitalists forcibly reduced them and their loved ones to commodities to be used for profit. The names of this power were not just Bennett, Hamilton, Lucas, and Kennedy. The names were also bank, guardhouse, and mill. Whites had to resort to dozens of killings and dozens more deportations to stuff the protest back into the mouths of the people.

Racism once again rolled over Black Charleston with the fog off the rivers. It dampened and weighed upon the hope for a revolutionary freedom that the rebels had been creating in their movement. It brought lingering persecution for 1822. A visitor to Charleston in 1825 found "a negro" in the city jail who had been part of "one of the recent conspiracies." He'd been spared hanging but had been sentenced to transportation out of the United States. Now three years after his conviction, he was still confined on the jail's upper floor, where "atrocious criminals" were kept two to a cell, overcrowded, "without ever being allowed to come into the open air." His slaver had simply not gotten together the arrangements to sell him into the West Indies. Like a ghost, he remained among any friends who knew where he was, present and possibly even able to see them through the windows.[18]

The tribunal banished more than a score of enslaved people, ordering them to be sold "beyond the limits of the United States," but it banished free Black people, too. Several went to Liberia and Sierra Leone. They and other Charlestonians, such as Susan Vesey (Denmark's widow) and Thomas C. Brown (a fellow carpenter and Vesey's acquaintance) also went to West Africa. Liberia and Sierra Leone were settler colonies of the United States and Britain, respectively. Those who ended up in the newly reorganized Liberia arrived in time for war with native Africans. Poorly armed, they would ironically have found themselves fighting other Black people—rather than whites. As one historian at the time put it, "At this period the colonists were in a sad condition." Those who went to Sierra Leone might have had it slightly better, because the colony was somewhat older. Any Charlestonians ending up there would have found exiles from Bussa's rebellion in Barbados, many of them skilled Creole artisans and mechanics. Other people in the colony were freed by English cruisers interdicting slave traffickers on the Atlantic—as in 1818 when thirty slaves onboard the *Cherub* were landed and placed in "Country Towns where they are free." To refugee to these places from the United States was to rebuild a life with a diverse Atlantic African population, which was a situation somewhat like what they had known in the settler colonial society of South Carolina. It was not a "return" to a West African ancestral homeland.[19]

Colonial projectors and boosters considered Liberia an excellent site for the colonization project. It was "on the very borders of [the] benighted heathen," sermonized one promoter. Religious revival, education, and a colonial freedom were fast developing, he claimed. Liberia had water, lumber, and excellent clay for bricks, and most important, "all [the] country [was] very fertile." One US Navy officer claimed that "the colonists are better off here than in America" because they had become "more independent, as healthy, and much happier." African American colonists, however, often lamented the conditions. Those who could sometimes returned to the United States.[20]

There were tensions with indigenous African communities in the area. Self-possessed and accomplished in significant craft skills and other cultural knowledge, they were not necessarily impressed with the African Americans, whom they sometimes called *"black-white* people," or with "their improvements" of the land influenced by their Anglo-American colonial experience. Freed US slave Frederick Clark wrote to his former master that "freedom is a great boon," but, he said, getting established was more expensive than expected. He and his family experienced "the acclimating process" and "Africa fever, which every emigrant has to go thro' more or less." It was some years more before he would profess himself entirely contented to have a 250-square-foot "farm house" and ten acres for a bare subsistence that seems only a little better than a Carolina slave cabin and garden plot. Thomas C. Brown, from Charleston and an acquaintance of Denmark Vesey's, had left the United States for the sole purpose of "escaping the oppressive laws of South Carolina." He had sold his property in South Carolina at a fraction of its real worth and traveled to Liberia with a large group of Charleston residents and Georgians. Although he felt well received, he believed the colony was terrible and a disappointment. He lost his savings and two of his children. His brother and sister also died. He insisted his case was not unusual. He may, in part, have been referring to his friend Susan Vesey when he said that more of the emigrants would return to the United States if they could. Susan Vesey also lost family in Liberia and eventually returned to Charleston, where she presumably still had family and friends. It was where all that remained of what she had known and loved could be found.[21]

In 1853, Hannah Vesey, Susan Vesey, and others who could remember the uprising movement participants and leaders still lived in Charleston when a white, British, antislavery-sympathizing painter named Eyre Crowe visited. He was touring the United States looking for subject matter. An unusual slave sale caught his attention. The newspaper ad described it as a sale of "Ninety-six NEGROES" experienced in "the culture of rice" on the Combahee River. They were going to be auctioned off near the waterfront. Crowe attended the auction and made a sketch that later became his painting *Slave Trade* (1854). A print based on the painting would be published in the years after his return to England. It shows a crowded scene centered on an active

FIGURE 4.2 *Slave Sale, Charleston, South Carolina* by Eyre Crowe, 1856. African-American History—1801s–8050s, Wallach Division Picture Collection, New York Public Library, NY.

auction on a balcony almost overflowing with people for sale as chattels (see fig. 4.2). In the image, one can see what the ad had promised: "These negroes are very orderly and well disciplined," the sellers promised in the pages of the *Charleston Mercury*. But in his painted version of the scene, Crowe interrupts that promised docility with a vignette of transgression in the right foreground. A Black man furtively handles a large book he is concealing from the crowd with his body. It is not possible to tell if he is putting the book in or taking it out of the bag he holds. But Crowe wanted us to notice it. Two other Black men seated beside the man with the book seem to be part of a small group. They may be free or enslaved. Perhaps they are part of the lot for sale, which included "carpenters" and "a cooper." It is even possible the men are a reference Crowe is making to the 1822 uprising movement and literate artisans such as Denmark Vesey and Monday Gell. But it is remarkable that the print completely removed these men and all suggestion of Black literacy or resistance from the scene. Perhaps Crowe or the magazine publisher of the print feared backlash. Regardless, the erasure of resistance activity from the rhetoric of his image reenacts the attempted erasure of the 1822 movement's resistance during these decades.[22]

Burials and Aftershocks 137

Both the painting and the edited print portray the Black community's apprehensions about separation from loved ones, which had been part of the 1822 movement's motivation. In the open street, at a time when any person just forty years old or older might remember the 1822 movement, we see a drama of a profitable liquidation of the Black friendships, families, and community whose labor had been productive but was no longer as expedient as their sale price. According to the newspaper ad, the men, women, and children were being "sold in families, with the exception of a few who are single." Yet a woman who holds a child stares intently at a man apparently making a bid to buy either her or her child but perhaps not both of them. In the painted version, there is a second auctioneer right behind her who has his hand on the head of another child, possibly also hers, attempting to prompt bidding from a different direction. Behind him a man looks warily back at the woman and child toward the same bidder. Is he a relative? The father? Though the sellers had claimed families would not be separated, the auctioneers unapologetically announced that cousins and others would be sold regardless of family connections. Whatever would become of this woman and her children, her community was being broken up. For many years, these ninety-six people had cultivated rice together. For the last five years they had been raising Sea Island cotton together. This was the last time many of them would ever see each other.[23]

Since the end of slavery, advocates of remembering antiracist, antislavery resistance have gradually won appreciable victories in Charleston. The statue of Denmark Vesey that has stood in Charleston's Hampton Park since 2014 is a triumph for several generations of community aspiration to commemorate the 1822 uprising. That the statue has been vandalized repeatedly demonstrates how far away a full reckoning with the real and suppressed Black history of the region may yet be. However, the statue itself isolates Vesey from his cohorts, offering him as a synecdoche of the movement by representing him without reference to the movement's other leaders, participants, and supporters in the community. This representation of Vesey as alone reflects the manner in which the white tribunal isolated him as the sole cause in its publishing campaign to malign Black freedom. After Vesey was executed alongside Rolla Bennett, Amaritta La Roche must have walked the city aware of the organizing role that Rolla had played. She and her people knew. Various friends and associates of Peter Poyas and Gullah Jack knew how central, loyal, and inspiring they had been. Both men died without naming anyone else in the community. They protected their community. Many Black Charlestonians knew Vesey had not been alone, that Vesey and the others had collaborated.

When the tribunal condemned Vesey to death, he reportedly shed a tear and returned to his cell to await death alone, but when he went to the scaffold he was in the presence of a Black community. His courageous silence even on the scaffold, when last-minute betrayals might have prevented his hanging, spoke loudly to the community of his affection for his fellows, as he had once called them.[24]

Remembering the revolutionary affections of 1822 fully means remembering the coalition of linguistically and spiritually diverse indigenous Africans and African Americans. The movement's leaders were a group of relatively equal people embedded in communities they loved as much as their own lives. Their uprising, as they and later generations called it, was not unlike the stories told in classic slave narratives, in which resistance is a collaborative act deeply aware of affectionate relationships. The uprising movement's community basis and coalition dynamics were consistent with what we know about many slave rebellions in which leaders were embedded in diverse religious and ethnic groupings.[25] Perhaps the current Vesey memorial could be joined by another memorial suggesting this unsettling of the tribunal's official story. A mural, plaque, or dedicated cemetery marker located on the campus of the Medical University of South Carolina where the public burial ground was in 1822 might acknowledge the rising's many organizers. Coincidentally, the Vesey statue faces the general direction of the 1822 public burial ground (as well as Haiti and Cuba). It is likely that the last, possibly undisturbed, graves of the old burial ground are at or near the corner of Bee and President Streets in the general vicinity of a garden and exercise yard. At least a few of the 1822 rebels were buried somewhere in the public burial ground by city ordinance and the tribunal's direction, including Vesey himself. Certainly, a large portion of the generation of the Black community that the rebel movement sought to free was buried there from 1822 until the cemetery closed in 1840.

If there are still people under that ground, it is important to commemorate them for several reasons. First, it is the final resting place of a significant number of people. Knowing they are there obliges us to respect and observe their relationship to us. Second, in 1822 the newspapers and the tribunal offered up the bodies of the executed to surgeons in the city for dissection. Though there is no evidence that any doctors accepted the offer, the fact of the offer matters. And at its founding in 1824, the medical school boasted of its students' access to the bodies of deceased free and enslaved Black people in the city. Third, the medical school's founding doctors and students likely treated some of the general population buried in the potter's field between 1808 and 1840. Though the burial ground was not exclusively a Black cemetery, it was likely and disproportionately the final resting place of enslaved and free Black Charlestonians, who were both the largest and the poorest population in the city. The story of the diversity of the Black community whose resistance and survival birthed the uprising movement could be enhanced at such a site. Buried somewhere on that ground were people who risked everything in the necessary effort to wrest their loved ones from slavery and take freedom from exploitation—a struggle that is ongoing.

Afterword
The Story of the Papers

> The complete Journal of these trials can at any time be seen by our citizens, and is kept as an official record for History.
> —Unsigned ad, *City Gazette*, August 1822

> Cash paid to Christopher Jeannerett for copying certain documents . . . $30.00.
> —Governor's contingent fund ledger, November 1822

The papers have their own story—like a field of battle. As a material artifact, the handwriting style, copy editing, page layout, paper stock, and ink mixture of the South Carolina House and Senate copies of the tribunal's proceedings has not been systematically interpreted. This physical evidence weaves together at least three stories pertaining to the archive and creates a new perspective on the 1822 uprising. First, there is the story of the origins of the record. A thirty-dollar payment made to Christopher Jeannerett and noted in the governor's contingent fund ledger, can be definitively shown to be compensation to Jeannerett for duplicating the June and July manuscript interrogation records at the behest of the governor. There can no longer be any doubt that the June and July tribunal's original records were lost and that the surviving investigatory records of its proceedings held in the South Carolina state archive are copies made by Jeannerett. Second, there is a story in the construction of the pages themselves that reveals how credible they are as a record of the proceedings. Visible copy edits and other features of the orthography demonstrate that Jeannerett tried to replicate the originals loyally, without editing or arranging them. Therefore, the pages are a guide to the chaotic condition of the originals as they appeared in the fall of 1822. Third, there is a story in the survival of the pages over two centuries that attests to the physical integrity of the collection. Page sequencing, ink bleed-through, rips and folds, and other material markers on the copies demonstrate that the South Carolina House and Senate copies of the first tribunal's records are likely almost as complete today as they were when Jeannerett made them. It is likely that very little—if anything—was lost or removed from the collections submitted to the legislature that November. These three stories of the papers have driven important aspects of the interpretation provided in this book: that the movement was not a fiction of the court and that the papers were not faked. Because we can examine these copies with more confidence and knowledge about their origins, we can show how the tribunal distorted some of the evidence in its published story to make Vesey the sole instigator. This new approach allows a more nuanced understanding of the power dynamics of the fight between the white investigators and the Black community. The community withheld more information than the court realized. The detainees and other people in the community deceived the court strategically. Denmark Vesey was not the lone instigator or sole leader of the movement, and it was community based.

The Writing

In late May of 1822, Intendant James Hamilton and city investigators started writing notes, orders, and correspondence about their investigation. They began by using randomly available pieces of paper. This informal method was common in a time when paper was not industrially standardized, cheap, and ubiquitous. Officials and people in business often had only loose, differently sized, scrap pieces of paper on hand. Besides, Hamilton and the other earliest investigators were not yet certain there was anything much to record about the report of rebellion they had received. But the ad hoc recordkeeping appears to have continued after the city made Lionel Kennedy and Thomas Parker the leaders of the formal tribunal. Throughout the investigation, it appears that Hamilton, Kennedy, Parker, and numerous others who witnessed or participated in the legal proceedings simply built an archive of happenstance pages and notebooks—perhaps in a pile stored in a satchel. This might simply have been the typical method of Lionel Kennedy, the lead magistrate for the June and July tribunal. Kennedy was a state legislator who sometimes wrote committee reports. Unlike some of his punctilious and precise colleagues, Kennedy's surviving, signed reports as committee chair are on scraps of paper, written inexpertly and hurriedly.[1] Likewise, Kennedy appears to have kept chaotic records of the 1822 tribunal's proceedings. We have two neat manuscripts in the House and Senate records only because they are copies. This appearance is a veneer.

Kennedy and Parker did not lead or participate in the August tribunal, which formed only after they and the three freeholders working with them had resigned. The August proceedings were brief and created irregular records, too. It appears that the existing papers from August might be originals. They were collected separately, were not copied, and were added to the state archive's collection after the June and July copies were submitted to the House and Senate. They may have been added during the legislative session of 1822–23 or possibly at any time in the nineteenth or twentieth century before the entire archive was unfortunately laminated for preservation. The focus of debate among historians has been the June and July materials, implicitly, because they cover nearly all of the investigation's most significant events, including all the proceedings against the known leaders, the most significant confessions, and nearly all of the executions. The June and July records comprise well over 100 pages, while the August papers amount to barely more than a dozen pages.

Copies of the June and July records were made at the order of the governor and by a clerk he hired before the legislature convened for the fall. Governor Thomas Bennett personally hired Christopher Jeannerett on his own authority. Jeannerett was a middling-class man who lived near Bennett's house and his mills on Bull Street. Jeannerett wrote in a refined and regulated hand, but if he had expected the tribunal to supply a tidy collection of notes when hired, he'd have been disappointed. Many documents had no dates and no page numbers and were out of sequence in the collection. He made a remarkable archival choice facing the daunting task of copying this pile: He copied the pages exactly as they were presented. He loyally reproduced their utterly disheveled state in his mannered and polite clerical style. He made a couple of his own errors, too, unfortunately. Monday Gell's July 13 confession starts with a dramatic sentence announcing that he knows he is about to die. The Senate copy of the record preserves that line, but the House copy omits it. It is the only truly glaring mistake Jeannerett made. In general, he approached the tedious task Bennett hired him for with devotion, skill, and precision. One great benefit of his work is that it reveals that the *Official Report* and the *Negro Plot* were not strictly loyal transcriptions of the tribunal's papers. Hamilton, Kennedy, and Parker filled in details from their own memories and notes when they published these accounts of the investigatory proceedings. And they omitted or changed some details.[2]

Governor Bennett revealed in his own message to the legislature that he was not entirely confident in the *Official Report*, but he never claimed the proceedings were faked or the uprising movement was not real or a threat. Knowing that this skeptic was the source of our only existing copy of the investigatory manuscripts deflects the wholesale fraud accusations against the tribunal's records that some historians have made. Bennett would not have cooperated with an invented story. In fact, Bennett might have resented the tribunal for disrupting his business by killing a couple of his enslaved workers—whose lives he pleaded (unsuccessfully) with the magistrates to spare. He quietly sought a formal opinion from the South Carolina attorney general on the legality of the proceedings and was disappointed to be told it was a lawful proceeding. He distanced himself from the court's decisions, privately and publicly, and gained new enemies in doing so. He refused, on a couple occasions, to help the court carry out some of its decisions, telling them they were "clothed" in sufficient power and insinuating that they do their jobs themselves. It is impossible that such a person would have suddenly decided to become an accessory to a complete fraud on the public by the tribunal. If the investigatory records were fake, then he and Jeannerett would have known it when the papers came into the governor's possession. He would have trumpeted the fraud. The origins of the existing copies stand as direct evidence against claims that (1) the investigatory proceedings never happened and (2) the tribunal records were faked.[3]

The Story from the Handwriting Evidence

The method for identifying handwriting by an unknown author requires comparing a sample of that author's handwriting with samples known to be from specific authors with certainty. It is best if the samples are large. However, only one short sample of Jeannerett's handwriting is known to survive. Fortunately, it is a document related to the Vesey affair. In June 1822, at the start of the investigations, a Captain Martindale received orders from Governor Bennett to mobilize his militia unit. However, Martindale discovered that a portion of the unit's weapons were in disrepair and hired a gunsmith named John Shirer to make emergency repairs. Martindale died before Shirer was fully paid. The justice of the peace who eventually approved the rest of the payment to Shirer in 1823 was Christopher Jeannerett. In ordering Shirer to be paid, Jeannerett gave us the only surviving, positively identified sample of his handwriting. He wrote the receipt by hand and signed it (see fig. 3.1). Though it is a small sample, because it is about the 1822 uprising events it has an unusually high density of words, characters, and numerals in common with the court records. "Martindale" was a unique name in the region at the time, and the name was written in a unique style in both Jeannerett's sample and in the tribunal record copies. Thomas Bennett's handwriting style does not match and neither does the writing of any of the clerks then active in government circles, such as Jervis Henry Stevens, James W. Rouse, and Martin Strobel.[4]

When he sat down to copy the tribunal's records, Christopher Jeannerett surely remembered the crisis and the executions vividly even though he had taken no part in the proceedings. He might even have been acquainted with Denmark Vesey. He lived at 21 Bull Street in 1822, directly across the street from Vesey. Coming and going, or even just looking out the window, Jeannerett would have had a view of Vesey's home. They must have seen each other on Bull Street nearly daily—must have even walked right past each other at times. The two men were about the same age. Both men rented their home. However, unlike Vesey, Jeannerett owned four enslaved people and he doubtless lived a more prosperous life on this basis. Jeannerett had more "middle class" jobs than Vesey. He was a bookkeeper, teacher, and bank teller. He sometimes held minor positions of public trust. It would not be surprising if he and Governor Bennett were well acquainted. Bennett lived just a couple blocks away at 19 Lynch Street and his mills were close by, too.[5]

Jeannerett's order to pay for the repair of the Charleston Neck Rangers' guns has words and characters in common with the 1822 investigatory records. Some of these words are relatively common. For example, Jeannerett writes the word "makes" on the 1823 receipt as *makes*, and it corresponds well to "make" *make* in the Charleston manuscript copies of the investigation records. Placing them next to each other, one can readily see they are nearly alike in penmanship. Specific characteristics to consider are the shapes of letters, how the letters are connected, how they are completed with dots and crosses, and how they are decorated with flourishes and curls. The first curl on the *m* in "makes" and "make" is identical. The attachment of the three letters *m-a-k* to each other is also the same. The method for forming the letter *a* is similar, and the *k* is the same. The *e* looks different because the word is plural in the first example and singular in the second. But even if the samples were for the exact same word, some variation is normal for any writer. Changes in pen, paper, ink, emotion, setting for doing the writing, and even health condition at the time of writing can change the appearance of a person's handwriting. Further, other clerks, such as Jervis Henry Stevens, also sometimes wrote common words, such as "of," "that," "to," and "the," similarly to those found in the official records (see table 5.1). As a result, common words likely cannot positively identify Jeannerett on their own. In fact, most features of the best clerks' handwriting will be similar because they often had similar training.

A key task for identifying the writer of the official records is to identify unique characteristics of the clerk who created the tribunal copies and see if there are any matches across the documents. There are very strong similarities

TABLE 5.1 Handwriting samples: The investigatory record copies and four clerks with similar handwriting

Handwriting source	Words beginning with "A" or "a"
Tribunal manuscript records	
Senate and House copies of tribunal's investigatory records, 1822	*Army, a'ffiand, and, Arsenal, as*
Martin Strobel (*presumably the governor's clerk*)	
Governor Bennett's official correspondence copies, 1822	*and*
Governor Bennett's contingent fund account, 1822	*Army, April, arsenal, as*
Jervis Henry Stevens	
Petition to South Carolina General Assembly, 1806	*An, as*
Signed comptroller receipt, 1821	n/a
James W. Rouse	
Signed comptroller clerk receipt, 1823	*as*
Signed letter about old account, 1828	*ant, as, and*
Christopher Jeannerett	
Signed receipt for South Carolina Comptroller General records, 1823	*and, affrand, above, Account*

Words beginning with "C" or "c"	Words beginning with "D" or "d"
Charleston Charleston Christopher Black.	day Domingo Denmark done
Charleston.	District
Charleston Ch Couling...	during detained don...
Comptroller Clerk	D
n/a	n/a
Clerk	n/a
Charleston Clerk	Dear declines
Christopher Charleston So Carolina — "C" in "So. Carolina"	D day date

TABLE 5.1 (continued)

Handwriting source	Words beginning with "J" or "j"
Tribunal manuscript records	
Senate and House copies of tribunal's investigatory records, 1822	*July John June*
Martin Strobel (*presumably the governor's clerk*)	
Governor Bennett's official correspondence copies, 1822	*John*
Governor Bennett's contingent fund account, 1822	*John Jeannerett June*
Jervis Henry Stevens	
Petition to South Carolina General Assembly, 1806	n/a
Signed comptroller receipt, 1821	*[signature]* "Jervis"
James W. Rouse	
Signed comptroller clerk receipt, 1823	n/a
Signed letter about old account, 1828	*January*
Christopher Jeannerett	
Signed receipt for South Carolina Comptroller General records, 1823	*July Jeannerett J. J. John*

Words beginning with "M" or "m"	Words beginning with "O" or "o"
Martindaly me Master Mr muskits	of Oath, over One
Martindale Marion	of
Mobile Mill M. Messenger making Master made	O. F over over on one
maillu Master "Master"	One of
	n/a
n/a	n/a
Mr M M	of of
Martindale Mr Muskits me	of Oath One

TABLE 5.1 (continued)

Handwriting source	Words beginning with "S" or "s"
Tribunal manuscript records	
Senate and House copies of tribunal's investigatory records, 1822	*Saturday, St Domingo, Sally, sworn*
Martin Strobel (*presumably the governor's clerk*)	
Governor Bennett's official correspondence copies, 1822	*State.*
Governor Bennett's contingent fund account, 1822	*Sixty, Schurer*
Jervis Henry Stevens	
Petition to South Carolina General Assembly, 1806	*Six, Salary*
Signed comptroller receipt, 1821	*[illegible]* "So. Carolina"
James W. Rouse	
Signed comptroller clerk receipt, 1823	n/a
Signed letter about old account, 1828	*Sir, State*
Christopher Jeannerett	
Signed receipt for South Carolina Comptroller General records, 1823	*Schurer, Sworn, Sworn, State of S. Carolina*

Words beginning with "T" or "t"	Words beginning with "W" or "w"
that the to	*witness who who work Wilson*
the to	*who*
n/a	*Wilson with witnesses work*
to to the	n/a
n/a	n/a
n/a	n/a
the that to	*whether which will*
that the to "to…"	*who sworn* "w" in "Sworn"

Note: In addition to these key individuals with similar handwriting, I also identified known writing samples from dozens more clerks and ruled them out: Lionel Kennedy, Thomas Parker, Thomas Bennett, Lyon Levy, William Roach, John S. Cogdell, Benjamin Elmore, Thomas Lee, David Ramsay, C. Canaday, Benjamin Elmore, Henry M. Reid, Charles L. Black, J. W. Mitchell, John Robinson, William Miller, William F. DeSaussure, William M. Scott, Robert Anderson, William Martin, C. G. Memminger, Alfred Huger, John Murphy, Job Johnson, John Gault, Robert Gantt, Benjamin H. Saxon, David E. Dunlap, Felix Warley, John Sandford Dart, and W. S. Smith.

between unique handwriting characteristics of the investigatory records and Jeannerett's known writing sample from the following year (1823). In the tribunal copies the capital M is often written in a highly unusual way. For example, the letter M in "Master" in the tribunal's investigatory records has sharply pointed peaks, with the second peak rising higher than the first. Nearly all of the clerks for whom I found handwriting samples did the opposite of what the tribunal copyist did nearly all the time: they typically rounded the peaks in the capital M, and they made the first peak higher than the second. Only Jeannerrett and one other of the forty samples I was able to find in an extensive search for handwriting samples in South Carolina archives made the capital M in this pointed way. This unusual M is virtually identical to that in Jeannerett's known handwriting sample. The capital M and the entire name "Martindale" is virtually identical in both the investigatory records and Jeannerett's receipt (see table 5.1). Another unusual characteristic in the handwriting of both the investigatory records clerk and Jeannerett is in the word "Charleston." Jeannerett writes the capital C with a nearly horizontal high oval curl in the 1823 receipt he signed. In the court records for June and July, that distinctive C and indeed the entire word "Charleston" are written virtually identically. Other writers did not write "Charleston" quite this way, especially when it came to the capital C (see table 5.1). Jeannerett's "Charleston" and "Martindale" are nearly identical to words in the investigatory records in curvature, lift points, letter connections, and dots and crosses on letters. Several more favorably similar comparisons between the receipt and the investigatory copies exist. See table 5.1 to compare individual letters, combinations of letters, and full words. The handwriting of dozens of other writers who clerked in the era matches some of the distinctive features of the tribunal copyist's writing sometimes, but Jeannerett is by far the best match for the full combination of unique characteristics in the handwriting of the investigatory records copyist.[6]

The handwriting analysis taken together with the fact that Bennett named Jeannerett as being hired for "copying certain [unspecified] documents" just before he presented copies of the tribunal's records to the legislature means we can be certain that Jeannerett made the existing collection of copies of the June and July tribunal records. Furthermore, Jeannerett made both the House and the Senate copies of the June and July papers. The handwriting in both chambers' copies matches Jeannerett's, with differences merely being a matter of, perhaps, the quality of the quill pen or how much water he had mixed with his ink powder. For example, a comparison of Joe La Roche's testimony as written in the Senate copy and the House copy reveals only

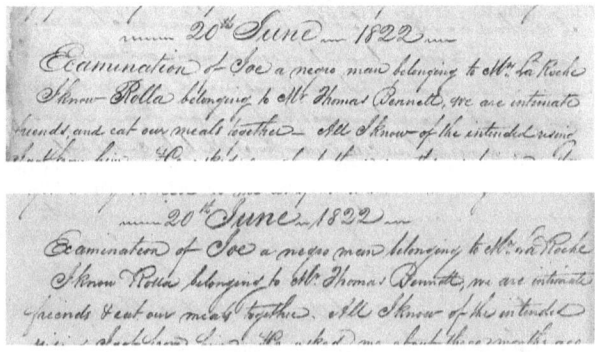

FIGURE 5.1 Lines from House and Senate copies of investigatory records, 1822. Governor's Messages, Court Proceedings and Testimony Regarding the Denmark Vesey Rebellion, South Carolina Department of Archives and History, Columbia.

superficial or very minor differences in the handwriting that do not indicate a different general style for making like words.

The differences are well within normal variability. All of the clerks working in public and private circles in the early nineteenth century had various ways of creating certain letters, and their writing also showed other minor variations due to changes in ink, paper, or other factors. Overall, these two samples are as similar as handwriting gets. They are by the same writer (see fig. 5.1).[7]

The Story from the Material Evidence of the Pages

Copy edits on the manuscript pages strengthen the conclusion that they were copied from an original that is now lost. There are copy edits that appear only in the House copy, such as striking the word "home" from William Colcock's confession. If we look at the same passage in the same testimony in the Senate copy, the word "home" does not appear at all. This might suggest that the Senate copy is the original. However, in other cases, an edit appears only in the Senate copy, such as a "were" inserted into Yorick Cross's confession. Such edits suggest that neither the Senate nor the House manuscript is the original. Rather, both have had different errors corrected against an authority that is now lost. An incomplete edit that appears in both copies further supports the claim that there was a lost original. In Billy Bulkley's testimony just before the tribunal adjourned on July 13, the words "Robert was coming" are inserted between lines in both copies. However neither copy has a caret indicating where the text should be inserted. Such a confusing failure to complete a correcting edit is unlikely to be done twice in the same place by the same fastidious clerk/teller/teacher in the same way, correcting the same error, in the same spot. Most likely, the caret was missing in a (now lost) original, and Jeannerett could not determine where to place the caret or the text so he just made a loyal copy of the confusingly incomplete edit. Lastly, that there was an original is suggested by the fact that Jeannerett's copies both share occasional elisions of simple facts. At the end of William Colcock's testimony, a phrase just before the start of the July 10 proceedings has an unresolved blank space in both the House and Senate copies: "crossing the ____ of Flinns Church." Jeannerett inserted an empty space, probably because he could not read the original's chicken scratch or because the original had a blank there for some reason.[8]

One can imagine the scene in which Jeannerett made the copies. At a desk, he has a stack of papers he has received. They are in a loose pile, perhaps wrapped by string or in a leather bag or paper envelope of some sort. Starting at the top of the pile, Jeannerett simply begins writing. He does not at first realize how odd it is that the records begin with an "examination" of Pompey Bryan without any context. When Pompey was detained on June 28, the investigatory hearings and proceedings had already been going on since June 19. By the twenty-eighth, several people had been imprisoned, tried, and convicted. But because there was no date on the manuscript, Jeannerett did not notice the incorrect order of the papers. He simply wrote the number 1 on the first sheet of paper and commenced copying. He kept that up for multiple pages, unwittingly reproducing eight or nine pages of undated and severely out-of-sequence "examinations" from June 24, then July 13, then July 5. Soon, Jeannerett stopped numbering his pages as the chaotic jumble of the original became clear. Jeannerett could have used the published versions of the investigatory records to insert dates, but doing so would have been arranging, even changing, the documents, not simply copying them. He was hired only to copy, and he would have known that it was illegal to alter or falsify a court record or judgment. The collection he created would have to reflect the randomness of the original.[9]

Ink and paper evidence further support the conclusion that the sequence of pages in the existing copies is likely the sequence as submitted to Jeannerett. Paper and ink were not standardized across batches before industrial manufacturing. People made their own ink from published recipes or else purchased powder from local suppliers to mix with water or other liquids. As a result of variation in the powders and in the mixing fluids, some inks were acidic and some more alkaline. The chemistry of any given batch might be almost unique. Iron gall ink, which was the most common type, oxidizes and fades from black to brown as time passes. Over time, its acids leach into the paper fibers adjacent to the pen strokes, compromising paper fibers as the ink oxidizes and acidifies. It also might leach acids onto any pages it rests against closely for prolonged periods of time. When iron gall ink is used, it is common to find shadows of the writing on adjacent pages due to this leaching. Much of the manuscript copies' ink has browned and most pages have acid stains from writing on adjacent pages. Searching the pages for evidence of whether any of the acid shadows reveal pages that have since been lost revealed none, though more work could be done in this regard.[10]

Either Jeannerett or the governor probably purchased the paper for the copies in Charleston, where they lived. There were options in the city. Foolscap was the most common type of writing paper in the era for business and government work. Clerks often used it for legal documents. But even foolscap was not standardized as to size or fiber source before industrialization. Its size as sold was often roughly sixteen by thirteen inches (40.6 × 33 cm). Cut in half, the paper created pairs of leaves approximately thirteen by eight inches (33 × 20.3 cm). However, because the sizes were not regulated and were not precision cut, the actual size of foolscap could vary a half inch or more between any two batches. Each supply of foolscap paper would have its own characteristics. And in fact, the copies of the June and July records appear to have been written on one or maybe two batches of foolscap, while the August records appear on differently sized foolscap paper stocks and scraps. Jeannerett, always the precise and regulated clerk/teller/teacher, had attempted to ensure he would have paper of consistent sizes for the entire copying job—a mark of his professionalism and experience.[11]

Evidence from the layout of the pages further reveals the condition of the original loose scraps and odd pages. First, in both copies there is a brief section of pagination starting with June 19 as page 1 and going up to page 11. But the content of the pages is slightly different between the Senate and House copies because of line spacing and character size differences. As a result, a given numbered page in the House copy is further into the proceedings than the same numbered page in the Senate copy, proving that the page numbers were not in the original but were an idea of Jeannerett's that he abandoned. Four-fifths of the collection is not paginated at all. Second, there are almost no page breaks in the House copy. The sequence of pages in the House copy is revealing. Because Jeannerett never started a new page from the original with a new page in his House copy but rather simply started writing a new line when he reached a new page in the original, the House copy reveals the order of pages as he encountered them in the lost original. Comparing the Senate copy's page and line breaks with the House copy confirms that it, too, recapitulated the sequence of documents in the House copy and—implicitly—the lost original. Therefore, records of the proceedings that are missing in the copies were missing in the lost original, too. An example of this is the proceedings against Denmark Vesey himself. The proceedings are mostly represented in the manuscript. However, the date, plea, and sentencing statement are missing. The sequence of documents in the House copy proves that Jeannerett never copied those parts of the proceedings, certainly because he never received them from the tribunal. Kennedy and Parker sent just enough of Vesey's trial to confirm how poorly they had preserved official records of these felony cases against both enslaved property and free Black people. The documents demonstrate the proceedings were real, but his own shoddy recordkeeping should have embarrassed Kennedy, who held a seat representing the Charleston area in the state legislature when these copies came over from the governor.[12]

The Story of Their Survival: Material Evidence of Preservation

At least three significant investigatory documents exist outside the state archives, but physical and handwriting evidence confirms they were never part of the Jeannerett copies. A version of John Enslow's statement is at the South Carolina Historical Society, and one of Bacchus Hammett's statements as well as another statement from John Enslow are held at Duke University. Neither collection is on paper stock of the same size as the House and Senate copies and neither matches Jeannerett's handwriting. It is possible that either the Enslow confession or the Bacchus confession were part of the tribunal's lost original pile of loose notes, but the handwriting does not match that of Lionel Kennedy or Thomas Parker. These documents might also be copies made by or for Bacchus's and John's slavers. The Jeannerett copies have always been stored in batches of papers, not as a bound book. Over time, the pages were lightly bound in three successive ways: (1) folded in batches, (2) bound with ribbon, and (3) laminated and bound with thread. The latter is how they are preserved today. Each method did new damage to the papers, but it appears that nothing has been lost from the collection that was presented to the legislature in the fall of 1822.[13]

At first, both the House and Senate copies of document B (the governor submitted the investigatory copies as item B in a series of documents labeled with letters) were unbound and folded into packets. The packets were ordered to be laid out on a table for legislators in each chamber to consult.[14] On document B there are two or three sets of folding marks. One set has a pair of shaded areas, probably where there were wide-radius, rounded edges created by folds in a thick stack of paper that collected dirt and friction wear over many years of storage. Some other parts of the records reveal thin, sharp folds like those of an envelope. Here the paper fibers long ago began to break and allow the pages to fragment into sections along the fold lines. Such deterioration indicates many years of storage in this folded manner. Each copy of exhibit B (House and Senate) has a pair of snake-eyes perforations in the margin for a ribbon to tie the pages together. Such a binding was in place long enough to wear the pages and badly tear some of them in irregular ways, as repeated paging through the collection expanded the perforations around the ribbon. All the June and July papers were bound this way. However, the governor's cover message has three holes instead of two. And the August investigatory records in the Senate copy have no holes for ribbon at all, suggesting they remained loose while the June and July investigatory records were bound together for years.[15]

It is remarkable that any of these pages survived given what the collection endured. They were stored for decades in the trifolded state in which they had lain on the table in the legislative chamber in late 1822 and early 1823. This long period resulted in staining, creasing, and stress tearing along the folds that permanently damaged the papers and may be why a couple pages that are in the House copy are missing from the end of the Senate copy. During the Civil War, Charleston was bombarded, burned, and looted. Among other things, all of Charleston's loose wills were lost. Many of Governor Bennett's papers also appear to have been lost, probably because they were stored with his family in Charleston. If Kennedy's family was preserving the original records of the tribunals, they, too, were perhaps destroyed in the war. Archivists in the state capital, Columbia, saved the Jeannerett copies from destruction when they moved the state records out of the city before fire and looting destroyed both public and private buildings in 1865. At some point in the late nineteenth century, perhaps an archivist unfolded the papers and "bound" them with ribbons. They stayed in this state for many years. In the mid-twentieth century, the entire collection was subjected to an acetate lamination process that has preserved them at the cost of requiring readers to view the pages through an ultrathin layer of transparent fibers.[16]

Conclusion

It is appropriate that such a collection of papers is so tortured. It is physically marked by the chaos and agony of a struggle to the death. Enslaved men and women protected themselves as well as beloved friends and relatives. Slavers enforced their desire to continue exploiting those very loves and relationships, generation after generation. The documents are marked by this conflict. Some of the accused appear to have sensed that they could not save themselves or anyone else. Feelings of fear, desolation, and anger in such moments of realization would have been immense. But for some, perhaps for many, such feelings may have been unfortunately very familiar. Strong emotions might not have been so confusing to the experienced and tactful. They were veterans who had been in such situations before and could better judge how to act because they knew better how to cope with their fear. Slavers beat, sold, or killed enslaved people in the presence of others frequently enough that many had seen it or experienced it dreadfully often. Denmark Vesey had perhaps experienced and seen it; so had Monday Gell, Peter Poyas, Gullah Jack, and Perault Strohecker—and Prudence Bussacre, Sally Howard, and Amaritta La Roche. Their experience informed a terrifying understanding but could also shape veteran strategies of silence, deception, and tactically incomplete truth-telling. It is ironic, but the incompleteness of the papers and distortions of the official story are traces of the success of these people's strategies. Maybe incompleteness and contortion are qualities such archives should have. It is also ironic that the collection only came into existence because a white political rival of the tribunal magistrates had it made. And in a last irony, it exists today only because archivists protected it from the ravages of the Civil War that ended the chattel slavery that the 1822 uprising movement had marked for destruction four decades earlier. What survives remains undoubtedly one of the most significant primary source collections on African American life and rebellion written in English during the era of slavery.

Acknowledgments

There are too many people to acknowledge as fully as deserved. My greatest thanks are to Wendy Gonaver, Doug Egerton, and the anonymous reviewers for the University of North Carolina Press for their commentary. I hope the final text reflects the improvements recommended. I wish to thank archivists and librarians Chuck Lesser, Harlan Greene, Molly Silliman, Wade Dorsey, and Gosha Domagala for their expert and generous assistance. I am grateful to Bernie Powers at the Center for the Study of Slavery in Charleston and to the Carolina Low Country in the Atlantic World Program at the College of Charleston for support and community over the years. Colleagues at the University of Ghana at Legon had a formative influence on the writing of this book when I was there in 2016 and 2018, especially Akosua Adomako Ampofo, Samuel Ntewusu, and Akosua Adoma Perbi. Several current and former colleagues at Soka University have also been formative in terms of theory, approach, and methods: Ryan Caldwell, Aneil Rallin, Shane Barter, Chika Esiobu, Monika Calef, and many more. I am grateful to the undergraduate research assistants who, over the last several years, have made direct contributions to this book, especially Khin Thazin, Jordyn Saito, Anjan Rana Magar, Keito Newman, and Siena Taylor. I want to express my gratitude for friends, community organizers, and collaborators in California with whom I have worked in praxis for so many years—particularly Chicanxs Unidxs de Orange County in Santa Ana and the Acjachemen Nation/Juaneño Band of Mission Indians in San Juan Capistrano. Essays featuring earlier versions of some of this research have been published by the *William and Mary Quarterly* and the University of South Carolina Press, and I am grateful for the commentary I received from peer reviews in each case. Last, I wish to acknowledge Soka University of America for the financial support that enabled several extended visits to archives in South Carolina.

Notes

Abbreviations

BHP	Benjamin Hammett Papers, Duke University Libraries, Durham, NC
CCPL	Charleston County Public Library, Charleston, SC
City Gazette	City Gazette and Commercial Daily Advertiser (Charleston, SC)
HL	Huntington Library, San Marino, CA
House Copy, SCDAH	Governor's Message, Evidence B, Court Proceedings and Testimony Regarding the Denmark Vesey Rebellion, South Carolina House of Representatives Copy, South Carolina Department of Archives and History, Columbia
SCDAH	South Carolina Department of Archives and History, Columbia
SCHS	South Carolina Historical Society, Charleston
Senate Copy, SCDAH	Governor's Message, Document B, Court Proceedings and Testimony Regarding the Denmark Vesey Rebellion, South Carolina Senate Copy, South Carolina Department of Archives and History, Columbia

Prologue

1. On June 16 the new moon was still a few days away. It was due on Wednesday, June 19. But rebels wanted a quiet Sabbath Sunday, not a busy Wednesday, for their revolution. On Sunday, June 16, the not-quite-new moon was past its last quarter. The waning sliver of a moon would not rise until an hour or so before dawn. Until then, the sky would be as dark as on a new moon night until well after midnight. Even when the sliver of the crescent moon rose, it would provide only the slightest illumination. See James R. Schenk, *City Directory* [...] *1822* (Charleston, SC, 1822). Similar, corroborating data is available in *The Connecticut Almanack* [...] *for 1822* (New Haven, CT, 1821), 6–7, https://archive.org/details/ConnecticutAlmanac1822. See also *Time's Telescope for 1822* [...] (London, 1822), 175; and *The Nautical Almanac and Astronomical Ephemeris* [...] *1822* (London, 1820), 61.

2. Some Black Charlestonians came to a conclusion that Kellie Carter Jackson observes McCune Smith came to in 1848 (himself also citing the 1822 Charleston Uprising Movement organizing): "Our white brethren cannot understand us unless we speak to them in their own language; they recognize only the philosophy of force," see *Force and Freedom: Black Abolitionists and the Politics of Violence* (Philadelphia: University of Pennsylvania Press, 2019), 2, 123–25; Vincent Brown, *Tacky's Revolt: The Story of an Atlantic Slave War* (Cambridge, MA: Belknap Press of Harvard University Press, 2020),

6–7; Manuel Barcia, *The Great African Slave Revolt of 1825* (Baton Rouge: Louisiana State University Press, 2012), 7–8, 97–119; Holly Jackson, *American Radicals: How Nineteenth Century Protest Shaped the Nation* (New York: Crown, 2019), 51–63; Manisha Sinha, *The Slave's Cause: A History of Abolition* (New Haven, CT: Yale University Press, 2016), esp. chaps. 5 and 6; Julius S. Scott, *The Common Wind: Afro-American Currents in the Age of the Haitian Revolution* (New York: Verso 2018), xvii, 2–3, 196; Walter C. Rucker, *The River Flows On: Black Resistance, Culture, and Identity Formation in Early America* (Baton Rouge: Louisiana State University Press, 2006), 5–9; Daniel Rasmussen, *American Uprising: the Untold Story of America's Largest Slave Revolt* (New York: Harper, 2011); Timothy Patrick McCarthy and John Stauffer, eds., *Prophets of Protest: Reconsidering the History of American Abolitionism* (New York: New Press, 2006); Steven Hahn, *A Nation under Our Feet: Black Political Struggles in the Rural South from Slavery to the Great Migration* (Cambridge, MA: Harvard University Press, 2003); Eric Williams, *Capitalism and Slavery*, 3rd ed. (Chapel Hill: University of North Carolina Press, 2021).

3. Douglas R. Egerton, *He Shall Go Out Free: The Lives of Denmark Vesey* (New York: Madison House, 1999), 49–50, 80–81. Denmark Vesey's former wives and his children remained enslaved. Egerton identifies Vesey's wives as Beck, Dolly, and Susan, in that order. He also had several children.

4. *City Gazette*, August 8, 1822, 3; "Confession of Monday Gell," July 13, 1822, Senate Copy, SCDAH; "Second Confession of Monday Gell," July 23, 1822, Senate Copy, SCDAH; Lionel H. Kennedy and Thomas Parker, *An Official Report of Sundry Negroes, Charged with an Attempt to Raise an Insurrection* [...] (Charleston, SC, 1822), 171; "Confession of Yorick Cross," Senate Copy, SCDAH.

5. Tiya Miles, *All That She Carried: The Journey of Ashley's Sack, a Black Family Keepsake* (New York: Random House, 2021), 3–4; Margaret Washington Creel, *"A Peculiar People": Slave Religion and Community-Culture among the Gullahs* (New York: New York University Press, 1988), 22, 148–66. Creel clearly appreciated that the events of 1822 had origins in the previous seven or so years and were of the character of a movement, the causes of which she found in Christianity and Gullah (African) ideology. Vincent Brown describes the local contingency and dynamics of any rebellion against slavery in *Tacky's Revolt*, 162–63.

Chapter One

1. My use of "arrived" here is meant specifically to evoke the meaning in the term *arrivant*, coined by the Afro-Caribbean poet Kamau Braithwaite to describe the position of African-descended people in the Americas. Jodi Byrd, Stephanie Smallwood, and others have recently proposed *arrivant* as an analytical concept for thinking about slavery and African American status relative to settler colonialism in America. This third category is useful for thinking about the radical potential of love and commitment to acquaintances, friends, and family. See Jodi Byrd, *The Transit of Empire: Indigenous Critiques of Colonialism* (Minneapolis: University of Minnesota Press, 2011), xix; and Stephanie E. Smallwood, "Reflections on Settler Colonialism, the Hemispheric Americas, and Chattel Slavery," *WMQ* 76, no. 3 (2019): 407–16. See also Vincent Brown, *Tacky's Revolt: The Story of an Atlantic Slave War* (Cambridge, MA: Belknap Press of Harvard University Press,

2020), 86 (on an eight-to-one ratio in Jamaica ca. 1750); and Carolyn Fick, *Making Haiti: The Saint Domingue Revolution from Below* (Knoxville: University of Tennessee Press, 1990), 278n14 (on a possible ten-to-one or wider ratio in 1789). Population data from Robert Mills, *Atlas of South Carolina* (Baltimore: F. Lucas Jr., 1825). Capture ad for Mary Woods from *City Gazette*, June 25, 1822, 2.

2. For evidence of family, friendship, and other social ties between Black women and men in Charleston, see the testimonies of Prudence Bussacre, Frank Ferguson, Sally Howard, Joe La Roche, Agrippa Perry, and others in House Copy, SCDAH; and in Senate Copy, SCDAH; Manisha Sinha, *Counter-Revolution of Slavery: Politics and Ideology in Antebellum South Carolina* (Chapel Hill: University of North Carolina Press, 2003), 12; and Saidiya Hartman, *Scenes of Subjection: Terror, Slavery, and Self-Making in Nineteenth-Century America* (New York: Oxford University Press, 1997), 277. Though the United States outlawed the slave trade in stages and completely by 1808, there was extensive smuggling and Charleston was a hub in the illicit networks, so there were possibly very recent African arrivals among the enslaved population in Charleston in 1822. See Ernest Obadele-Starks, *Freebooters and Smugglers: The Foreign Slave Trade in the United States after 1808* (Fayetteville: University of Arkansas Press, 2007), 9–10, 17, 20–22, 64–65; Michael A. Gomez, "Africans, Culture, and Islam in the Lowcountry," in *African American Life in the Georgia Lowcountry: The Atlantic World and the Gullah Geechee*, ed. Philip Morgan (Athens: University of Georgia Press, 2010), 104–5, 111, 119–21; and Leonardo Marques, *The United States and the Transatlantic Slave Trade to the Americas, 1776–1867* (New Haven, CT: Yale University Press, 2016). For most of a century before 1808, Charleston newspapers sometimes identified the places of origin of enslaved people. More than 120,000 enslaved persons' African origins can be identified. See William S. Pollitzer, "The Relationship of the Gullah-Speaking People of Coastal South Carolina and Georgia to Their African Ancestors," in *The Legacy of Ibo Landing*, ed. Marquetta L. Goodwine (Atlanta: Clarity, 1998), 54; and Douglas Chambers, *Murder at Montpellier: Igbo Africans in Virginia* (Jackson: University of Mississippi Press, 2005), 38.

3. As Saidiya Hartman has pointed out — alongside Hortense Spillers, Jennifer Morgan, and others — reproductive labor was central to slave labor in the United States during the slaving era and since. Saidiya Hartman, "Belly of the World: A Note on Black Women's Reproductive Labors," *Souls* 18, no. 1 (2016): 167; Jennifer L. Morgan, *Laboring Women: Reproduction and Gender in New World Slavery* (Philadelphia: University of Pennsylvania Press, 2004), 10, 112–45. In 1822, the white authorities in Charleston convened a special tribunal of magistrates and freeholders to investigate the claims of insurrectionary conspiracy as well as conduct trials, decide guilt, and order and carry out sentences. Throughout this book, because of the menacing and informal nature of the tribunal's authority over the accused as well as irregularities in the tribunal records, I represent statements attributed to the uprising movement's members in italics rather than in quotation marks to emphasize that the words are possibly only paraphrases and not necessarily precise. For a clear example of the tribunal changing the words of a confession, compare Bacchus Hammett's first and second confessions in the manuscript with what the tribunal published in its official report, discussed in chapter 3 of this book. "Examination of Joe La Roche," House Copy, SCDAH.

4. Harriet Jacobs, *Incidents in the Life of a Slave Girl* [...], ed. Jean Fagan Yellin (1861; Cambridge, MA: Harvard University Press, 1987), 100–101; Mary Prince, *The History of Mary Prince, a West Indian Slave: Related by Herself* [...] (London, 1831), 21. As Tiya Miles proposes, love is contingent on local, cultural, and historical "moments," and in Charleston in 1822 it layered gendered constructions of the "new solidarities" and a sense of "belonging" that Vincent Brown discusses. See Tiya Miles, *All That She Carried: The Journey of Ashley's Sack, a Black Family Keepsake* (New York: Random House, 2021), 207, 308n18; and Brown, *Tacky's Revolt*, 244–46. On fugitivity, see Fred Moten, "The Case of Blackness," *Criticism* 50, no. 2 (2008): 187–88; Tina Campt, *Listening to Images* (Durham, NC: Duke University Press, 2017), 32; Judith Butler and Athena Athanasiou, *Dispossession: The Performative in the Political* (Cambridge, UK: Polity, 2013), 21; Leigh Patel, "Fugitive Practices: Learning in a Settler Colony," *Educational Studies* 55, no. 3 (2019): 253–61; and Karen Cook Bell, *Running from Bondage: Enslaved Women and their Remarkable Fight for Freedom in Revolutionary America* (Cambridge: Cambridge University Press, 2021), 137–59. See also Neil Roberts, *Freedom as Marronage* (Chicago: University of Chicago Press, 2015), 73–74. On cultural capital—and social, economic, and symbolic capital—see Pierre Bourdieu, *Distinction: A Social Critique of the Judgment of Taste* (Cambridge, MA: Harvard University Press, 1984).

5. "William Paul Testimony," June 19, 1822, House Copy, SCDAH.

6. Sarah Paul was Denmark Vesey's stepdaughter from a previous marriage, and historians have identified her as "Sarah Vesey." However, William Paul, who was enslaved in the same household as Sarah, identifies the Paul family as her slavers. If so, she would have been known by that name and not by "Vesey" no matter how she or Denmark might have felt. Naming her Vesey would have been a little like reassigning the Paul family's property to Denmark Vesey. So the family name "Paul" is probably how she was referred to when necessary. Using the name "Sarah Paul" represents this ugly, oppressive situation and underscores what Denmark Vesey had in common with the enslaved rebels. Denmark's family was not entirely "his" family, because parts of it were held as other people's property. See "William Paul Testimony," June 19, 1822, House Copy, SCDAH; and Frederick Douglass, *Narrative of the Life of Frederick Douglass* (Boston, 1845), 106–7. On the political economy of slavery, see Eric Williams, *Capitalism and Slavery*, 3rd ed. (Chapel Hill: University of North Carolina Press, 2021), 29.

7. Lionel H. Kennedy and Thomas Parker, *An Official Report of Sundry Negroes, Charged with an Attempt to Raise an Insurrection* [...] (Charleston, SC, 1822), 110; Jeff Strickland, *Unequal Freedoms: Ethnicity, Race, and White Supremacy in Civil War-Era Charleston* (Gainesville: University Press of Florida, 2010), 3.

8. Sven Beckert and Seth Rothman, *Slavery's Capitalism: A New History of American Economic Development* (Philadelphia: University of Pennsylvania Press, 2016), 10–12; Adam Rothman, *Slave Country: American Expansion and the Origins of the Deep South* (Cambridge, MA: Harvard University Press, 2005), 86–98, 198–99 (Charleston slavery exports into the Mississippi River Valley were significant but the largest in volume); John Craig Hammond, "Slavery, Settlement, and Empire: The Expansion and Growth of Slavery in the Interior of the North American Continent, 1770–1820," *Journal of the Early Republic* 32, no. 2 (2012): 200. Hundreds of thousands of Africans—perhaps almost 800,000—were smuggled into the United States by slave traffickers from 1808

to 1861. See Obadele-Starks, *Freebooters and Smugglers*, 8–10; Stephanie Smallwood, *Saltwater Slavery: A Middle Passage from Africa to American Diaspora* (Cambridge, MA: Harvard University Press, 2007), 34–36, chap. 2; Michael Ralph and Maya Singhal, "Racial Capitalism," *Theory and Society*, December 20, 2019; and Cedric Robinson, *Black Marxism: The Making of the Black Radical Tradition* (1983; Chapel Hill: University of North Carolina Press, 2000).

9. Emma Hart, *Building Charleston: Town and Society in the Eighteenth-Century British Atlantic World* (Charlottesville: University of Virginia Press, 2009), 193.

10. Hart, *Building Charleston*, 193–94.

11. On the Ashley River ferry team boat, see William Faux, *Memorable Days in America* [. . .] *November 27, 1818–July 21, 1820* (London, 1823), 73; Karl Bernhard, Duke of Saxe-Weimar-Eisenach, *Travels through North America, during the Years 1825 and 1826, in Two Volumes* (Philadelphia, 1828), 2:4; and *City Gazette*, December 8, 1818, 2; May 8, 1819, 2; January 5, 1822, 2.

12. *City Gazette*, January 1, 1822, 2; May 22, 1822, 2; December 24, 1822, 2.

13. There is no direct evidence of Bennett's mill expansion being completed by the end of the 1810s, but the inference is strong. Using surveyor plats, published maps, and passing references in newspapers from the 1810s and early 1820s that describe features of the expanded mill complex—such as more than one sawmill near Boundary Street and a wharf at Bull Street—the picture of a complete redesign by about 1818 emerges. For example, in 1821 Bennett advertised his mills on the west side of town as the site of a wharf that was the embarkation point for passengers and freight leaving for St. Augustine (*City Gazette*, July 9, 1821, 3). There was no wharf at the site before the expansion and rebuild. Jonathan Lucas and Thomas Bennett disputed the boundary between their Ashley River expansion millponds from at least 1811 until at least 1838, revealing numerous details of the rebuilding process. See John Diamond, ["Plats of Charleston Neck,"] 1807, 32-47-10/12, Maps/Plats, SCHS; *City Gazette*, May 19, 1817, 1; March 3, 1818, 4; September 15, 1818, 3; January 18, 1822, 3; and March 4, 1823, 3; mill complex plats, 1838 and n.d., both in McCrady Plat Collection, SCDAH; plat of 1813 survey (copy), no. 7913, McCrady Plats Collection, Charleston Registry of Deeds, Charleston, SC; Henry S. Tanner, *New Map of South Carolina*, 1836, David Rumsey Historical Map Collection, accessed June 27, 2020, www.davidrumsey.com/static/maps2782.html; and G. Bonnor, "Plan of the City of Charleston, South Carolina, 1802," 33-65-14, Maps/Plats, SCHS.

14. Records of the Commissioners of Streets and Lamps and the Board of Commissioners for Opening and Widening of Streets, Lanes and Alleys, 1806–66, 26–27, City of Charleston Records, CCPL; *City Gazette*, June 3, 1819, 3; February 19, 1821, 3; April 1, 1822, 3; April 2, 1822, 2; November 20, 1822, 3; Schenk, *City Directory*, 79.

15. *City Gazette*, June 3, 1820, 3 (Egleston); June 26, 1820, 1 (Chieffell); October 4, 1820, 3 (Coats and West); February 23, 1821, 3 (Egleston expansion).

16. For Ceasar Smith description, see "Further Confession of Bacchus," July 13, 1822, Senate Copy, SCDAH. Marsh Street, Vernon Street, and Inspection Street, southeast of the corner of Boundary and East Bay Streets, appear to have been streets in name only until at least 1822. Concord, right beside Gadsden's busy wharf, shows signs of substantial and active occupation in the records as early as 1805. Gadsden's own plans had been

dealt a setback by his early death in the first decade of the nineteenth century, leading to the sale of the land to satisfy claims against the estate. *City Gazette*, June 20, 1805, 3 (development at Concord Street); March 2, 1807, 3 (sale of Gadsden, deceased, lands).

17. Joseph Purcell. "[Plat of Sans Souci] 1799," 32-43-10, Maps/Plats, SCHS. For a sample of fugitive slave ads that feature waterman knowledge by the enslaved, see *City Gazette*, January 4, 1821, 4; November 30, 1821, 1; April 25, 1822, 1; August 8, 1822, 3; October 21, 1822, 3; February 10, 1823, 3. David S. Cecelski, *The Waterman's Song: Slavery and Freedom in Maritime North Carolina* (Chapel Hill: University of North Carolina Press, 2001), 127–29, 132–33.

18. Bernhard, *Travels through North America*, 2:13.

19. Walter Rucker refers to "ethnic enclaves" of indigenous Africans, slaves from Saint-Domingue, and Gullahs in which Akan, Mande, and Igbo cultural resources frequently became part of everyday life. See Walter C. Rucker, *The River Flows On: Black Resistance, Culture, and Identity Formation in Early America* (Baton Rouge: Louisiana State University Press, 2006), 5–9, 13 (Charleston was no exception, as Rucker suggests). See also Pollitzer, "Relationship," 54; and Michael A. Gomez, *Exchanging Our Country Marks: The Transformation of African Identities in the Colonial and Antebellum South* (Chapel Hill: University of North Carolina Press, 1998), 3–4.

20. Douglas R. Egerton and Robert L. Paquette, *The Denmark Vesey Affair: A Documentary History* (Gainesville: University Press of Florida, 2017), 16–17; Isaria N. Kimambo, Gregory H. Maddox, and Salvator S. Nyanto, *A New History of Tanzania* (Dar es Salaam, Tanzania: Mkuki na Nyota, 2017), 83–84; Eva-Marie Ström, "The Situation of Ndengeleko: A Coastal Tanzanian Language," in *Selected Proceedings of the 38th Annual Conference on African Linguistics: Linguistic Theory and African Language Documentation*, ed. Masangu Matondo, Fiona McLaughlin, and Eric Potsdam (Somerville, MA: Cascadilla Proceedings Project, 2009); Julius O. Adekunle, "East African States," in *Africa*, ed. Toyin Falola, vol. 1, *African History before 1885* (Durham, NC: Duke University Press, 2000), 191–206; Malyn Newitt, *A History of Mozambique* (Bloomington: Indiana University Press, 1995), 49–50, 244–51; Margaret Washington Creel, *"A Peculiar People": Slave Religion and Community-Culture among the Gullahs* (New York: New York University Press, 1988). Creel discusses theories of Gullah Jack's origins and supports the identification of Angola in West Central Africa as the region and "BaKango peoples" as the source of his ethnicity (16–17).

21. Kimambo et al., *New History of Tanzania*, 83–84; Ström, "Situation of Ndengeleko"; Adekunle, "East African States," 191–206; Newitt, *History of Mozambique*, 49–50, 244–51. Daniel L. Schafer believes Gullah Jack may have been of Ndonde, Ngingo, or Makua ethnicity, based on a Charleston newspaper ad that announced the arrival of the *Gustavia*'s cargo in 1806. See Daniel L. Schafer, *Zephania Kingsley Jr. and the Atlantic World* (Gainesville: University Press of Florida, 2013), 80–81. Gullah Jack may have been Ndengereko, a people of the Rufiji River area of Tanzania south of Dar Es Salam and Zanzibar. Another theory is that Jack was Ngoni—an inference from the fact that many Yao and Makua in the region of Mozambique and Tanzania practiced scarification and tooth filing, whereas the Ngoni seemed to emphasize distinctive facial hair for men's country marks. No evidence suggests Jack had marks other than the distinctive facial hair to which he was by all accounts powerfully attached.

22. James Hamilton, *Negro Plot: An Account of the Late Intended Insurrection among a Portion of the Blacks of the City of Charleston, South Carolina*, 2nd ed. (Charleston, 1822), 24, 50; Kennedy and Parker, *Official Report*, 105, 178–79; Ann Beck, "Traditional Healer in Tanzania," *Issue* 9, no. 3 (1979): 2–5; John M. Janzen, *Ngoma: Discourses of Healing in Central and Southern Africa* (Berkeley: University of California Press, 1992), 27, 68, 70, 110, 117, 212; Bryan Edwards, *An Abridgement of Mr. Edwards's Civil and Commercial History of the British West Indies* [...] (London, 1794), 390–96, as cited in Milton C. Sernett, *Afro-American Religious History: A Documentary Witness* (Durham, NC: Duke University Press, 1985), 21. Fiddler crabs of coastal South Carolina and the ghost crab found in eastern Tanzania have characteristics consistent with the claws Gullah Jack distributed: most important, they have one smaller and one larger claw—a feature limited to male fiddler crabs and more pronounced in the male ghost crab. Hamilton's account of the investigations was first published as *An Account of the Late Intended Insurrection among a Portion of the Blacks of the City* (Charleston, SC, 1822). Later that year he published an edited version with a new title. I have worked closely with this slightly later version he entitled *Negro Plot: An Account of the Late Intended Insurrection among a Portion of the Blacks of the City of Charleston, South Carolina*.

23. "Confession of Yorick Cross," Senate Copy, SCDAH; Creel, *"Peculiar People,"* 16–25, esp. 22.

24. Beck, "Traditional Healer in Tanzania," 2–5.

25. Janzen, *Ngoma*, 27, 68, 70, 110, 202. This role, and the simultaneously spiritual and sociopolitical way Gullah Jack practiced it, has significant similarity to the *nganga* role in Kongolese society. See, e.g., Linda M. Heywood, *Njinga of Angola: Africa's Warrior Queen* (Cambridge, MA: Harvard University Press, 2017), 32–34. It resonated well with how the Kongolese people in South Carolina who had converted to Christianity would have seen the purpose of religion. Jason Young argues it was in opposition to "the very theoretical and religious underpinnings that supported and justified enslavement in the first place." See Jason Young, *Rituals of Resistance: African Atlantic Religion in Kongo and the Lowcountry South in the Era of Slavery* (Baton Rouge: Louisiana State University Press, 2007), 101–2. Jack's practice also resonates with the "dueling revelations" perspective on traditional religion and Kongolese Christianity in Sylvester A. Johnson, *African American Religions, 1500–2000: Colonialism, Democracy, and Freedom* (Cambridge: Cambridge University Press, 2015), 70–75; and Rijk van Dijk, Ria Reis, and Marja Spierenburg, eds., *The Quest for Fruition through Ngoma: The Political Aspects of Healing in Southern Africa* (Oxford, UK: James Currey, 2000), 4–5, 18–19, 34, 99–100.

26. Edwards, *Abridgement*, 21.

27. Jack Frazier, "Sea Turtles in Tanzania," *Tanzania Notes and Records*, no. 77–78 (1976): 11–14; Mpho Rinah Setlalekgomo, "Ethnozoological Survey of Traditional Medicinal Uses of Tortoises in Lentsweletau and Botlhapatlou Villages in Kweneng District of Botswana," *Scientific Journal of Zoology* 2, no. 4 (2013): 36–39; Janzen, *Ngoma*, 117.

28. Frazier, "Sea Turtles in Tanzania," 11–14; Setlalekgomo, "Ethnozoological Survey," 36–39 (uses on 38); Janzen, *Ngoma*, 117.

29. Thomas Bennett, Governor's Message 2, November 28, 1822, Governors' Messages, SCDAH; "Further Confession of Bacchus," July 13, 1822, Senate Copy, SCDAH; Kennedy and Parker, *Official Report*, 175n; "Proceedings against William Garner," Senate Copy,

SCDAH; "Confession of Monday Gell," July 13, 1822, House Copy, SCDAH; "Second Confession of Monday Gell," July 23, 1822, House Copy, SCDAH. Sometime around 1800, Hugh Crow reported on *dibia* priests and Obia at Bonny, claiming they were people powerful enough to defy or overrule kings. See Hugh Crow, *Memoirs of the Late Hugh Crow of Liverpool* [...] (London, 1830), 226–27, 229. See also Kathleen O'Connor, "Talking to God: Divination Systems," in *Africa*, ed. Toyin Falola, vol. 2, *African Cultures and Societies before 1885* (Durham, NC: Duke University Press, 2000), 95–105; David Eltis and David Richardson, eds., *Routes to Slavery: Direction, Ethnicity and Mortality in the Atlantic Slave Trade* (New York: Routledge, 1997), 73–74; Brown, *Tacky's Revolt*, 105–7; Gomez, *Exchanging Our Country Marks*, 128–30, 145–49; and Rucker, *River Flows On*, 39–43.

30. O'Connor, "Talking to God," 95–105.

31. "Confession of Monday Gell," July 13, 1822, House Copy, SCDAH; "Second Confession of Monday Gell," July 23, 1822, House Copy, SCDAH. The Nri region of Igbo land was one of the most significantly affected areas in the slave trade. See Gomez, *Exchanging Our Country Marks*, 125–26; Chambers, *Murder at Montpellier*, 30; Crow, *Memoirs*, 44; and Ebere Nwaubani, "Acephalous Societies," in *Africa*, ed. Toyin Falola, vol. 1, *African History before 1885* (Durham, NC: Duke University Press, 2000), 275–94.

32. The *Official Report* claims that Perault's family traded inland "as far as Hassou," but searches for that place name or ethnic name have failed. A Mr. James Delaire was in business on the Charleston wharves in the 1800s until 1813—last at Motte's Wharf. See *City Gazette*, April 12, 1813, 3; June 26, 1813, 1; and Kennedy and Parker, *Official Report*, 110. See also Rucker, *River Flows On*, 173–74.

33. An alternative interpretation suggests that Denmark Vesey was born in St. Thomas. However, Egerton and Paquette's volume of documents (*The Denmark Vesey Affair*) helps demonstrate that Denmark was born in Africa. "Africa" and "Coromantee" (on the Gold Coast) are the only names given in any of the nineteen documents to identify where Denmark was from. When St. Thomas is mentioned in the archive, it is only to identify it as the place where Joseph Vesey purchased Denmark—not to suggest that St. Thomas was where Denmark was born. In addition, St. Thomas was a Danish colony, and the Danish were active slave traders on the Gold Coast in the period. In fact, even the name of the likely slaving vessel *Fredensborg* was also the name of a Danish Gold Coast slave trading fort—the ruins of which are now a UNESCO World Heritage site in the greater Accra region of Ghana. Other documents also corroborate Denmark's African origins. Joseph Vesey bought Denmark on St. Thomas in 1781 as part of a cargo of 390 enslaved people. Further, though we do not know when Joseph Vesey arrived in St. Thomas, we know he had made it to his next destination of Saint-Domingue by April 24, 1782, when an ad appeared announcing his arrival. The French-language ad identifies Vesey's cargo as having come from the Côte-d'Or ("the Gold Coast"). Egerton and Paquette, *Denmark Vesey Affair*, 1 ("Côte-d'Or"), 2–3, 749–50 ("Coromantee"), 777 (Vesey "brought from Africa"). Egerton asserts Vesey was most likely born in St. Thomas. Douglas R. Egerton, *He Shall Go Out Free: The Lives of Denmark Vesey* (New York: Madison House, 1999), 3–4. Rucker (*River Flows On*, 162) accepts St. Thomas as Vesey's likely birthplace but suggests a possible Gold Coast (Akan) ethnicity. And Gomez (*Exchanging Our Country Marks*, 1) considers both Africa or the Americas plausible. Others have surmised an African birth for Vesey.

See Herbert Aptheker, *American Negro Slave Revolts* (New York: Columbia University Press, 1943), 268.

34. William Hutton, *A Voyage to Africa* [...] (London, 1820), 98 (quote). On June 2, 1781, the *Rio Volta* arrived from Africa with 391 enslaved people, 24.3 percent of whom were mere boys. Though the place of origin was not officially recorded, the name of the vessel references the Volta River on the Gold Coast. On November 11, 1781, the *Fredensborg* arrived with 510 enslaved people from the Gold Coast. The *Fredensborg*'s cargo was 10.8 percent boys. Voyage ID 35007 and voyage ID 35008, in Slave Voyages: The Trans-Atlantic Slave Trade Database, accessed July 1, 2022, www.slavevoyages.org/voyage/database. On October 8, 1799, the lottery drew ticket number 1884 for the grand prize of $1,500. Denmark Vesey had purchased the ticket and used the money to bargain for his freedom from his master. His manumission was dated Saturday, December 7, 1799, and recorded on December 31. In mid-to-late December, he received his prize money and paid $600 to his owner Mary Clodner, who was Joseph Vesey's wife. See Miscellaneous Records of the Secretary of State, book 3M, 427–28, SCDAH. I am indebted to Nic Butler for this citation and explanation. See Nic Butler, host, *Charleston Time Machine*, podcast, episode 54, "Denmark Vesey's Winning Lottery Ticket," CCPL, February 23, 2018, www.ccpl.org/charleston-time-machine. Kennedy and Parker's *Official Report* incorrectly identifies the year of Vesey's emancipation as 1800 (42). Brown, *Tacky's Revolt*, 234–35.

35. Rucker, *River Flows On*, 157. For the cultural and political beliefs of Akan speakers in the Gold Coast, see Gomez, *Exchanging Our Country Marks*, 105–13. Vesey was probably from the Gold Coast, but it is not absolutely certain. If he was from the Gold Coast, an Akan background is possible. However, he was still a child when he was trafficked, which likely limited his community education in Africa.

36. Several other important individuals have thinner biographies than this but were nonetheless pivotal, such as Peter Poyas and Charles Drayton.

37. "Rolla Bennett Proceedings," House Copy, SCDAH (Amaritta); Olwell, *Masters, Slaves, and Subjects: The Culture of Power in the South Carolina Low Country, 1740–1790* (Ithaca, NY: Cornell University Press), 166–78; Wendy Gonaver, "Race Relations: A Family Story, 1765–1867," (master's thesis, College of William and Mary, 2001); Amrita Chakrabarti Myers, *Forging Freedom: Black Women and the Pursuit of Liberty in Antebellum Charleston* (Chapel Hill: University of North Carolina Press, 2011), 78–80.

38. Natasha Lightfoot, "'Their Coats Were Tied Up Like Men': Women Rebels in Antigua's 1858 Uprising," *Slavery and Abolition* 31, no. 4 (2010): 537. Instead of referring to Beck by the name "Beck Vesey," I am using the name of Beck's slaver at the time she and Denmark were married. I use "Barker" because that is likely how she was referred to during her marriage to Denmark. She would have been "Mr. Barker's Beck." About the time she and Denmark separated, she and her son Robert were purchased by James Evans. So thereafter she would have been "Mr. Evans's Beck," but that is too awkward to write and not explain. For Beck's biographical information, see Egerton and Paquette, *Denmark Vesey Affair*, 361n4; and Egerton, *He Shall Go Out*, 77 (Egerton refers to her as Beck Vesey). See also Gonaver, "Race Relations."

39. Prudence Bussacre examination; Sally Howard examination; and William Paul examination (on Sarah cooking in Denmark's yard), all in House Copy, SCDAH. For Sarah Paul (aka Vesey) biographical information, see Egerton, *He Shall Go Out*, 78.

40. In *Tacky's Revolt*, Vincent Brown has a similar interest in how resistance develops a new geography of space and place (see esp. 243). Anthony E. Kaye demonstrates how community construction of neighborhoods affected neighborhood solidarities and decisions about aiding or exposing runaways. Anthony E. Kaye, *Joining Places: Slave Neighborhoods in the Old South* (Chapel Hill: University of North Carolina Press, 2007), 119–51. Jennifer Morgan argues for a nuanced understanding of gender and resistance in their personal, political, social, and cultural dimensions in *Laboring Women: Reproduction and Gender in New World Slavery* (Philadelphia: University of Pennsylvania Press, 2004), 169–70.

41. William Faux, *Memorable Days in America* [. . .] *November 27, 1818–July 21, 1820* (London, 1823), 65–66. Chinaberry (*Melia azedarach*) has lilac-like flowers and yellow bead-like seeds that whiten over time. Faux made this reflection after traveling between his hotel and Patrick Duncan's house and gardens on Rutledge Street in Cannonborough. Most of the city was not paved this well, and many areas still had dirt streets and wooden sidewalks (if any).

42. Adam Hodgson, *Letters from North America, Written during a Tour in the United States and Canada* (London: Hurst, Robinson, 1824), 1:41 (garden) and 55 (slave sale).

43. Christina R. Butler, *Lowcountry at High Tide: A History of Flooding, Drainage, and Reclamation in Charleston, South Carolina* (Columbia: University Press of South Carolina, 2020).

44. In September 1819, Mr. John Duncan's "extensive Mill Pond" adjacent to the "head of Beaufain Street" did "not appear to be discharged of its contents once or twice a day like other tide mills, there not being sufficient vent, or employment for the force of water." A recommendation was made that the city take measures to prevent "so large a body of water" from remaining stagnant so close to the city and order it drained once or twice a week, according to the season. Records of the Commissioners of Streets and Lamps and the Board of Commissioners for Opening and Widening of Streets, Lanes and Alleys, 1806–66, 26–27, City of Charleston Records, CCPL. See also Christina R. Butler, *Lowcountry at High Tide*.

45. On slavery's role in the resiliency of the Charleston economy, see Hart, *Building Charleston*. Smith's Wharf in Mazycboro is mentioned in *City Gazette*, May 7, 1820, 3; August 7, 1821, 3; and frequently from 1823 onward. But Charlestonians continued to refer to his former wharf near Broad Street in the center of the old city using his name. Not until 1823 did the ownership of his old wharf change and become associated with another person. See *City Gazette*, June 3, 1823, 3.

46. In 1817, Hibben's Ferry appears to have been located at the public landing past the Vendue Range at the end of Queen Street. This is where Gibbs and Harper's Wharf was. See Records of the Commissioners of Streets and Lamps and the Board of Commissioners for Opening and Widening of Streets, Lanes and Alleys, 1806–18, 316–18, City of Charleston Records, CCPL. The 1825 Mills Atlas identifies a Matthews Ferry in the vicinity of Hibben's Ferry, but it does not appear to have started operating until about January 1823; *City Gazette*, January 18, 1823, 4. In 1821, an article identified the village of Mount Pleasant as the eastern terminus of Hibben's Ferry; *City Gazette*, January 12, 1821, 3.

47. Advertisement regarding Patrick in *City Gazette*, October 29, 1822, 1. Hodgson, *Letters*, 1:41; *City Gazette*, June 28, 1820, 3. Cecelski, *Waterman's Song*, 127–29, 132–33.

48. Hodgson, *Letters*, 1:111.

49. Noah Davis, *Narrative of the Life of Rev. Noah Davis, a Colored Man* (Baltimore, 1859), 15-16, 17. Douglass, *Narrative*, 38, 43-44.

50. The location of John Gell's livery stable can be mapped quite accurately from surviving records: With the stable listed at 127 Church Street in the 1822 *City Directory*, John Gell was close to the Planter's Hotel (now the Dock Street Theater) at 135 Church Street, as 136 Church Street was "nearly opposite" the hotel; *City Gazette*, November 22, 1821, 2. An ad for the sale of 127 Church Street (*City Gazette*, February 9, 1824, 3) claimed it was opposite John Billings's stables, which the *City Directory* identifies as being at 122 Church Street. Being almost next door to the Planter's Hotel and running a livery stable suggests that Monday would not have been able to hold meetings about the uprising—or even allow casual conversations—for fear of discovery by his master or customers from the Planter's Hotel. James R. Schenk, *City Directory* [. . .] *1822* (Charleston, SC, 1822).

51. A cluster of evidence triangulates the location of Monday's shop and residence. That Monday lived and worked in a central location is suggested by how frequently he told people to come to his shop when they wanted news about the movement. The specific location can be identified with some precision using other evidence: Kennedy and Parker's *Official Report* (44) says that Monday kept his shop on Meeting Street separate from his master John Gell's livery stable on Church Street. In the tribunal's investigatory records, George Vanderhorst says that Monday Gell and Gullah Jack lived next to each other; Yorick Cross's testimony suggests that Monday's and Jack's doors were just six steps apart in a backyard "by a mahogany shop"; and Dick Sims's testimony adds that there was a cabinetmaker's lot next to Monday's place. The *City Directory* also lists a cabinetmaker named John Cowan at 123 Meeting Street (odd numbers were on the east side of Meeting Street). There was a lumberyard on the north side at 44 Market Street, according to the 1822 *City Directory* and ads in the *City Gazette*. The lumberyard was associated with several people, including Henry Sifley and William White. This address had space for 30,000 cypress shingles at one point in the summer of 1822 (*City Gazette*, July 30, 1822, 3), but I found no evidence of mahogany on the site in 1822. Nonetheless, "the cabinetmaker" and "the mahogany shop" might be different terms for the same place: A cabinetmaker engaged exclusively in making mahogany furniture in 1822. Taken together, these data points indicate that Monday's house/shop and Jack's house were likely located at or near Meeting and Market Street.

52. Bernhard, *Travels through North America*, 2:7.

53. "It is a species of vulture, black, with a naked head. Seen from a distance they resemble turkeys, for which reason they are denominated turkey-buzzards." Bernhard, *Travels through North America*, 2:7. On buzzards and dying, see Johann Shoepf, *Travels in the Confederation* [. . .] *1783-1784* (1788; Philadelphia: 1911), 195; and Nic Butler, host, *Charleston Time Machine*, podcast, episode 25, "The Rise of the Urban Vultures," CCPL, July 28, 2017, www.ccpl.org/charleston-time-machine.

54. Records of the Commissioners of Streets and Lamps and the Board of Commissioners for Opening and Widening of Streets, Lanes and Alleys, 1806-66, 21-23 (Zig Zag Alley), City of Charleston Records, CCPL; Christina R. Butler, *Lowcountry at High Tide*, 42-43 (Bedon's Alley, Stoll's Alley, and East Bay Street), 52-54 (Gadsden's development).

55. Daniel Payne, *Recollections of Seventy Years* (Nashville, 1888), 11-13, 15.

56. Charles Drayton statement at Dick Sims proceedings, in Egerton and Paquette, *Denmark Vesey Affair*, 320.

57. Lucas to master of the Workhouse, July 31, 1854, Duncan McKercher Papers, HL.

58. Edw. S. Lucas certificate, November 3, 1855, Duncan McKercher Papers, HL.

59. Kennedy and Parker, *Official Report*, 49–50 (stroll), 105 (whiskers); Bacchus Hammett fourth confession, BHP.

60. William Faux, *Memorable Days in America* [. . .] *November 27, 1818–July 21, 1820* (London, 1823), 103; "Stopped from a Negro," *City Gazette*, March 6, 1822, 1 (a box of candles had been seized); Christine Walker, *Jamaica Ladies: Female Slaveholders and the Creation of Britain's Atlantic Empire* (Chapel Hill: University of North Carolina Press, 2020), 62–63; Jeff Strickland, *All for Liberty: The Charleston Workhouse Slave Rebellion of 1849* (New York: Cambridge University Press, 2022), 27.

61. Abiel Abbot, "The Abiel Abbot Journals: A Yankee Preacher in Charleston Society, 1818–1827 (Continued from April)," ed. John Hammond Moore, *South Carolina Historical Magazine* 68, no. 3 (1967), 118–19. On smuggling, see Obadele-Starks, *Freebooters and Smugglers*, 10, 17, 20–22, 64–65. For more on the Workhouse, see Strickland, *All for Liberty*, 123.

62. "Jack the Slave of Col Cattell," Senate Copy, SCDAH; Egerton and Paquette, *Denmark Vesey Affair*, 363; Timothy James Lockley, *Maroon Communities in South Carolina: A Documentary Record* (Columbia: University Press of South Carolina, 2009), 78–79; Sylviane A. Diouf, *Slavery's Exiles: The Story of the American Maroons* (New York: New York University Press, 2014), 1, 2, 4–5.

63. *City Gazette*, November 30, 1821, 1.

64. This ethic may have developed on the notion that Charleston was like one large, diverse, constantly changing "neighborhood" of Black people, in which even unknown enslaved people might be understood by strangers in the city as possibly someone's kin and therefore as someone to be left alone or aided—but almost certainly not reported to whites. The urban environment, therefore, created a contrast with plantations, where strangers might be reported by the enslaved themselves. See Kaye, *Joining Places*, 132–34.

65. *City Gazette*, August 8, 1822, 3.

66. The reward amount seemed to vary a little based on the skill level and experience of the enslaved, as well as how difficult it might be to capture them. See *City Gazette*, March 7, 1817, 3 (five dollars for capture of Rob, a sawyer); January 21, 1822 (ten dollars for capture of Daniel, a cabinetmaker and carpenter); April 25, 1822, 1 (ten dollars for capture of Sam, who escaped from a steamboat with a forged pass); and June 27, 1822, 3 ($100 for capture of the carpenter Jacob, who may have escaped the state).

67. *City Gazette*, December 22, 1820, 4.

68. *City Gazette*, January 12, 1821, 3.

69. *City Gazette*, April 25, 1822, 1 (Jim Hadden and Watson); June 27, 1822, 3 (Jacob).

70. *City Gazette*, April 25, 1822, 1 (Fanny); October 21, 1822, 3 (Isaac).

71. *City Gazette*, November 30, 1821, 1 (Ruth); January 6, 1823, 1 (Margery).

72. *City Gazette*, May 8, 1820, 3.

73. *City Gazette*, December 22, 1820, 4.

74. *City Gazette*, August 8, 1822, 3.

75. *City Gazette*, February 10, 1823, 7.

76. The locations of these church buildings have never been precisely identified with property records or plats. However, newspaper ads and other records identify them as being in Hampstead. And an 1820 petition declares that the main church was called Zion and located at Hanover and Reid Streets. The tribunal's records establish only the general locations of the Anson Street and Cow Alley praise houses. *City Gazette*, December 30, 1817, 2; April 5, 1822, 2; August 14, 1822, 3; Kennedy and Parker, *Official Report*, 76, 115; "To the Honorable the Speaker, and Members of the House of Representatives of [South Carolina]," n.d. [ca. 1820], petition 1893, series S165015, Petitions to the General Assembly, SCDAH, as cited in Egerton and Paquette, *Denmark Vesey Affair*, 34.

77. This agency, creation of a new social geography, emphasizes the will of free and enslaved Black people and the communities they built—the opposite of a "social death" is a social struggle such as this. See Vincent Brown, "Social Death and Political Life in the Study of Slavery," *American Historical Review* 114, no. 5 (2009): 1231–49. Cecelski, *Waterman's Song*, 127–29, 132–33.

78. Jacobs, *Incidents in the Life*, 100–101. As Vincent Brown (*Tacky's Revolt*, 248–49) puts it, slavery itself produced the antagonisms that generated slave rebellion. Michael Nicholls, *Whispers of Rebellion: Narrating Gabriel's Conspiracy* (Charlottesville: University of Virginia Press, 2012), 11. In social movement theory, I am working along similar lines as James Jasper on "a concern for the microfoundations of social and political action." See James Jasper, "Social Movement Theory Today: Toward a Theory of Action?," *Sociology Compass* 4, no. 11 (2010): 965. But this book attempts no particular intervention in the vast body of social science literature known as "social movement theory." On intimacy and power, I work from an interpretation of Ann Laura Stoler and Michel Foucault. See Michel Foucault, *The History of Sexuality*, vol. 1, *An Introduction* (New York: Pantheon 1978), 61–62, 66–67, 92–94; and Ann Laura Stoler, ed., *Haunted by Empire: Geographies of Intimacy in North American History* (Durham, NC: Duke University Press, 2006), 13–16, 19–20.

79. Bernard E. Powers, *Black Charlestonians: A Social History, 1822–1885* (Little Rock, AR: University of Arkansas Press, 1994), 20–21; Egerton and Paquette, *Denmark Vesey Affair*, 55–58 (petition). (Powers was among the first scholars to identify the formation of the African Church as "a rebellious act of revolutionary proportions.") On the walkout and the early development of and attacks against Methodists in Charleston, see Robert L. Paquette, "Revisiting Vesey's Church," in *Fugitive Movements: Commemorating the Denmark Vesey Affair and Black Radical Antislavery in the Atlantic World*, ed. James O'Neil Spady (Columbia: University of South Carolina Press, 2022), 179–96; and John Saillant, "Before 1822: Anti-Black Attacks on Charleston Methodist Churches from 1786 to Denmark Vesey's Execution," *Common Place* 16, no. 2 (2016) n.p. On the burial ground, memorialized and preserved in the twenty-first century as the African Burial Ground, see J. A. Gilmore, A. A. Ofunniyin, O. L. Oubré, R. E. Fleskes, and T. G. Schurr, "The Dead Have Been Awakened in the Service of the Living: Activist Community-Engaged Archaeology in Charleston, SC," *American Antiquity*, no. 89 (2024): 165–84; and R. E. Fleskes, G. S. Cabana, J. K. Gilmore, et al., "Community-Engaged Ancient DNA Project Reveals Diverse Origins of 18th-Century African Descendants in Charleston, South Carolina," *Proceedings of the National Academy of Science* 120, no. 3 (2023): 3.

80. Payne, *Recollections of Seventy Years*, 11–13, 15, 16.

81. There is some controversy among scholars about Denmark Vesey's church membership. The only evidence for his being a member of the African Church is the tribunal's records, which arouses suspicion among scholars skeptical of the tribunal. There is reason for skepticism. The tribunal pinned sole responsibility on Vesey for instigating the uprising plot and blamed the only Black-led church in the city as the sole seedbed. Perhaps the court exaggerated in some way, but completely inventing a general fact pattern was not one of their tactics, and several different people told the tribunal that Vesey was a member of the African Church. It is also true that no evidence has survived to show that Vesey left Second Presbyterian—if he ever did. However, even if Vesey remained a member of Second Presbyterian, nothing would have stopped him from attending meetings of the African Church and the Circular Church as well. He was a prominent, educated, elder, free Black craftsman long established in the city, and it is therefore likely he would have been welcomed in the pews of either the African Church or the Circular Church regardless of whether his membership at Second Presbyterian had lapsed. If he made such visits often enough, attendees of the African Church may have come to regard him as a member. "Examination of Frank Ferguson," House Copy, SCDAH; Hamilton, *Negro Plot*, 31; Kennedy and Parker, *Official Report*, 22–24, 87; Egerton and Paquette, *Denmark Vesey Affair*, 186n6; Michael P. Johnson, "Denmark Vesey's Church," *Journal of Southern History* 86, no. 4 (2020): 805–48; Paquette, "Revisiting Vesey's Church," 179–96; Saillant, "Before 1822." Jeremy Schipper's *Denmark Vesey's Bible: The Thwarted Revolt That Put Slavery and Scripture on Trial* (Princeton, NJ, 1822) is a meditation on Vesey's reported biblical citations, the reaction of Charleston whites to that reading, and the influence the reading had on the subsequent debates among white divines over Christianity and slavery in the years after 1822, and it is the most authoritative such treatment in print.

82. Quotes, in order, are from Hutton, *Voyage to Africa*, 28–30; MacGregor Laird, *Narrative of an Expedition into the Interior of Africa* (London, 1837), 39; and William T. Hamilton, *A Word for the African* (Newark, NJ, 1825), 21. "Examination of Frank Ferguson," Senate Copy, SCDAH.

83. "Examination of Frank Ferguson," House Copy, SCDAH; Hamilton, *Negro Plot*, 31; Kennedy and Parker, *Official Report*, 22–24, 87; Egerton and Paquette, *Denmark Vesey Affair*, 186n6. See also Kevin G. Lowther, *The African American Odyssey of John Kizell: A South Carolina Slave Returns to Fight the Slave Trade in His African Homeland* (Columbia: University of South Carolina Press, 2012), 226–27. Creighton ran repeatedly to Sierra Leone and at least one Black Charlestonian, the free man Prince Graham, left with Creighton's August 1822 voyage. It is because of the difficulty in taking people with you that Vesey reportedly told others that he did not go "with Creighton to Africa" because he thought he should stay in Carolina to help his fellows. Kennedy and Parker, *Official Report*, 87–88, 163; Kennedy and Parker, *Official Report*, 87–88, 163; "Examination of Frank Ferguson," Senate Copy, SCDAH; *City Gazette*, October 3, 1821, February 2, August 7, 14, 1822.

84. Payne, *Recollections of Seventy Years*, 57.

85. Peter Hinks, *David Walker's Appeal to the Colored Citizens of the World* (University Park: Pennsylvania State University Press, 2000), xx–xxi; Peter Hinks, *To Awaken My Afflicted Brethren: David Walker and the Problem of Antebellum Slave Resistance* (University

Park: Pennsylvania State University Press, 1997), 29; David Walker, *Walker's Appeal* [...] *to the Colored Citizens of the World* (Boston, 1829).

86. Hinks, *David Walker's Appeal*, xx–xxi; Hinks, *To Awaken*, 29–30. Hinks believes that Walker must have been in Charleston "at least through 1821." The *Columbia* was one of three vessels making the trip to Goose Creek but probably the only steamboat. A schooner named *Sophia* made runs from Mey's Wharf, and a barge named *President's Barge* departed repeatedly from "the foot of Vendue Range," probably from Gibbs and Harper's Wharf near the Hibben's Ferry dock. *City Gazette*, April 16, 1821, 3.

Chapter Two

1. Jamie Monson describes the value of Tanzanian medicine in armed conflict as practice exhibiting a "narrative efficacy." See Jamie Monson, "War of Words: The Narrative Efficacy of Medicine in the Maji Maji War," in *Lifting the Fog of War*, ed. James Giblin and Jamie Monson (Boston: Brill, 2010), 31–69.

2. South Carolina inherited the legal definition of conspiracy that was in force in 1822 from 1712 English common law. Seemingly any two individuals could form a criminal conspiracy simply by pledging an oath or making some other "alliance." Throughout its proceedings, the tribunal treated moments when the accused reportedly said they would join the movement as the moments they made an oath or alliance as members of the uprising movement, which the magistrates and freeholders on the tribunal viewed as criminal conspiracy. On the law of conspiracy, see Thomas Cooper, ed., *The Statutes at Large of South Carolina* (Columbia, SC, 1837), 2:423. I am grateful to Marion C. Chandler, an archivist in the South Carolina Department of Archives and History, for this citation. Many historians since 1822 have also labeled the events a conspiracy, "the Denmark Vesey conspiracy," or the "Denmark Vesey rebellion." Most recently, Douglas Egerton and Robert Paquette have proposed calling it "the Denmark Vesey affair." I follow their lead when describing the total set of associated events, because this term captures the breadth of it: the controversy, the politics, the uprising movement, the investigation, the white perspectives, and the memory and memorialization of the events. But when focusing on the perspectives of the enslaved and free Black people themselves and their collective organizing, movement terminology is more accurate than conspiracy discourse. For recent examples continuing the focus on Vesey as the sole center of the events, see Jeremy Schipper's *Denmark Vesey's Bible: The Thwarted Revolt That Put Slavery and Scripture on Trial* (Princeton, NJ: Princeton University Press, 2022), which centers primary agency on Vesey when it discusses the events of 1822, calling it "Vesey's cause" (23) and Vesey "the man behind the insurrection plot" (7). Edward Pearson, "Denmark Vesey and the Culture of Resistance in Early Nineteenth-Century Charleston," in *The Enslaved and Their Enslavers: Power, Resistance, and Culture in South Carolina, 1670–1825* (Philadelphia: University of Pennsylvania Press, 2024), 331–64; Lionel H. Kennedy and Thomas Parker, *An Official Report of Sundry Negroes, Charged with an Attempt to Raise an Insurrection* [...] (Charleston, SC, 1822), xiii–xiv (quotes), 50.

3. Tiya Miles, *All That She Carried: The Journey of Ashley's Sack, a Black Family Keepsake* (New York: Random House, 2021), 20, 308n18. Reading against the grain means paying close, nuanced attention to how the relations of power constructed what got

recorded in the archive. See chap. 3, note 7, in this book for an outline of my approach and method on this point.

4. Tim Lockley, "Foreshadowing Vesey: The Camden Slave Conspiracy of 1816," *American Nineteenth Century History* 23, no. 2 (2022): 185–201. In 1797 an insurrection scare in Charleston ended with executions even though there had been no actual attack. The convictions were merely for sedition. The rebel plan had been to burn Charleston. Some of the men were "French negroes," who whites argued were Haitian Revolution veterans. Betrayed by an enslaved person named Figaro, white authorities hanged several men and sentenced Figaro to be transported to Surinam for sale. For this and other 1790s incidents, see Henry William Desaussure affidavit, December 4, 1798; and John Desbeaux, "Petition for the loss of Figaro," December 12, 1798, both in Petitions to the General Assembly, SCDAH. (I wish to thank Wade Dorsey of the South Carolina Department of Archives and History for his help with these citations.) See also Bernard E. Powers, *Black Charlestonians: A Social History, 1822–1885* (Little Rock: University of Arkansas Press, 1994), 28–29, which cites "Slave Conspiracy in Charleston Manuscript, South Caroliniana Library"; and Walter C. Rucker, *The River Flows On: Black Resistance, Culture, and Identity Formation in Early America* (Baton Rouge: Louisiana State University Press 2006), 155.

5. For Monday Gell's opinion, see "Smart Anderson Confession," House Copy, SCDAH. That slavery was the cause of rebellion was something understood by the author-activist David Walker, who visited Charleston around 1821 and denounced the subservient Christianity taught to the enslaved and Black community there. See David Walker, *Walker's Appeal [. . .] to the Colored Citizens of the World* (Boston, 1829), 5 (slavery as cause), 44–45 (Charleston visit). Broad evidence of the desire for freedom in the era can be found in other incidents ongoing in the region in the 1820s, see Robert Paquette, "From Rebellion to Revisionism: The Continuing Debate about the Denmark Vesey Affair," *Journal of the Historical Society* 4, no. 3 (2004): 307–9; John Oliver Killens, *The Trial Record of Denmark Vesey* (Boston: Beacon, 1970), 20, 21–22; Lionel H. Kennedy and Thomas Parker, *An Official Report of Sundry Negroes, Charged with an Attempt to Raise an Insurrection [. . .]* (Charleston, SC, 1822), 146; and "Inhabitants of Claremont, Clarendon, St. John, St. Stevens, and Richland Districts to South Carolina Senate, ca. 1824" and "Petition of John Jonah Murrell et al. to the Speaker and Members of the South Carolina House of Representatives, 1829," in Loren Schweninger, ed., *The Southern Debate Over Slavery: Petitions to Southern Legislatures, 1778–1864* (Urbana: University of Illinois Press, 2001), 83–85, 108. The problem that Monday Gell and the others recognized—that they were people reduced to chattels—is what Walter Johnson calls the "chattel principle" in *Soul by Soul: Life inside the Antebellum Slave Market* (Cambridge, MA: Harvard University Press, 1999), 19–20.

6. This paragraph's broad description of ideological statements attributed to movement members summarizes the statements quoted in this chapter's epigraphs and other statements attributed to several of the leaders. The epigraphs are statements attributed to named and unnamed individuals, preserved in the manuscript records of the tribunal. The white court's words should not be represented as the direct speech of the rebel detainees using quotations, except perhaps in a very few unambiguous or independently corroborated cases. Evidence demonstrates that the tribunal did not always accurately

record what was said by a speaker. Therefore, I represent the words attributed to the uprising movement members in italics, not in quotes. For the statement attributed to Peter Poyas, see "Robert Harth Examination," June 21, 1822, House Copy, SCDAH. For the statement attributed to Vesey, see "Examination of Frank Ferguson," June 27, 1822. Denmark Vesey was also said to have declared that *all men have equal rights, blacks as well as whites*, see "Benjamin Ford's Statement," House Copy, SCDAH. For statement attributed to Gullah Jack, see "Confession of Yorick Cross," Senate Copy, SCDAH. For the statement attributed to any of a group of five or six men headed to an organizing meeting at Thayer's farm in March 1822., see "Examination of Billy Bulkley," July 11, 1822, Senate Copy, SCDAH; "Smart Anderson Confession," House Copy, SCDAH; Douglas R. Egerton and Robert L. Paquette, *The Denmark Vesey Affair: A Documentary History* (Gainesville: University Press of Florida, 2017), 301; and Michael A. Gomez, *Exchanging Our Country Marks: The Transformation of African Identities in the Colonial and Antebellum South* (Chapel Hill: University of North Carolina Press), 2.

7. Frederick Douglass, *Narrative of the Life of Frederick Douglass* (Boston, 1845); Harriet Jacobs, *Incidents in the Life of a Slave Girl* [. . .], ed. Jean Fagan Yellin (1861; Cambridge, MA: Harvard, 1987).

8. Vincent Brown, *Tacky's Revolt: The Story of an Atlantic Slave War* (Cambridge, MA: Belknap Press of Harvard University Press, 2020), 244.

9. Daniel Payne, *Recollections of Seventy Years* (Nashville, 1888), 11–13, 15–16; Robert L. Paquette, "Revisiting Vesey's Church," in *Fugitive Movements: Commemorating the Denmark Vesey Affair and Black Radical Antislavery in the Atlantic World*, ed. James O'Neil Spady (Columbia: University of South Carolina Press, 2022), 195–96; *City Gazette*, December 30, 1817, 2; "Bacchus Hammett Confession," July 17, 1822, Senate Copy, SCDAH; Egerton and Paquette, *Denmark Vesey Affair*, 32–34 (petition).

10. Emma Hart, *Building Charleston: Town and Society in the Eighteenth-Century British Atlantic World* (Charlottesville: University of Virginia Press, 2009), 110–12; Edward Perry, Kit Perry, and Doll Perry statements in "Trial of Agrippa Perry," July 23–24, 1822, Senate Copy, SCDAH. Kit Perry made the statement about all the hands having gone to Charleston; hiring out had clearly separated family members on the Perry plantation.

11. Mary Prince, *The History of Mary Prince, a West Indian Slave: Related by Herself* [. . .] (London, 1831), 2–4; petition of John Jonah Murrell et al. to the Speaker and Members of the South Carolina House of Representatives, 1829, 84–85 in Schweninger, *Southern Debate Over Slavery*, 83–85. (In 1821, the petitioners claimed, crop prices having declined, some Christ Church planters sent redundant enslaved workers to Charleston for sale.)

12. The 1800 regulations tried to control the spread of Black freedom merely by requiring multiple sworn character endorsements. The free Black community continued to grow. The best accounts of Catherine's story are in Nic Butler, host, *Charleston Time Machine*, podcast, episode 191, "Freedom Won and Lost: the Story of Catherine in Antebellum Charleston, Part 1," CCPL, February 19, 2021, www.ccpl.org/charleston-time-machine/freedom-won-and-lost-story-catherine-antebellum-charleston-part-1; Nic Butler, host, *Charleston Time Machine*, podcast, episode 192, "Freedom Won and Lost: the Story of Catherine in Antebellum Charleston, Part 2," CCPL, February 26, 2021, www.ccpl.org/charleston-time-machine/freedom-won-and-lost-story-catherine-antebellum-charleston-part-2; and Karen Cook Bell, *Running from Bondage: Enslaved*

Women and Their Remarkable Fight for Freedom in Revolutionary America (Cambridge: Cambridge University Press, 2021), 125. See also Amrita Chakrabarti Myers, *Forging Freedom: Black Women and the Pursuit of Liberty in Antebellum Charleston* (Chapel Hill: University of North Carolina Press, 2011), 1–2.

13. *City Gazette*, October 3, 18, November 6, 1821. In April, it was reported that the *Calypso* had arrived in Sierra Leone and been sold to the American Colonization Society; *City Gazette*, April 22, 1822. Later, the *Calypso* was reported as making runs to the American Colonization Society's colony of Cape Mesurado; *City Gazette*, August 19, 1822. Creighton ran repeatedly to Sierra Leone. Promoters of colonization promoted places such as Freetown in Sierra Leone by praising its appearance, numerous public buildings, and schools for African and freed people's children. It had a prison, a hospital, and hundreds of kids learning to read and write each year. A visitor to Monrovia described Cape Mesurado as "picturesque." The colonization project was viewed as an insult by some activists nonetheless. William Hutton, *A Voyage to Africa [...]* (London, 1820), 28–30; MacGregor Laird, *Narrative of an Expedition into the Interior of Africa* (London, 1837), 39; *City Gazette*, October 3, 1821; *City Gazette*, July 20, 1822, 3 (William Garner and Jack Lopez relationship).

14. Butler, *Charleston Time Machine*, episode 191; Butler, *Charleston Time Machine*, episode 192.

15. That there were women who knew about the plan is not entirely speculative, as we will see in chapter 3. "Examination of Frank Ferguson," Senate Copy, SCDAH; "Second Confession of Monday Gell," July 23, 1822, House Copy, SCDAH; "Robert Harth Examination," June 21, 1822, House Copy, SCDAH; "Smart Anderson Confession," House Copy, SCDAH; and "Bacchus Hammett Further Confession," July 17, 1822, House Copy, SCDAH. See also Egerton and Paquette, *Denmark Vesey Affair*, 442.

16. In fact, the term "uprising" was significant enough that as late as 1936 it was still used by a former Charleston slave to describe the events of 1822, which he claimed people still talked about in the antebellum decades (secretly, most likely). See Jeff Strickland, *All for Liberty: The Charleston Workhouse Slave Rebellion of 1849* (New York: Cambridge University Press, 2022), 23, 213n54. Although the tribunal's *Official Report* emphasized the African Church as the seedbed of the movement, it does not appear that any of the organizing occurred in the church itself. "Robert Harth examination," June 21, 1822, House Copy, SCDAH; "Smart Anderson Confession," House Copy, SCDAH; "Bacchus Hammett Further Confession," July 17, 1822, House Copy, SCDAH. For examples of uses of "the business" by Black and white workers in the Atlantic world as a term of resistance, see Peter Linebaugh and Marcus Rediker, *The Many-Headed Hydra: Sailors, Slaves, Commoners, and the Hidden History of the Revolutionary Atlantic* (Boston: Beacon, 2001), 116, 133, 204, 324.

17. Rolla Bennett said that Vesey told him he was *the leader of the plot*, and this statement, right at the beginning of the tribunal's investigation, confirmed a strong bias by the court, spurring them to ignore contradictory evidence suggested in other testimony and devise a more nuanced argument about leadership. George Vanderhorst in his examination called Gullah Jack the head of all and the head of the Gullah Company; Yorick Cross's confession identifies Gullah Jack as the head man. The manuscript court record attributes to Billy Bulkley the statement that Gullah Jack and Robert Robertson

were "the principal men" and that Jack was the head man and Robert his second; Richard Lucas reportedly said Batteau Bennett was the *one at the head*. Frank Ferguson reportedly said that Vesey said *he (Vesey), Ned Bennett, Peter Poyas, and Monday Gell were the principals and that he was the head man and that they all went about to organize the people.* Yorick Cross said Monday Gell acknowledged he was the head of "his" countrymen, the Igbos. Robert Harth said that Peter Poyas called himself "the Captain" to take the lower guardhouse and arsenal. Frank Ferguson said Vesey told him that Gullah Jack would lead them, that there was a group of principal men including Monday Gell and Ned Bennett, and that Vesey said he was the head man ("Examination of Frank Ferguson," House Copy, SCDAH). Jack Purcell in a gallows confession blamed Vesey for bringing *him* into the movement, but he did *not* declare Vesey the sole originator of the movement. "Examination of Billy Bulkley," July 11, 1822, Senate Copy, SCDAH; "Robert Harth Examination," June 21, 1822, House Copy, SCDAH; "Confession of Yorick Cross," Senate Copy, SCDAH.

18. For a debate about the meaning of Vesey's association with the Second Presbyterian Church, see Michael P. Johnson, "Denmark Vesey's Church," *Journal of Southern History* 86, no. 4 (2020): 805–48; and Paquette, "Revisiting Vesey's Church," 179–96.

19. "Robert Harth Examination," June 21, 1822, House Copy, SCDAH; "Benjamin Ford Statement," June 26, 1822, House Copy, SCDAH; Douglas R. Egerton, *He Shall Go Out Free: The Lives of Denmark Vesey* (New York: Madison House, 1999).

20. *City Gazette*, November 15, 1821, 3; November 6, 1821, 3.

21. US military stores were being held at Mey's Wharf, adjacent to Pritchard's Wharf, in late 1821 and 1822. "US Military Stores," in Schenk, *City Directory* [...] *1822* (Charleston, SC, 1822); John Enslow confession, 11/331, folder 10, Henry Ravenel Papers, SCHS.

22. "Confession of Monday Gell," July 13, 1822, House Copy, SCDAH. (In a later confession, Monday added Rolla Bennett to his list of initial Vesey associates.) Monday actually tells this story as if it were all Vesey's idea. He insists that he (Monday) was skeptical and refused to join. Monday made these statements after Vesey had been executed and after he himself was arrested, tried, convicted, sentenced to death, and then placed in confinement with Charles Drayton specifically to elicit more testimony. Therefore, his claims about who did the most "criminal" things must be treated with added skepticism, according to the method I am using. We might expect that Monday downplayed his own role and elevated the role of the already executed Vesey to protect both himself and others—perhaps people who were never named. He needed to deflect on "culpability" while offering basic facts that would not be contradicted. However, he would need to deflect guilt from himself in order to persuade the court to spare his life.

23. Walter Rucker was the first to approach the African dimensions in the rebellion effort in the Denmark Vesey affair as central rather than as an incidental or additional subtheme. Walter Rucker, "'I Will Gather All Nations': Resistance, Culture, and Pan-African Collaboration in Denmark Vesey's South Carolina," *Journal of Negro History* 86, no. 2 (2001): 132–47; Rucker, *River Flows On*, 152–79; James Ferguson to Thomas Parker, September 16, 1822, in Kennedy and Parker, *Official Report*, 28; "Smart Anderson Confession," House Copy, SCDAH; "Bacchus Hammett Further Confession," July 17, 1822, House Copy, SCDAH.

24. "Confession of Yorick Cross," Senate Copy, SCDAH; "Tom Russell Proceedings," July 15, 1822, House Copy, SCDAH; "William Paul Testimony," June 19, 1822, House Copy, SCDAH; "Confession of Monday Gell," July 13, 1822, Senate Copy, SCDAH; "Second Confession of Monday Gell," July 23, 1822, Senate Copy, SCDAH. Drivers were reported on both sides, as supporters and as opponents of the uprising movement. See James Ferguson to Thomas Parker, September 16, 1822, in Kennedy and Parker, *Official Report*, 28; and Egerton and Paquette, *Denmark Vesey Affair*, 317.

25. Adam Hodgson, *Letters from North America, Written during a Tour in the United States and Canada* (London: Hurst, Robinson, 1824), 1:50–51; Egerton, *He Shall Go Out*, 138–39.

26. [James Matthews,] "Recollections of Slavery by a Runaway Slave," *The Emancipator* (New York), August 23, September 13, September 20, October 11, and October 18, 1838; Susanna Ashton, "Re-collecting Jim," *Commonplace* 15, no. 1 (2014).

27. *City Gazette*, August 8, 1822, 3 (Robin and January); "Jack the Slave of Col Cattell," Senate Copy, SCDAH; Egerton and Paquette, *Denmark Vesey Affair*, 363.

28. *City Gazette*, June 25, 1822, 2.

29. *City Gazette*, August 8, 1822, 3.

30. The ad mentions a specific house on South Bay Street, one belonging to a "Mr. Lampson," but the *City Directory* has no such listing in 1822 — no "Lampson" at all in the city. The was a merchant named David Lamb at the bottom of King Street almost at the corner of South Bay, and there was a factor named James H. Ladson at Craft's South Wharf and living on Church Street, which also intersects South Bay. *City Gazette*, June 18, 1822, 3. Schenk, *City Directory*, 53.

31. On speaking Gullah for secrecy, see "James Mall Statement," House Copy, SCDAH; and Perault Strohecker, "The testimony in the case of Nero the Slave of Mr. Haig," in Egerton and Paquette, *Denmark Vesey Affair*, 355.

32. "Examination of Joe La Roche," House Copy, SCDAH; "Examination of Rolla Bennett," House Copy, SCDAH; "Confession of Yorick Cross," Senate Copy, SCDAH.

33. "Examination of Joe La Roche," House Copy, SCDAH; "Examination of Rolla Bennett," House Copy, SCDAH; "Confession of Yorick Cross," Senate Copy, SCDAH; Killens, *Trial Record*, 41–47.

34. Help from Africa is something Rolla Bennett reportedly invoked. It is, however, also possible that the rebels might have found welcome at places such as Accra (in modern Ghana), where other enslaved people returned as refugees from the Americas during the nineteenth century. Into the twenty-first century there has been an Afro-Brazilian community in Accra. Gullah Jack, Peter Poyas, and Harry Haig each told Yorick Cross that a major goal was to keep fighting until the English could join them in the fight against the United States; "Confession of Yorick Cross," Senate Copy, SCDAH. "Examination of Joe La Roche," House Copy, SCDAH; "Examination of Rolla Bennett," House Copy, SCDAH; and "William Paul Examination," House Copy, SCDAH. Manuel Barcia notes exaggeration as an organizing strategy in Cuba in 1825, as well. Manuel Barcia, *The Great African Slave Revolt of 1825* (Baton Rouge: Louisiana State University Press, 2012), 101.

35. "Examination of Joe La Roche," House Copy, SCDAH.

36. "Examination of Joe La Roche," House Copy, SCDAH; "Testimony of Mrs. La Roche," House Copy, SCDAH; "Examination of Sambo La Roche," House Copy, SCDAH.

37. A claim that Yorick might have been culturally closer to Peter Poyas than to Gullah Jack rests on four points of evidence: Jack was from a region few Carolina slaves ever came from; Peter was the first to approach Yorick; Yorick treated Jack's East African word for his crab claws as if it were a foreign word; and Peter was the one to threaten to turn Yorick's "country people" against him if he did not join. That latter threat would likely have had little force if Yorick did not believe Peter held sway with people from his home region. "Confession of Yorick Cross," Senate Copy, SCDAH.

38. "Confession of Yorick Cross," Senate Copy, SCDAH.

39. "Confession of Yorick Cross," Senate Copy, SCDAH.

40. "Confession of Yorick Cross," Senate Copy, SCDAH.

41. "Confession of Yorick Cross," Senate Copy, SCDAH.

42. "Confession of Yorick Cross," Senate Copy, SCDAH; "Second Confession of Monday Gell," July 23, 1822, House Copy, SCDAH.

43. "Robert Harth Examination," June 21, 1822, House Copy, SCDAH; "John Enslow Confession (Alternate)," BHP; John Enslow confession, 11/331, folder 10, Henry Ravenel Papers, SCHS; "Confession of Yorick Cross," Senate Copy, SCDAH.

44. "Lot Forrester on his trial," in Egerton and Paquette, *Denmark Vesey Affair*, 317; John Enslow confession (alternate), BHP; John Enslow confession, 11/331, folder 10, Henry Ravenel Papers, SCHS.

45. "Confession of Monday Gell," July 13, 1822, Senate Copy, SCDAH; "Examination of Joe La Roche," House Copy, SCDAH. That women knew any details is an inference from testimony given to the tribunal on a few occasions, such as when Edwin Paul told the court that *even the women* wondered why Denmark Vesey and Monday Gell were not taken up earlier than they were. Edwin Paul testimony at Pompey Bryan proceeding; William Paul examination; Prudence Bussacre examination; and Sally Howard examination, all in House Copy, SCDAH.

46. "Second confession of Monday Gell," July 23, 1822, House Copy, SCDAH.

47. "Second confession of Monday Gell," July 23, 1822, House Copy, SCDAH; "Stopped from a Negro," *City Gazette*, March 6, 1822, 1. On the cluttered streets, see Records of the Commissioners of Streets and Lamps and the Board of Commissioners for Opening and Widening of Streets, Lanes and Alleys, 1806–18, 316–18, City of Charleston Records, CCPL of the Streets records.

48. Ada Ferrer, *Freedom's Mirror: Cuba and Haiti in the Age of Revolution* (New York: Cambridge University Press, 2014), 329–35, 338 ("free soil"); Ousmane K. Power-Greene, *Against Wind and Tide: The African American Struggle against the Colonization Movement* (New York: New York University Press, 2014), 32–41; *City Gazette*, October 3, 1821; Paul Gilroy, *The Black Atlantic: Modernity and Double Consciousness* (New York: Verso, 1993), 16–18. Liberia was only just being established in 1822, but there were US colonists in Mesurado, which would become Liberia. I use "Liberia" for convenience only.

49. That these were *ngoma* gatherings is plausible on the basis of Gullah Jack's probable origins as an East African and as a *mganga* (healer) who would have been adept at officiating such ceremonies. John M. Janzen, "Theories of Music in African 'Ngoma' Healing," in *Musical Healing in Cultural Context*, ed. Penelope Gouk (London: Ashgate, 2000), 46–66; John M. Janzen, *Ngoma: Discourses of Healing in Central and Southern Africa* (Berkeley: University of California Press, 1992), 117, 122–26; Andrew Apter, "On

African Origins: Creolization and Connaissance in Haitian Vodou," *American Ethnologist* 29, no. 2 (2002). Billy Bulkley claimed that Adam Robertson, Robert Robertson, John Robertson, Dick Sims, Pollydore Faber, Peter Poyas, and Gullah Jack attended several meetings before and after April 27. See "Examination of Billy Bulkley," Senate Copy, SCDAH; "Examination of Frank Ferguson," Senate Copy, SCDAH; "Confession of Monday Gell," July 13, 1822, Senate Copy, SCDAH; "Second Confession of Monday Gell," July 23, 1822, Senate Copy, SCDAH; and Kennedy and Parker, *Official Report*, 139–40, 171. The records offer hints about why the plantation where Billy Bulkley lived—where these ceremonies took place—was apparently not monitored by white people. Egerton and Paquette identify Stephen Bulkley as Billy's slaver. The city directory for 1822 lists three Bulkleys all living at 261 King Street, which was also their business address. Stephen is listed without a profession, and Ashbel and Erastus Bulkley are listed as "merchant" and "dry goods," respectively. Schenk, *City Directory*, 28. The Bulkleys also appear to have split their residential life between New York and Connecticut, shuttling between the two via ship in the pursuit of a family business in fine furniture. See *City Gazette*, May 2, 1817, 3; June 26, 1822, 3; July 7, 1825, 6. Billy Bulkley examination, in Kennedy and Parker, *Official Report*, 171.

50. They also referred to the Gullah Society as the *Gullah Band*. Many slave narratives feature references to the power of healers or spiritualists, such as those of Frederick Douglass and William Welles Brown. William Grimes, enslaved in Savannah in the 1820s, believed that one of his fellow enslaved people was a witch, and he believed that she sometimes would "ride" him at night, endeavoring to harm, frighten, or kill him. William L. Andrews and Regina E. Mason, eds., *Life of William Grimes, the Runaway Slave* (1825; New York: Oxford University Press, 2008), 52–53; "Evidence of Billy Belonging to Mr. Bulkley," Senate Copy, SCDAH; "Examination of Frank Ferguson," Senate Copy, SCDAH; "William Paul Testimony," June 19, 1822, Senate Copy, SCDAH; "Confession of Monday Gell," July 13, 1822, Senate Copy, SCDAH; "Second Confession of Monday Gell," July 23, 1822, Senate Copy, SCDAH; Kennedy and Parker, *Official Report*, 139–40, 171; Rucker, *River Flows On*, 43; Janzen, "Theories of Music," 55.

51. "Confession of Monday Gell," July 13, 1822, Senate Copy, SCDAH; "Second Confession of Monday Gell," July 23, 1822, Senate Copy, SCDAH.

52. The buzzards were commonplace for generations. "It is a species of vulture, black, with a naked head. Seen from a distance they resemble turkeys, for which reason they are denominated turkey-buzzards." Karl Bernhard, Duke of Saxe-Weimar-Eisenach, *Travels through North America, during the Years 1825 and 1826, in Two Volumes* (Philadelphia, 1828), 2:7.

53. "Confession of Monday Gell," July 13, 1822, Senate Copy, SCDAH; "Second Confession of Monday Gell," July 23, 1822, Senate Copy, SCDAH.

54. "Confession of Yorick Cross," Senate Copy, SCDAH.

55. "Confession of Monday Gell," July 13, 1822, House Copy, SCDAH.

56. "Confession of Monday Gell," July 13, 1822, House Copy, SCDAH.

57. "Confession of Monday Gell," July 13, 1822, House Copy, SCDAH.

58. "Second Confession of Monday Gell," July 23, 1822, House Copy, SCDAH.

59. Bernhard, *Travels through North America*, 2:4; William Faux, *Memorable Days in America* [...] *November 27, 1818–July 21, 1820* (London, 1823), 73.

60. Bernhard, *Travels through North America*, 2:4; Faux, *Memorable Days in America*, 73.

61. For almanac data on relevant sunrise, moon phase, moonrise, and tides, see Schenk, *City Directory*. For Bastille Day, see Egerton, *He Shall Go Out*, 138–39.

62. Peter Poyas told Yorick Cross that the attackers would come in groups from James Island, Johns Island, and Christ Church Parish. "Confession of Yorick Cross," Senate Copy, SCDAH. Joe La Roche gave a similar description of the targets. See "Examination of Joe La Roche," House Copy, SCDAH; and Kennedy and Parker, *Official Report*, 63. For one example of ads for guns sold at Duquercron's Store that ran during the fall, see *City Gazette*, October 18, 1821, 3.

63. Kennedy and Parker, *Official Report*, 63.

64. "Robert Harth Examination," June 21, 1822, House Copy, SCDAH; John Enslow confession (alternate), BHP; John Enslow confession, 11/331, folder 10, Henry Ravenel Papers, SCHS.

65. "Robert Harth Examination," June 21, 1822, House Copy, SCDAH; records of the Commissioners of Streets and Lamps and the Board of Commissioners for Opening and Widening of Streets, Lanes and Alleys, 1806–66, City of Charleston Records, CCPL.

66. "Petition of John Jonah Murrell et al. to the Speaker and Members of the South Carolina House of Representatives, 1829," in Loren Schweninger, ed., *The Southern Debate Over Slavery: Petitions to Southern Legislatures, 1778–1864* (Urbana: University of Illinois Press, 2001), 84–85; James Ferguson to Thomas Parker, September 16, 1822, in Kennedy and Parker, *Official Report*, 28; Carolyn E. Fick, *Making of Haiti: The Saint Domingue Revolution from Below* (Knoxville: University of Tennessee Press, 1990); Laurent Dubois, *Avengers of the New World: The Story of the Haitian Revolution* (Cambridge, MA: Belknap, 2004), 286–88.

67. Perault Strohecker repeatedly mentioned Smith's Wharf. Specifically, and most meaningful, Perault claimed at the proceedings against Dick Sims that he had once met Dick *between Craft's and Smith's Wharf*. Perault also testified that Naphur, Adam, and Bellisle Yates had a group of men with whom they were going to sleep at the cooper James Mitchel's place on Smith's Wharf on East Bay Street the night the rebellion was to begin, because that was where they were going to commence the fight. The court's record of Perault's claims identifies only a "Mr. Mitchell," but the 1822 *City Directory* notes James Mitchel had a cooperage operation in and around Smith's Wharf on East Bay Street. The location of Smith's Wharf can mean only the wharves near Broad Street—not the Smith's Wharf up in Mazycboro on the Neck. In 1822, William Smith Jr. was in the process of moving his operations to new facilities farther up the peninsula, but the move was still incomplete. For years he had just the one wharf, just south of Broad Street along East Bay Street. Known generally as "Smith's Wharf," by 1820 it had begun to confine his business, and Smith took steps to expand. He acquired marshland north of Boundary Street, north of Gadsden's Wharf in Mazycboro. There he began to have a new, much larger wharf complex built that could sustain shipbuilding and other enterprises. As early as May 1820, his wharf in Mazycboro was operating, referred to in the newspapers sometimes as Smith's "North" Wharf, with the one on East Bay Street as Smith's "South" Wharf. By mid-1823 these distinctions disappeared, and Smith's South Wharf was completely taken over by another person under a new name. For mentions of Smith's Wharf in Mazycboro, see *City Gazette*, May 7, 1820, 3; August 7,

1821, 3; and frequently in 1823 and onward. The first citation of Smith's South Wharf is in *City Gazette*, March 16, 1821, 3. The last citation is in *City Gazette*, April 3, 1823, 3. The first citation of Smith's North Wharf in the *City Gazette* is March 27, 1821, 3; the last is December 18, 1822, 3. The first citation of Kiddell's Wharf is in *City Gazette*, June 3, 1823, 3. It is described in an ad as "formerly" Smith's Wharf. Kiddell would still be operating from the wharf in the mid-1830s.

68. John Enslow confession (alternate), BHP; John Enslow confession, 11/331, folder 10, Henry Ravenel Papers, SCHS.

69. Vincent Brown (*Tacky's Revolt*, 17–41, 85–86, 108–11) writes that Jamaican maroons participated in a "transatlantic struggle" (18) and "adapted their military tactics to the landscape" (111) — tactics they had inherited from the Atlantic slave war that had started in various regions of West Africa and Central Africa. Samuel Ntewusu, "Arrows of Power: Festival of Slave Resistance and Abolition in Ghana, Africa," in *Fugitive Movements: Commemorating the Denmark Vesey Affair and Radical Antislavery in the Atlantic World*, ed. James O'Neil Spady (Columbia: University Press of South Carolina, 2022) 161–78; Joseph E. Inikori, "The Struggle against the Transatlantic Slave Trade," in *Fighting the Slave Trade: West African Strategies*, ed. Sylviane A. Diouf (Athens: Ohio University Press, 2003), 171–93.

70. John Beaty and Ralph Bailey, *A Historic Archaeological Survey of the Upper Peninsula, Charleston South Carolina* (Atlanta: Brockington, 2004), 28–29 (Payne's Farm), 30 (powder magazine). Payne's Farm was smaller than Bulkley's, at 11.5 acres, but it was busy. Between 1818 and 1822, William Payne and Sons advertised in the *City Gazette* approximately 2,000 times, very often for sale of slaves, though also for sales of real estate or other property. In one issue of the *City Gazette* in 1821, for example, William Payne and Sons ran eight ads in the paper's auctions section. Six of their eight ads included the sale of enslaved people. In the rest of the auctions section, only three of fifteen ads featured slaves for sale.

71. Billy Bulkley examination, in Kennedy and Parker, *Official Report*, 171; Schenk, *City Directory*, 68 (Payne family listing). For powder magazine locations north of the Lines, see Hartman Bache, James D. Graham, C. M. Eakin, W. M. Boyce, and William James Stone, *Charleston Harbour and the Adjacent Coast and Country, South Carolina, Surveyed at Intervals, 1823, 1824, and 1825* (Washington, DC, 1825); R. P. Bridgens and Robert Allen, *An Original Map of the City of Charleston, South Carolina* (Washington, DC, 1852); Elaine B. Herold, Martha A. Zierden, and Joanne A. Calhoun, *An Archaeological Preservation Plan for Charleston, South Carolina* (Charleston, SC: Charleston Museum, 1982), 22–25; and Beaty and Bailey, *Historic Archaeological Survey*, 30.

72. *City Gazette*, December 17, 1810, 4 (powder magazine construction contract); September 18, 1813, 3 (damaged powder at the magazine).

73. "Examination of Frank Ferguson," House Copy, SCDAH; "Richard and Bram Lucas Testimony," House Copy, SCDAH; Kennedy and Parker, *Official Report*, 88–89; William Faux, *Faux's Memorable Days in America, 1819-1820* (Cleveland, OH: Arthur H. Clark, 1905), 67, www.loc.gov/item/05007750. "Mr. Duncan's Trees" was probably a well-known grove belonging to Patrick Duncan outside the city limits. I am indebted to Nic Butler, historian at the Charleston County Public Library, for this identification. Butler believes it is also possible that the "Mr. Duncan" referred to might be the John Duncan who lived

on Bull Street near Vesey in 1822. However, John Duncan lived within the boundaries of the city, putting all four men at risk of arrest by the patrol, and John Duncan did not have the reputation for grand trees that Patrick Duncan enjoyed. Egerton and Paquette (*Denmark Vesey Affair*, 281n3) identify Mr. Duncan as John Duncan.

74. Sally E. Hadden, *Slave Patrols: Law and Violence in Virginia and the Carolinas* (Cambridge, MA: Harvard University Press, 2001), 58–59.

75. Roy Williams III and Alexander Lucas Lofton, *Rice to Ruin: The Jonathan Lucas Family in South Carolina, 1783-1929* (Columbia: University Press of South Carolina, 2018).

76. "Confession of Yorick Cross," Senate Copy, SCDAH.

77. In Rolla Bennett's second confession, he claims that Vesey told him that "the best way... for us to conquer the whites, is to set the town on fire in several places, at the Governor's Mills, and near the Docks, and for every servant in the yards to be ready with axes and knives and clubs, to kill every man, as he came out when the bells began to ring." Kennedy and Parker, *Official Report*, 67; John Enslow confession, 11/331, folder 10, Henry Ravenel Papers, SCHS; "Robert Harth Examination," June 21, 1822, House Copy, SCDAH.

78. "Robert Harth Examination," June 21, 1822, House Copy, SCDAH.

79. *Distances between United States Ports*, 13th ed. (Washington, DC: US Department of Commerce 2019), 10, table 1; "Confession of Monday Gell," July 13, 1822, House Copy, SCDAH; "Second Confession of Monday Gell," July 23, 1822, House Copy, SCDAH; "Examination of Joe La Roche," House Copy, SCDAH. For the quote about lovers of freedom going to Haiti, see *Columbian Sentinel*, July 4, 1821, as quoted by Power-Greene, *Against Wind and Tide*, 27–28, 29; Ada Ferrer, "Haiti, Free Soil, and Antislavery in the Revolutionary Atlantic," *American Historical Review* 117, no. 1 (2012): 40–66. Jean-Pierre Boyer became president of a reunited Haiti after the death of Alexandre Pétion in the South and the suicide of King Henri Christophe in the North in 1820. Sara Fanning, "The Roots of Early Black Nationalism: Northern African Americans' Invocations of Haiti in the Early Nineteenth Century," *Slavery and Abolition* 28, no. 1 (2007): 61–85; Gilroy, *Black Atlantic*, 16–18; Sylvia R. Frey, *Water from the Rock: Black Resistance in a Revolutionary Age* (Princeton, NJ: Princeton University Press, 1991), 229–332; Ferrer, *Freedom's Mirror*, 329–35, 338; Power-Greene, *Against Wind and Tide*, 32–41.

80. Kennedy and Parker, *Official Report*, 50.

81. Frederick Douglass, *Narrative of the Life of Frederick Douglass* (Boston, 1845), 64; Harriet Jacobs, *Incidents in the Life of a Slave Girl* [...], ed. Jean Fagan Yellin (1861; Cambridge, MA: Harvard, 1987), 239–41; Solomon Northrup, *Twelve Years a Slave* (Auburn, NY, 1853), 57–58, 68–72; Kennedy and Parker, *Official Report*, 50.

82. An "Intendant" of a city is its chief administrator—an office with some functions in common with a mayor but generally with less executive authority. For Peter Prioleau's statement see: Kennedy and Parker, *Official Report*, 49–50.

83. Thomas Bennett, Governor's Message 2, November 28, 1822, Governors' Messages, SCDAH; Kennedy and Parker, *Official Report*, 35, 80.

84. For the Sunday churchgoers' arrivals in boats, see Kennedy and Parker, *Official Report*, 38–39. After the plan was exposed, Hamilton had the number of slaves entering the city counted on successive Sundays. He "directed the numbers of those who came over in such boats on Sundays from the Islands to be counted." And "even at that time

[of fear due to trials], upwards of five hundred entered the city on one Sunday." "Smart Anderson Confession," House Copy, SCDAH.

Chapter Three

1. The epigraph for this chapter comes from Lionel H. Kennedy and Thomas Parker, *An Official Report of Sundry Negroes, Charged with an Attempt to Raise an Insurrection* [...] (Charleston, SC, 1822), 52. The last sentence in this paragraph reflects a Gullah proverb that says that not every shut eye means a person is sleeping and not every grin means a person is laughing. Guy B. Johnson, "Proverbs," in *Folk Culture on St. Helena Island, South Carolina* (1930; Hatboro, PA: Folklore, 1968), 160–61.

2. For the culling the Black population rumor, see "Robert Harth Examination," June 21, 1822, House Copy, SCDAH; and Kennedy and Parker, *Official Report*, 21–22. See also [Thomas Pinckney,] *Reflections Occasioned by the Late Disturbances in Charleston* (Charleston, SC, 1822), 10–12, in which Pinckney proposes, ironically, reducing the slave majority in the city of Charleston as a response to the Denmark Vesey affair—though without killing the enslaved, whom, of course, he and others of his class regard as valuable property. On conditions in the Workhouse, which would see its own rebellion in the 1840s, see Jeff Strickland, *All for Liberty: The Charleston Workhouse Slave Rebellion of 1849* (New York: Cambridge University Press, 2022), 30–32.

3. Prudence Bussacre examination; Sally Howard examination; and "Robert Harth examination," June 21, 1822, all in House Copy, SCDAH; Karen Cook Bell, "The Missing Black Women in Denmark Vesey's Conspiracy," *Black Perspectives*, August 30, 2022, www.aaihs.org/the-missing-black-women-in-denmark-veseys-conspiracy.

4. "Robert Harth Examination," June 21, 1822, House Copy, SCDAH; "Further Confession of Bacchus," July 13, 1822, Senate Copy, SCDAH; "William Colcock Confession," Senate Copy, SCDAH; William Paul statement, in Kennedy and Parker, *Official Report*, 85.

5. William Faux, *Memorable Days in America* [. . .] November 27, 1818–July 21, 1820 (London, 1823), 65–66.

6. Karl Bernhard, Duke of Saxe-Weimar-Eisenach, *Travels through North America, during the Years 1825 and 1826, in Two Volumes* (Philadelphia, 1828), 2:7; Abiel Abbot, "The Abiel Abbot Journals: A Yankee Preacher in Charleston Society, 1818–1827 (Continued from April)," ed. John Hammond Moore, *South Carolina Historical Magazine* 68, no. 3 (1967), 123.

7. The credibility of the detainees' statements has been debated by scholars. I have previously published a method for approaching their credibility centering on five questions that guide this book: (1) How early was the testimony given? (2) Was testimony given voluntarily (or at least by individuals who were never imprisoned)? (3) Was testimony potentially self-incriminating or against self-interest (for example, a speaker admitted they would join if there was "force enough")? (4) Did the speaker have an intimate social bond of loyalty with the accused (student/teacher, close friend, or family)? (5) Did a white owner or lawyer witness the testimony or cross-examine the witness? The most credible statements were given early, voluntarily, against self-interest, and with more powerful whites present who sought to preserve the life of the detainee, who him or herself had a close social relationship with the accused. The

statements attributed to enslaved and free Black people that best passed these tests for acceptable credibility were used to counterbalance the remainder of the information. These were statements by Smart Anderson (pleaded guilty), Prudence Bussacre (not arrested), Yorick Cross (not arrested), John Enslow (pleaded guilty), Robert Harth (not arrested), Sally Howard (not arrested), Joe La Roche (volunteer informant), Bram Lucas (not arrested), Richard Lucas (not arrested), Peter Prioleau (volunteer informant), and George Wilson (volunteer informant). These can be used to corroborate other, less credible statements, except as to the "guilt" or "innocence" of any particular person. Some of the less credible statements were perfectly useful on basic matters of fact, such as locations, meeting dates, description of events or places, and more. With all statements, I apply journalistic conventions of skepticism, attribution, and independent confirmation as much as possible. I have explicated these topics elsewhere. See James O'Neil Spady, "Belonging and Alienation: Gullah Jack and Some Maroon Dimensions of the Denmark Vesey Conspiracy," in *Maroons and the Marooned: Runaways and Castaways in the Americas*, ed. Richard Bodek and Joseph Kelly (Jackson: University Press of Mississippi, 2020), 30–54; and James O'Neil Spady, "Power and Confession: On the Credibility of the Earliest Reports of the Denmark Vesey Slave Conspiracy," *William and Mary Quarterly* 68, no. 2 (2011): 287–304.

8. For a short summary of historians' debate on the Denmark Vesey affair, see note 82 of this chapter. In this book, I generally refer to the "trials" with alternate terms such as "proceedings" or "hearings." This is both because the tribunal recorded much more than just the "trials" and because the proceedings against the detainees were not really trials in the sense that many readers will assume if I use that term. The detainees were not considered innocent until proven guilty, and the five tribunal members were simultaneously investigators, prosecutors, jury members, and judges. These were, at best, informal proceedings that mimicked proper trials in only a few respects. The tribunal's own official report discusses this problem, and it also uses both "proceedings" and "trials" as descriptors. Kennedy and Parker, *Official Report*, vi–vii, 49–50 (Prioleau's statement); "Examination of George Wilson," House Copy, SCDAH; "Examination of Joe La Roche," House Copy, SCDAH.

9. Solomon Northrup, *Twelve Years a Slave* (Auburn, NY, 1853); Mary Prince, *The History of Mary Prince, a West Indian Slave: Related by Herself* [. . .] (London, 1831).

10. Because of the anomalous nature of the "trials," I generally refer to them not as trials but as proceedings. Similarly, I have decided to code the arrests as detentions and avoid terms such as "guilty," "convict," "sentence," and "judge" as much as possible to avoid the connotations of a criminal proceeding. To the whites it was a criminal trial, for sure, but to the rebel movement it was a set of proceedings designed to repress their effort to take freedom—which to them was not a crime. Abbot, "Journals," 123; Powers, *Black Charlestonians*, 32. On the fears among the white population, Powers cites Catherine McBeth to her brother, October 4, 1822, Malcolm McBeth Collection, SCHS. For the 1740 act, see Kennedy and Parker, *Official Report*, xii–xiii. Enslaved people did not have access to the rights of English common law that the United States had inherited: judges, juries, and habeas corpus. Whites had created a novel category in the law for the enslaved. In the 1822 proceedings, both enslaved and free people were judged by a special tribunal under the 1740 South Carolina slave code. The law required

a minimum of two white men to approximate the prosecution, the judge, and the jury. Free Black people such as Denmark Vesey, Prince Graham, and Saby Gaillard would also be treated like slaves because of their race, as prescribed in section 14 of the 1740 slave code. Free and enslaved Black people had reason to be afraid of this tribunal, because "their sentence is final." There would be no appeals. Thus, the documents of the Workhouse fight offer a representation of the proceedings in which the free and enslaved Black rebel defendants can never speak without a thought of the white elite's power, as Saidiya Hartman has observed. Therefore, these texts should be read "against the grain" and as evidence of struggle and contestation, not as a transparent window offering a legible and unmediated view of the past. Saidiya Hartman, *Scenes of Subjection: Terror, Slavery, and Self-Making in Nineteenth-Century America* (New York: Oxford University Press, 1997), 12–15.

11. Bennett's best single statement about the totality of the events is his published circular, in which he argued that the planning was real but unlikely. In somewhat lower-profile critiques, such as a cover letter he sent to the legislature, he was more critical of the tribunal—though he never wavered in his belief that the movement was real and a heavy police response warranted. He believed that a justice of the peace should be involved, which was regulated by the state. See David James McCord, ed., *The Statutes at Large of South Carolina: from 1814 to 1838* [. . .] (Columbia, SC: A. S. Johnston, 1839), 6:116; and Thomas Bennett, "Circular of Governor Thomas Bennett Jr.," August 10, 1822, and Bennett to Robert Y. Hayne, July 1, 1822, both in Douglas R. Egerton and Robert L. Paquette, *The Denmark Vesey Affair: A Documentary History* (Gainesville: University Press of Florida, 2017), 147–48, 467–71.

12. Tim Lockley, "Foreshadowing Vesey: The Camden Slave Conspiracy of 1816," *American Nineteenth Century History* 23, no. 2 (2022): 185–201. "Account of the Contingent Fund of Gov. Thomas Bennett," 1822, Governor's Messages, S165009, SCDAH. John Mill was a bookseller at 34 Broad Street in 1822. *City Gazette*, April 22, 1822, 3; James R. Schenk, *City Directory* (Charleston, SC, 1822), 60. A John Wilkes advertised substantial quantities of foolscap paper for sale throughout 1822, including in October and November (e.g., in *City Gazette*, October 10, 1822, 3), and there were other sellers.

13. Jeannerett receipt, 1823, item 54, series S165015, Petitions to the General Assembly, SCDAH; Giles Bergel, "Authorship in Script and Print: The Example of Engraved Handwriting Manuals of the Eighteenth Century," in *Pen, Print, and Communication in the Eighteenth Century*, ed. Caroline Archer-Parré and Malcolm Dick (Liverpool, UK: Liverpool University Press, 2020), 38–40; L. C. Hector, *The Handwriting of English Documents* (London: Edward Arnold, 1966), 63–64. Bennett may have supplied Jeannerett with paper, too. He had just used public money to pay $83.84 for a large quantity of stationery from John Mill two days earlier. Bennett made two other payments for small quantities of stationery in October and November, but each was less than two dollars. "Account of the Contingent Fund of Gov. Thomas Bennett," 1822, Governor's Messages, S165009, SCDAH.

14. For a further and extended discussion of these findings, see the afterword of this book. On Jeannerett, see "Louisa Martindale and Charles O'Neale, executors of James C. Martindale, Petition and Supporting Papers Asking to be Paid back Money

Expended by James Martindale to Arm the Charleston Neck Rangers," series S165015, Petitions to the General Assembly, SCDAH. Egerton and Paquette speculate that the transcripts were created at Governor Bennett's direction and that clerks hired by the legislature's branches made the copies. See Egerton and Paquette, *Denmark Vesey Affair*, xv–xvi, 336n1.

15. Jeannerett's chaotic copies must be a mimic of the original. If the tribunal records had been in great order when the governor received them and were then presented to the legislature in disarray like this, there would have been a scandal because both Kennedy and Hamilton held seats in the chamber. If the governor had discovered evidence of fraud in the manuscripts, there would have been a different scandal, because the tribunal would have destroyed significant property of the governor. In short, because we can prove that the copies come from the governor and not the tribunal and that Kennedy and Hamilton were in a position to review the copies presented to them as legislators, we know the manuscript contains loyal copies. Therefore, the manuscript can authoritatively interrogate the published reports in specific and significant ways. How Bennett got the originals into his possession is unknown, but he may have been responding to a public boast in the *City Gazette* in late August. An anonymous writer, probably a member of the tribunal, almost dared any skeptic to request the documents, writing, "The complete *Journal* of these trials can at any time be seen by our citizens, and is kept as an official record for History." Perhaps Bennett took them at their word; see *City Gazette*, August 21, 1822, 2. In *The Denmark Vesey Affair* (e.g., 296n1), Egerton and Paquette speculate that the transcripts were made by a clerk, or clerks, working for the legislature. They contend that the clerk made numerous guesses about missing information and that clerical guessing explains many of the differences between the sources. But it was unlawful to modify court records, which is what Jeannerett was copying. He was required to make a loyal copy. In the afterword in this book, I analyze the physical and orthographic evidence of the manuscripts and argue that the best explanation for all the evidence is that Jeannerett tried to exactly copy every page in the exact form and order handed to him. Jeannerett may have made some errors (leaving out a line, e.g.), but he was not trying to introduce any information and risk falsifying a court record. Jeannerett was a more precise writer than Kennedy, which probably explains Jeannerett's long career as a bank teller and professional clerk and schoolmaster. The most likely conclusion covering all the evidence is that most of the contradictions between the manuscript and the published reports originate in the *Official Report* and *Negro Plot* and that most losses to the manuscripts were suffered *before* reaching Jeannerett. The tribunal's incomplete narrative resulted from the court's inability to learn the full story from Black Charlestonians unwilling to give up friends, family, and acquaintances. There was also political competition and self-promotion among the whites. An article in the *City Gazette* in late August, just as Hamilton's account of the investigations appeared in print, specifically singled out Kennedy for praise for his leadership and his speech upon sentencing Gullah Jack to death. *City Gazette*, August 21, 1822, 2.

16. Abbot, "Journals," 118–19.

17. Adam Hodgson, *Letters from North America, Written during a Tour in the United States and Canada* (London: Hurst, Robinson, 1824), 1:98.

18. Mary Lamboll Beach to Eliz. Gilchrist, July 5, 1822, Mary Lamboll Thomas Beach Papers, SCHS. Lacy Ford asserts, I think correctly, that the Denmark Vesey affair was not invented out of whole cloth but was exaggerated for political gain. Lacy Ford, "An Interpretation of the Denmark Vesey Insurrection Scare," in *Proceedings of the South Carolina Historical Association*, ed. Robert Figueira and Stephen Lowe (Charleston: South Carolina Historical Association, 2012), 16.

19. Wendy Gonaver cites a character reference for Lionel Kennedy, who in late 1822 was seeking a judicial appointment. The reference was polite but unenthusiastic as to Kennedy's skills and readiness. Wendy Gonaver, "Race Relations: A Family Story, 1765–1867," (master's thesis, College of William and Mary, 2001), 117n75. Robert Y. Hayne wrote to John C. Calhoun on December 7, 1822, about Kennedy and the judicial position: "I have also heard today that Mr. L. H. Kennedy has made an application. He is also a respectable man, of good principles, amiable character, & worthy of public confidence. But on the score of talents and learning I should consider him inferior to several of the applicants." W. Edwin Hemphill, ed., *The Papers of John C. Calhoun*, vol. 7, *1822–1823* (Columbia: University Press of South Carolina, 1973), 376–77. Kennedy did not get the appointment. Prohibition and condemnation of interracial unions such as those in Kennedy's extended family was common in North America, though perhaps less so in Jamaica and perhaps elsewhere in the Caribbean. Christine Walker, *Jamaica Ladies: Female Slaveholders and the Creation of Britain's Atlantic Empire* (Chapel Hill: University of North Carolina Press, 2020), 218–20.

20. Parker is a more obscure figure than Kennedy. He was a member of Charleston's elite St. Cecelia Society, and he was a part owner of a summer vacationing retreat called the Cabins Tract in backcountry South Carolina (Abbeville District). Nicholas Michael Butler, *Votaries of Apollo: The St. Cecelia Society and the Patronage of Concert Music in South Carolina, 1766–1820* (Columbia: University of South Carolina Press, 2007), 277. Parker died in 1844, and his will and estate inventory were recorded in Abbeville, South Carolina, in the probate court. In his inventory he was reported to own books, a cotton gin, lots of livestock, and several families of enslaved people.

21. "Examination of George Wilson," House Copy, SCDAH; "Examination of Joe La Roche," House Copy, SCDAH. "Examination of Rolla Bennett," House Copy, SCDAH.

22. "Examination of George Wilson," House Copy, SCDAH; "Examination of Joe La Roche," House Copy, SCDAH. Though George appears to have spoken first, he did not know much. He told the tribunal that Joe brought Rolla to him on or about June 14 to share the secret of a planned insurrection. According to George, Rolla warned him of the uprising in coded language. George understood the innuendo and flatly refused to join. He wept. Rolla would not abandon the movement. That was about all George knew.

23. Natasha Lightfoot points out that women in Antigua in 1858 (after emancipation) also played a central role by communicating information. See Natasha Lightfoot, "'Their Coats Were Tied Up Like Men': Women Rebels in Antigua's 1858 Uprising," *Slavery and Abolition* 31, no. 4 (2010): 537. "Examination of Joe La Roche," House Copy, SCDAH; "Examination of Rolla Bennett," House Copy, SCDAH; "Examination of Sambo La Roche," House Copy, SCDAH; Killens, *Trail Record*, 45–47. The examinations of Mr. La Roche and three of Thomas Bennett's slaves (Peter, March, and Sampson) on Rolla's behalf were recorded as taking place June 22, 1822.

24. "Examination of Joe La Roche," House Copy, SCDAH; Douglas R. Egerton, *He Shall Go Out Free: The Lives of Denmark Vesey* (New York: Madison House, 1999), 55–56, 97, 144.

25. In another example, "in 1822" a maroon community formed that lasted into 1829. See "petition of John Jonah Murrell et al. to the Speaker and Members of the South Carolina House of Representatives, 1829," and "Inhabitants of Claremont, Clarendon, St. John, St. Stevens, and Richland Districts to South Carolina Senate, ca. 1824," in Loren Schweninger, ed., *The Southern Debate Over Slavery: Petitions to Southern Legislatures, 1778-1864* (Urbana: University of Illinois Press, 2001), 83–85, 108; Sally E. Hadden, *Slave Patrols: Law and Violence in Virginia and the Carolinas* Cambridge, MA: Harvard University Press, 2001), 115–17; "Examination of Sambo La Roche," House Copy, SCDAH; Robert Paquette, "From Rebellion to Revisionism: The Continuing Debate about the Denmark Vesey Affair," *Journal of the Historical Society* 4, no. 3 (2004): 307–9 (on a variety of assaults and small-scale rebellions during the summer and fall of 1822); and Killens, *Trial Record*, 20, 21–22, 42–43. On the awareness among the enslaved in the city of the fugitives in the backcountry, see the conversation Monday Gell claims to have had with Jack Cattell, in "Jack the Slave of Col Cattell," Senate Copy, SCDAH; and Egerton and Paquette, *Denmark Vesey Affair*, 363. Whether or not Monday was correct or honest about information passing between Jack and him, he was correct about backcountry fugitives. Sylviane A. Diouf, *Slavery's Exiles: The Story of the American Maroons* (New York: New York University Press, 2014), 1, 2, 4–5.

26. "Examination of Rolla Bennett," House Copy, SCDAH; "Examination of Joe La Roche," House Copy, SCDAH. Rolla's postsentencing confession was given to a visiting minister and is therefore not in the manuscript proceedings. See Kennedy and Parker, *Official Report*, 67–68.

27. James Hamilton, *Negro Plot: An Account of the Late Intended Insurrection among a Portion of the Blacks of the City of Charleston, South Carolina*, 2nd ed. (Charleston, 1822), 19.

28. Hamilton, *Negro Plot*, 14.

29. "Robert Harth Examination," June 21, 1822, House Copy, SCDAH. Smart Anderson made a similar claim about the movement originating from the earliest attacks on the African Church, but he attributed the desire to Gullahs, whose language he spoke (perhaps he was Gullah). See "Smart Anderson Confession," House Copy, SCDAH. Gullah Jack, Smart Anderson, and Tom Russell spoke Gullah. See James Mall testimony, in Egerton and Paquette, *Denmark Vesey Affair*, 310.

30. Hamilton's *Negro Plot* says the trial was on the twenty-seventh, but the manuscript records indicate that testimony against Vesey specifically—that is, not testimony merely mentioning him—began being taken on June 26. Scholars have sometimes concluded that the manuscripts do not include the trial records for Vesey, but there is an untitled section on June 26 and 27 that includes all of the witnesses listed in the *Official Report*'s representation of Vesey's trial. In fact, there is more in the manuscript than in the *Official Report*. All that is missing from the manuscript is a heading and date. My account of Vesey's trial follows the manuscript. Vesey's trial had an outsized significance for the court, which noted that Vesey's personal defense counsel, William Cross, cross-examined witnesses against Vesey. Nonetheless, despite the importance to the tribunal, the manuscript records very casually represent the proceedings. When William Paul and Joe La Roche testified against Vesey, the tribunal's notetaker did not even record

their statements. Instead, in the manuscript, we read only that they testified "much as before." In the *Official Report,* Kennedy and Parker simply inserted statements given by both men *before* Vesey's trial as if they had been given live in court, when in fact the men might have said similar but not identical things. Indeed, the hedging phrase "much as before" suggests they did not say *exactly* the same things. What was different? We will never know. The manuscript also makes no effort to represent the cross-examinations. Though Monday Gell names Vesey a lot, he never says Vesey instigated the plan on his own or that he was the sole leader or overall commander. Though Monday shows that Vesey was a central figure, he does not even acknowledge Vesey as his own commander, captain, or general. Kennedy and Parker, *Official Report,* 22 ("absolutely necessary" quote); Trial of Denmark Vesey, June 26–27, 1822, House Copy, SCDAH.

31. "Trial of Denmark Vesey," June 26–27, 1822, House Copy, SCDAH; "Benjamin Ford Statement," June 26, 1822, House Copy, SCDAH.

32. "Frank Ferguson Testimony," House Copy, SCDAH; "Adam Ferguson Testimony," House Copy, SCDAH.

33. "Jesse Blackwood Testimony," House Copy, SCDAH. Jesse Blackwood's proceeding, from arraignment to sentence, took place on June 28. See Egerton and Paquette, *Denmark Vesey Affair,* 295n1.

34. Kennedy and Parker, *Official Report,* 177–78. In their sentences of Gullah Jack and then a group of ten men, the tribunal echoed some of this language and amplified the racism of it by declaring that "such men as you, are in general, as ignorant as you are vicious, without any settled principles, and possessing but few of the virtues of civilized life; you would soon, therefore, have degenerated into a horde of barbarians, incapable of any government" (180).

35. Daniel J. Flanigan, "Criminal Procedure in Slave Trials in the Antebellum South," *Journal of Southern History* 40, no. 4 (1974): 542. For the outcome for Rev. Morris Brown, see Hamilton, *Negro Plot,* 31, 45; and Egerton and Paquette, *Denmark Vesey Affair,* 665–67.

36. "Yorick Cross Testimony," Senate Copy, SCDAH.

37. Fifty years later, William L. King remembered the location of the July 2 execution as being "on a hill East of the Meeting Street Road, about eight hundred yards North of the street, now known as Line Street." William L. King, *The Newspaper Press of Charleston, S.C.: A Chronological and Biographical History, Embracing a Period of One Hundred and Forty Years* (Charleston, 1872), 61–62, as cited in Egerton and Paquette, *Denmark Vesey Affair,* 168n12. The site is probably somewhere along what is now Stuart Street, east of Meeting Street, because Stuart is approximately 800 yards north of Line Street. The area was often referred to as "Blake's Lands," a rather large area north of Line Street and Blake Street. It was also the site of the New Market Races, the city's racecourse before the Washington Racecourse was established in what is now Hampton Park; *City Gazette,* March 5, 1790, 2, 3. The New Market Races, no longer a racecourse, had been used in February 1822 for a slave auction of 100 people by Payne and Company; *City Gazette,* February 7, 1822, 3. It also had a tavern.

38. *City Gazette,* July 3, 1822, 1.

39. *City Gazette,* July 3, 1822, 1.

40. "Examination of Sally Howard," Senate Copy, SCDAH. In this sense, Sally recognized Jesse as a burden in the sense that Anthony Kaye discusses such burdens. Anthony

E. Kaye, *Joining Places: Slave Neighborhoods in the Old South* (Chapel Hill: University of North Carolina Press, 2007), 134–35. In fact, there may have been more close family connections among the uprising movement members than we realize: Jesse Blackwood's brother had married Sally Howard's mother, but Jesse had himself married a woman whose sister was married to Sandy Vesey. See E. P. Simon sworn testimony, Sandy Vesey proceedings, in Egerton and Paquette, *Denmark Vesey Affair*, 314.

41. Hamilton, *Negro Plot*, 47; "Sally Howard Examination," House Copy, SCDAH.

42. "Examination of Joe La Roche," House Copy, SCDAH.

43. "Examination of Joe La Roche," House Copy, SCDAH; "Examination of Sambo La Roche," House Copy, SCDAH; Killens, *Trial Record*, 42–43; Egerton, *He Shall Go Out*, 55–56, 97, 144; Robert Olwell, *Masters, Slaves, and Subjects: the Culture of Power in the South Carolina Low Country, 1740–1790* (Ithaca, NY: Cornell University Press), 166–78.

44. "Testimony of Mrs. La Roche," Senate Copy, SCDAH.

45. "William Paul Examination," House Copy, SCDAH (Denmark Vesey and Sarah Paul relationship); "Sally Howard Examination," House Copy, SCDAH (Sally Howard and Jesse Blackwood relationship); E. P. Simon sworn testimony, Sandy Vesey proceedings, in Egerton and Paquette, *Denmark Vesey Affair*, 314; Kennedy and Parker, *Official Report*, 124 (Sandy Vesey and Jesse Blackwood relationship).

46. William was arrested and he was intimidated, but he was the first to be detained and there was no one else in custody to coordinate his story with. These are among the reasons to consider his testimony relatively credible. "William Paul Examination," House Copy, SCDAH. William even identifies someone named Jim Bennet, who may not have existed. Kennedy and Parker, *Official Report*, 52 (quotes).

47. "William Paul Examination," House Copy, SCDAH.

48. Billy Bulkley describes Gullah Jack (and Robert Robertson) as principal leaders for "Gullah Jack's party." See "Trial of Robert," July 16, 1822, House Copy, SCDAH.

49. "Yorick Cross testimony," Senate Copy, SCDAH.

50. "Yorick Cross testimony," Senate Copy, SCDAH.

51. "Yorick Cross testimony," Senate Copy, SCDAH.

52. Hamilton, *Negro Plot*, 20.

53. Kennedy and Parker, *Official Report*, 179. In a separate sentence brought down on ten men, the tribunal echoed some of this language and amplified the racism of it by declaring that "such men as you, are in general, as ignorant as you are vicious, without any settled principles, and possessing but few of the virtues of civilized life; you would soon, therefore, have degenerated into a horde of barbarians, incapable of any government" (180).

54. Hamilton, *Negro Plot*, 21; Kennedy and Parker, *Official Report*, 58.

55. Kennedy and Parker, *Official Report*, 58.

56. The full list of new detainees: Tom Russell, Smart Anderson, Bacchus Hammett, Pharo Thompson, Pollydore Faber, Perault Strohecker, Billy Bulkley, John Enslow, Buonaparte Mulligan, Peter Ward, Sandy Curtis, Charles Shubrick, Isaac Trapier, Cuffy Graves, William Adger, Smart Ward, Mungo Lowndes, Thomas Ward, Bob Hibben, Butcher Gibbes, John Taylor, Louis Cromwell, Seymour Kunhardt, Saby Gaillard, Isaac Harth, and Scipio and Dick Sims as well as Adam, John, and Robert Robertson. Hamilton, *Negro Plot*, 47–49.

57. Hamilton, *Negro Plot*, 20.

58. Monday, by his own declaration, was not very close to Gullah Jack, Tom Russell, or the Gullah-speaking group, all of whom had close ties to the countryside and died without naming names. That Monday was part of the "Ebo" company and Tom and Gullah Jack part of the separate Gullah company gets a suggestive confirmation in a description of their sociability in the proceedings against Tom Russell and several others. Monday says that he spoke with Perault often (Perault was with Monday's group) but rarely with Tom. "Confession of Mr. Hammet's Bacchus on 12th July 1822," House Copy, SCDAH; "Tom Russell proceedings," July 15, 1822, House Copy, SCDAH; "Confession of Monday Gell," July 13, 1822, Senate Copy, SCDAH; "Second Confession of Monday Gell," July 23, 1822, Senate Copy, SCDAH.

59. "Sentence of Jack," in Kennedy and Parker, *Official Report*, 179.

60. Writes Hamilton of these six, "These individuals were important witnesses in all the apprehensions and trials subsequent to the 13th of July." Hamilton, *Negro Plot*, 27.

61. "Confession of Monday Gell," July 13, 1822, Senate Copy, SCDAH.

62. The thirty-seven named individuals in Monday Gell's two confessions (listed alphabetically; an asterisk indicates that someone was named only in the second confession): Adam (a "free man," probably Creighton), Smart Anderson, Paris Ball, Ned Bennett, Rolla Bennett*, William Colcock, Charles Drayton, Adam Ferguson, Frank Ferguson, Lot Forrester, Saby Gaillard, William Garner, Jack Glen, Gullah Jack, Bacchus Hammett, Isaac Harth, Mingo Harth, Albert Inglis, John Enslow, Edward Johnson, Joe Jore, Denbow Martin, Billy Palmer, William Paul, Peter Poyas, Jack Purcell, Luis Remoussin, Tom Russell, Scipio Sims, Stephen Smith, Perault Strohecker, Pharo Thompson, Denmark Vesey, Vesey's eldest stepson*, Vesey's mulatto boy [his son-in-law]*, Sandy Vesey, and John Vincent. "Confession of Monday Gell," July 13, 1822, Senate Copy, SCDAH; "Second Confession of Monday Gell," July 23, 1822, House Copy, SCDAH.

63. Hamilton, *Negro Plot*, 45; "Confession of Monday Gell," July 13, 1822, Senate Copy, SCDAH; "Second Confession of Monday Gell," July 23, 1822, House Copy, SCDAH.

64. "Second Confession of Monday Gell," July 23, 1822, House Copy, SCDAH.

65. "Second Confession of Monday Gell," July 23, 1822, House Copy, SCDAH.

66. The phrase in italics, *what they could expect*, is a paraphrase of how the court abstracted Monday's words to Charles Drayton when Charles reproached him after they were sentenced to death. The words in both Hamilton's *Negro Plot* (20) and Kennedy and Parker's *Official Report* (57) is "what they had a right to expect."

67. "Confession of Monday Gell," July 13, 1822, House Copy, SCDAH; "Second Confession of Monday Gell," July 23, 1822, House Copy, SCDAH; Egerton and Paquette, *Denmark Vesey Affair*, 214n1, 425.

68. "Tom Russell on His Trial," Senate Copy, SCDAH; Egerton and Paquette, *Denmark Vesey Affair*, 309–10.

69. Bacchus confessed for a third time on July 17. And there is a fourth, undated version of Bacchus's confession held at Duke University ("Confession of Bacchus, the Slave of Mr. Hammet," BHP). Within that document is enclosed an additional confession of John Enslow ("The Confession of Mr. Enslows Boy John," BHP). The Duke manuscript of Bacchus's confession is significantly different from the confessions found in the Jeannerett manuscripts. Compare to "Confession of Bacchus Hammet," July 12, 1822,

House Copy, SCDAH; "Further Confession of Bacchus Hammet," July 13, 1822, House Copy, SCDAH; and "Third Confession of Bacchus Hammett," July 17, 1822, House Copy, SCDAH. The Enslow document held at Duke is very similar to Enslow's confession in the Jeannerett manuscripts.

70. The published report ignores Bacchus's third confession (July 17) recorded in the Jeannerett manuscripts. Compare "Third Confession of Bacchus Hammett," July 17, 1822, House Copy, SCDAH to Kennedy and Parker, *Official Report*, 141–45; and "Confession of Bacchus, the Slave of Mr. Hammet," BHP.

71. "Confession of Bacchus, the Slave of Mr. Hammet," BHP.

72. "Confession of Bacchus, the Slave of Mr. Hammet," BHP.

73. The first half of Bacchus's confession in the *Official Report* comes from the July 12 confession Bacchus gave to Benjamin Hammett and witnesses in the Workhouse before the proceeding against Bacchus convened. In the Jeannerett manuscripts, the July 12 statement is presented as a copy of an affidavit of sorts that Hammett presented to the tribunal (with the signatures and format of the original document recapitulated). The *Official Report*, however, deletes these signatures and format. Then, the report attaches the July 13 "further confession" to the July 12 confession without revealing that they were different documents. For a sense of the importance of changing third to first person, compare the quote about transporting the keg of powder in the *Official Report* to this text from the July 12 confession found in the House Copy: "That he Bacchus took the keg of Powder out of the back Store of his master—and he carried it in a bag to Denmark." For the various versions in the Jeannerett manuscripts held in South Carolina, see "Confession of Bacchus Hammett," July 12, 1822, House Copy, SCDAH; "Further Confession of Bacchus Hammett," July 13, 1822, House Copy, SCDAH; and "Third Confession of Bacchus Hammett," July 17, 1822, House Copy, SCDAH. Compare these to loyal copies in Egerton and Paquette (*Denmark Vesey Affair*, 298–303) and to the deceptive edits and omissions in Kennedy and Parker, *Official Report*, 141–45. The undated version of Bacchus's confession held at the Duke University Libraries is possibly a version written down by someone close to Hammett, perhaps a minister who visited Bacchus or Francis S. Belzer, Benjamin Hammett's lawyer in the Bacchus case. Belzer or a surrogate may have witnessed the interrogations. The text refers to both Bacchus and Benjamin Hammett in the third person. Included with the undated version of Bacchus's confession at Duke is a manuscript confession by John Enslow. Unlike Bacchus's confession, however, the content of the Enslow document ("The Confession of Mr. Enslows Boy John," BHP) is very much like the one found in Jeannerett's copies. See also Egerton and Paquette, *Denmark Vesey Affair*, 321–24 (undated Bacchus confession), 324–25 (John Enslow); and Michael P. Johnson, "Denmark Vesey and His Co-Conspirators," *William and Mary Quarterly*, 3rd ser., 58, no. 4 (2001): 926.

74. Included with the undated version of Bacchus's confession held at the Duke University Libraries is a manuscript confession by John Enslow. Unlike Bacchus's confessions, however, the content of the Enslow document ("The Confession of Mr. Enslows Boy John," BHP) is very much like the one found in Jeannerett's manuscript. "Confession of Bacchus Hammett," July 12, 1822, House Copy, SCDAH; "Further Confession of Bacchus Hammett," July 13, 1822, House Copy, SCDAH; "Third Confession

of Bacchus Hammett," July 17, 1822, House Copy, SCDAH. Compare these to Kennedy and Parker, *Official Report*, 141–45. See also Egerton and Paquette, *Denmark Vesey Affair*, 321–24 (undated Bacchus confession), 324–25 (John Enslow); and Michael P. Johnson, "Denmark Vesey," 926.

75. "Nero Haig Proceedings," Senate Copy, SCDAH. I am following Egerton and Paquette on the date of the proceeding against Nero Haig. See Egerton and Paquette, *Denmark Vesey Affair*, 356n1.

76. "Proceedings against Agrippa Perry," July 23–24, 1822, Senate Copy, SCDAH; "Trial of SCIPIO," in Kennedy and Parker, *Official Report*, 133–35.

77. Agrippa appeared at Scipio's proceedings as a defense witness. He said that he requested that Scipio hire a horse for him so he could go into the country. He said it was about the last day of the first week in June. Scipio took him to Perault, he says, but he did not know Perault and in his statement was unable to name him. He and Scipio went on horseback to the Perry plantation at a place called the Horse Savannah. The purpose was to get Agrippa's tools. He says they returned the next day, a Sunday. On cross-examination Agrippa's was able to name Perault and say that he lives *on the green*. Agrippa says he paid Perault two dollars in hand and another dollar when he returned. When he received the horse, Scipio was not with him yet. He says he had a pass. Scipio's name was not on the pass. He retrieved his mallet, chisel, and ax. They left town on Saturday about 10 a.m. "Proceedings against Agrippa Perry," July 23–24, 1822, Senate Copy, SCDAH; "Trial of SCIPIO," in Kennedy and Parker, *Official Report*, 133–35.

78. "Proceedings against Agrippa Perry," July 23–24, 1822, Senate Copy, SCDAH.

79. "Scipio Sims Proceedings," July 18–19, 1822, Senate Copy, SCDAH; "Trial of SCIPIO," in Kennedy and Parker, *Official Report*, 133–35; "Trial of Agrippa Perry," July 23–24, 1822, Senate Copy, SCDAH.

80. "Trial of Agrippa Perry," July 23–24, 1822, Senate Copy, SCDAH.

81. "Scipio Sims Proceedings," July 18–19, 1822, Senate Copy, SCDAH.

82. "Trial of Agrippa Perry," July 23–24, 1822, Senate Copy, SCDAH; "Scipio Sims Proceedings," July 18–19, 1822, Senate Copy, SCDAH.

83. An explicit engagement with the scholarly debate about the 1822 archive's veracity and reliability is not part of the scope of this work, but the debate has deeply affected my approach. As early as 1964, historians published doubts about the tribunal's records. A noteworthy example was the rarely discussed work of Marina Wikramanayake. Her 1973 book *A World in Shadow* argued that the court's assessments of the plot were "dubious" and that the court's records did "not quite tally" with each other. She was right. In 2001, historian Michael Johnson returned to this theme with a more ambitious conclusion. He contended that anxious, racist, white Charlestonians fabricated the slave testimony at the heart of the case and framed Vesey and his coconspirators. It was all a white conspiracy to lynch Black people and demolish their church. To fabricate sufficient evidence, they intimidated prisoners and encouraged the coordination of false information among the accused. The enslaved complied out of mortal fear of the gallows, and the tribunal faked its records. I agree that relations of power were constitutive of the responses from the enslaved, but false betrayal was not their only response. Slavery and slavery's racism meant they became practiced, skilled, and tactful in discourse with powerful whites. I argue that even in betrayals they told strategic

truths and that even when they lied it was sometimes to protect themselves and surviving friends, acquaintances, and loved ones. To recover the heart of the debate, see Egerton and Paquette, *Denmark Vesey Affair*; Douglas Egerton, *He Shall Go Out Free: the Lives of Denmark Vesey*, rev. and updated ed. (Lanham, MD: Rowman and Littlefield, 2004); Michael P. Johnson, "Denmark Vesey," 915–76; and Paquette, "From Rebellion to Revisionism," 291–334. For some different responses since, see P. A. Cramer, "'Diabolical Design': The Charleston Elite, the 1822 Slave Insurrection, and the Discourse of the Supernatural," in *The Memory of Catastrophe*, ed. Peter Gray and Kendrick Oliver (Manchester, UK: University of Manchester Press, 2004), 31–45; Walter C. Rucker, *The River Flows On: Black Resistance, Culture, and Identity Formation in Early America* (Baton Rouge: Louisiana State University Press, 2006), 163; and Joseph Kelly, *America's Longest Siege: Charleston, Slavery, and the Slow March toward Civil War* (New York: Overlook, 2013), 132–69; Kellie Carter Jackson, *Force and Freedom: Black Abolitionists and the Politics of Violence* (Philadelphia: University of Pennsylvania, 2019), 13, 131n3; and John Garrison Marks, *Black Freedom in the Age of Slavery: Race, Status, and Identity in the Urban Americas* (Columbia: University Press of South Carolina, 2020), 73. See also Richard Wade, "The Vesey Plot: A Reconsideration," *Journal of Southern History* 30, no. 2 (1964): 143–61; and Marina Wikramanayake, *A World in Shadow: The Free Black in Antebellum South Carolina* (Columbia: University of South Carolina Press, 1973).

84. Catherine Clinton, *Harriet Tubman: The Road to Freedom* (New York: Little, Brown, 2004), 79–97; "Trial of Julius Forrest," House Copy, SCDAH; "Examination of George Wilson," House Copy, SCDAH; "Confession of Yorick Cross," Senate Copy, SCDAH. In their published narratives, both Douglass and Jacobs cited family and friends repeatedly as motivation and also constraint in their plans to escape their enslavement. Jacobs tells her own story as a narrative of family affection, and she relates the stories of others. See Harriet Jacobs, *Incidents in the Life of a Slave Girl* [. . .], ed. Jean Fagan Yellin (1861; Cambridge, MA: Harvard University Press, 1987), 77–79, 129–30, 204, 276–77. Douglass notes the constraints repeatedly; see Frederick Douglass, *Narrative of the Life of Frederick Douglass* (Boston, 1845), 18–19, 45–46. He writes,

> It is impossible for me to describe my feelings as the time of my contemplated start drew near. I had a number of warm-hearted friends in Baltimore,—friends that I loved almost as I did my life,—and the thought of being separated from them forever was painful beyond expression. It is my opinion that thousands would escape from slavery, who now remain, but for the strong cords of affection that bind them to their friends. The thought of leaving my friends was decidedly the most painful thought with which I had to contend. The love of them was my tender point, and shook my decision more than all things else (106–7).

85. Sarah Bradford, *Scenes from the Life of Harriet Tubman* (Auburn, NY, 1869), 24–25; Clinton, *Harriet Tubman*, 91. "Trial of Julius Forrest," House Copy, SCDAH; "Examination of George Wilson," House Copy, SCDAH; "Confession of Yorick Cross," Senate Copy, SCDAH.

86. "William—Mrs. Colcock—Arraigned Plea Not Guilty on His Trial—Mr D D Bacot Attends," July 16, 1822, House Copy, SCDAH; "William Colcock's Confession," House Copy, SCDAH. Monday had named William in his first confession on July 13,

but he had not said he had joined the movement. Seeing him face-to-face, he cleared him instead of making up a story.

87. Evidence of uncertainty and distortions by the court in the general interpretation of the events is significant. See Kennedy and Parker, *Official Report*, 26 (admitting their incomplete knowledge). Similarly, the intendant ("mayor") James Hamilton (*Negro Plot*, 30) in his narrative of the events observed about "the probable causes of this conspiracy" that it is "a matter of speculation" and we should not "speak without reserve."

88. Kennedy and Parker, *Official Report*, 25–26, 59, 99, 175.

89. "Further Confession of Bacchus Hammett," July 13, 1822, House Copy, SCDAH; Kennedy and Parker, *Official Report*, 145; Hamilton, *Negro Plot*, 49; Egerton and Paquette, *Denmark Vesey Affair*, 337n1; Thomas Bennett, Governor's Message 2, November 28, 1822, Governors' Messages, SCDAH.

90. W. E. B. Du Bois, *The Souls of Black Folk* (Chicago: A. C. McClurg, 1903), 106.

91. "The State of South Carolina vs. William Allen," in Kennedy and Parker, *Official Report*, ii–v. Regarding the cases of three additional white men tried for the misdemeanor of inciting insurrection, see Kennedy and Parker, *Official Report*, i–x; Philip Rubio, "'Though He Had a White Face, He Was a Negro in Heart': Examining the White Men Convicted of Supporting the 1822 Denmark Vesey Slave Insurrectionary Conspiracy," *South Carolina Historical Magazine* 113, no.1 (2012): 50–67.

92. Kennedy and Parker, *Official Report*, 23.

Chapter Four

1. Fred Moten, "The Case of Blackness," *Criticism* 50, no. 2 (2008): 177–218 (epigraph on 215); *City Gazette*. For the free Black man Thomas C. Brown's memory of burials in the potter's field, see Douglas R. Egerton and Robert L. Paquette, *The Denmark Vesey Affair: A Documentary History* (Gainesville: University Press of Florida, 2017), 750.

2. The existence of the public burial ground and the city's reaction to unburied bodies found around town on occasion demonstrate that the tribunal was never going to simply dump the bodies in a marsh or river somewhere: *City Gazette*, April 21, 1818, 2 (inquest report on a Black child's body found in a marsh). But managing white health and property interests should not be confused with concern for Black bodies or community feelings. The ghastly offer of giving the bodies to surgeons "if requested" was repeated in the *City Gazette*. It certainly was not the fate of more than a few of the bodies, if any, given Charleston's limited capacity to process or store cadavers (the Medical College was founded in 1824). "Tribunal Sentences and Orders Meeting," July 22, 1822, Senate Copy, SCDAH; and *City Gazette*, July 27, 1822, 1. On August 27, after the tribunals' investigations had ended, the city responded to a complaint about the bodies buried at the Lines becoming a nuisance. The city addressed the problem immediately, but we do not know what it ordered. See Egerton and Paquette, *Denmark Vesey Affair*, 483. There has been some confusion among scholars as to where the burial ground was in 1822. In 1807 the city designated land at Bee and Doughty Streets as public burial ground. It served until the 1840s and received paupers, orphans, sailors, foreigners, and slaves. There were 445 burials there in 1822—one of the busiest years for the cemetery. Historians have often incorrectly identified the site as being at or near the Citadel. Charles

Pinckney, *Remarks Addressed to the Citizens of Charleston on the Subject of Internments* [...] (Charleston, 1839), 4, 26, 27; Michael Trinkley, Debi Hacker, and Nicole Southerland, *The Silence of the Dead: Giving Charleston Cemeteries a Voice* (Charleston, SC: Chicora Foundation, 2010), 3–6; Egerton and Paquette, *Denmark Vesey Affair*, 749, 753n10; M. Patrick Hendrix, *Down and Dirty: the Archaeology of the South Carolina Lowcountry* (Charleston, SC: History Press, 2006), 53. A historical marker on Reid Street says that the "African Society" had a burial ground there. See also *City Gazette*, August 14, 1822, 3; and Christina R. Butler, *Lowcountry at High Tide: A History of Flooding, Drainage, and Reclamation in Charleston, South Carolina* (Columbia: University Press of South Carolina, 2020), 36 (1807 ordinance against dumping bodies). See *Charleston (SC) Courier*, September 26, 1825, 2, for a description of the use of bodies of the "coloured population" for the Medical College of South Carolina, which opened in 1824. I am indebted to Brooke Fox of the Waring Historical Library for this reference.

3. Potter's field plat, Records Related to Charleston Arsenal, South Carolina, Series Plans of Military Posts in the United States, 1840-1947, Records of the Office of the Chief of Engineers, 1789-1999, RG 77, National Archives and Records Administration, Washington, DC.

4. There were 445 burials there in 1822—one of the busiest years for the cemetery. Pinckney, *Remarks Addressed*, 4, 26, 27. Hendrix (*Down and Dirty*, 53) describes the area around the Citadel and the Medical College (today the Medical University of South Carolina) as a vast potter's field burial ground for paupers, sailors, orphans, and slaves. This is only partly correct. In 1807 the city designated a potter's field—the site bounded by Bee, President, Doughty, and Thomas Streets that it defined as the new public burial ground that served until the end of the 1830s or maybe 1840. By ordinance it received paupers, orphans, sailors, strangers, free Black people, and the enslaved. Trinkley et al., *Silence of the Dead*, 3–6. The potter's field site was sold to the federal government in 1838. See "Resolution Consenting to the Purchase of Potters Field in Charleston by the Federal Government for an Extension of the Arsenal," 1838, Resolutions of the General Assembly, S165018, SCDAH.

5. Suzanne McIntosh, "Construction is Halted," *Charleston (SC) Evening Post*, April 19, 1968; Trinkley et al., *Silence of the Dead*, 3–6.

6. "A Remarkable Will Case," *Charleston (SC) Daily News*, March 28, 1873, 1; Egerton and Pauquette, *Denmark Vesey Affair*, 718n3 (Hannah Vesey), 721 (Delany); Ethan Kytle and Blain Roberts, "Freedom Fighter or Attila the Hun? How Black and White Charlestonians Remembered Denmark Vesey, 1822–2014," in *Fugitive Movements: Commemorating the Denmark Vesey Affair and Black Radical Antislavery in the Atlantic World*, ed. James O'Neil Spady (Columbia: University of South Carolina Press, January 2022), 212–13 (Delany).

7. Solomon Northrup, *Twelve Years a Slave* (Auburn, NY, 1853), 248; Kerry Walters, *American Slave Revolts and Conspiracies: A Reference Guide* (Santa Barbara, CA: ABC-CLIO, 2015), 129–31.

8. That iron gall ink was used for the Vesey archive is evidenced by the condition of the archive itself. Iron gall ink distinctively damages paper over time if it is not adequately deacidified. It sometimes browns in color. Remaining acids can stain adjacent pages. Sometimes, perhaps because a particular batch is especially acidic, the ink

burns through paper. Examples of all these effects of iron gall ink can be found on the 1822 manuscript archive's pages. For an example of an ad for the sale of ink powder in Charleston, see *City Gazette and Daily Commercial Advertiser*, February 10, 1821, 1. On iron gall ink, see Joe Nickell, *Pen, Ink, and Evidence: The Study of Writing and Writing Materials for the Penman, Collector, and Document Detective* (Lexington: University Press of Kentucky, 1990), 35–37.

9. [Edwin C. Holland,] *A Refutation of the Calumnies Circulated against the Southern & Western States, Respecting the Institution and Existence of Slavery among Them* [. . .] (Charleston, SC: A. E. Miller, 1822), 83–84; [Thomas Pinckney,] *Reflections Occasioned by the Late Disturbances in Charleston* (Charleston, SC, 1822).

10. [James Hamilton,] *Memorial of the Citizens of Charleston to the Senate and House of Representatives of the State of South Carolina* (Charleston, 1822), in John R. Commons, Ulrich B. Phillips, Eugene A. Gilmore, Helen L. Sumner, and John B. Andrews, eds., *A Documentary History of American Industrial Society* (Cleveland, OH: Arthur H. Clark, 1910), 2:104–6, as quoted in Michael Alan Schoeppner, "Navigating the Dangerous Atlantic: Racial Quarantines, Black Sailors, and United States Constitutionalism" (PhD diss., University of Florida, 2010), 33–35nn24–28.

11. "An Act for the Better Regulation and Government of Free Negroes and Persons of Color," in Egerton and Paquette, *Denmark Vesey Affair*, 594–96.

12. Manisha Sinha, *Counter-Revolution of Slavery: Politics and Ideology in Antebellum South Carolina* (Chapel Hill: University of North Carolina Press, 2003), 14–15 (on new policing measures as the first nullification); Stratford Canning to John Quincy Adams, February 13, 1823, in Notes from the British Legation in the US to the Department of State, 1791–1906, roll 13 (September 29, 1820–July 1, 1823), Malcolm A. Love Library, San Diego State University, CA; Benjamin Faneuil Hunt, Henry Elkison, Francis Gottier Deliesseline, and US Circuit Court, *The argument of Benj. Faneuil Hunt* [. . .] (Charleston, SC, 1823), www.loc.gov/item/45031209; Schoeppner, "Navigating the Dangerous Atlantic," 33–35; Philip M. Hamer, "Great Britain, the United States, and the Negro Seamen Acts, 1822–1848," *Journal of Southern History* 1, no. 1 (1935): 3–28; Joseph Kelly, *America's Longest Siege: Charleston, Slavery, and the Slow March toward Civil War* (New York: Overlook, 2013), 167–68. Kelly discusses this act, hinting at its similarity to nullification, though not using the term.

13. Lionel H. Kennedy and Thomas Parker, *An Official Report of Sundry Negroes, Charged with an Attempt to Raise an Insurrection* [. . .] (Charleston, SC, 1822), 22; Karl Bernhard, Duke of Saxe-Weimar-Eisenach, *Travels through North America, during the Years 1825 and 1826, in Two Volumes* (Philadelphia, 1828), 2:5. It is unclear who told Karl Bernhard, the visitor, this version of the story. While staying at Jehu Jones's hotel in Charleston he received visits from a variety of people from the city and visiting the city. Some of those who visited him from the city were Mr. Lowndes, to whom he says he had introductory letters; Dr. Johnson, who Bernhard says is the mayor of the city; two French merchants; the French consul; Mr. Bacott, probably a man from Charleston; and Major Massias.

14. W. E. B. Du Bois, "Of Mr. Booker T. Washington and Others," in *The Souls of Black Folk* (Chicago: A. C. McClurg, 1903), 47–48.

15. Du Bois, "Of Mr. Booker T. Washington and Others," in *Souls of Black Folk*, 47.

16. Du Bois, "Of Our Spiritual Strivings," in *Souls of Black Folk*, 2.

17. Du Bois, "Of Mr. Booker T. Washington and Others," in *Souls of Black Folk*, 47–48.

18. Bernhard, *Travels through North America*, 1:8.

19. Sir Charles MacCarthy to Thomas Clarkson, December 23, 1818, box 1, folder 49, Thomas Clarkson Papers, HL; See Kennedy and Parker, *Official Report*, 184–88; and James Hamilton, *Negro Plot: An Account of the Late Intended Insurrection among a Portion of the Blacks of the City of Charleston, South Carolina*, 2nd ed. (Charleston, 1822), 47–50 for some of the enslaved people who were banished, which included George Bampfield, Louis Cromwell, John Vincent, Charles Drayton, Monday Gell, Seymour Kunhardt, Harry Haig, Isaac Harth, Paris Ball, Peter Cooper, Dublin Morris, Billy Palmer, Billy Robinson, and Sandy Schnell. Samuel Wilkeson, *A Concise History of [. . .] Liberia* (Washington, DC, 1839), 13; *The Latest Official Accounts from Sierra Leone* (London, 1830), 23–24; Hilary Beckles, *Black Rebellion in Barbados: The Struggle against Slavery* (Bridgetown, Barbados: Antilles, 1984), 96. Beckles reports on two central primary documents for Bussa's rebellion: *Remarks on the Insurrection in Barbados and the Bill for Registering Slaves* (London, 1816); and *Report from a Select Committee of the House of Assembly [. . .]* (London, 1818).

20. William T. Hamilton, *A Word for the African* (Newark, NJ, 1825), 21; Thomas Clarkson, "A Few Places on the Coast of Africa Fit for Colonization," ca. 1820, box 2, folder 19, Thomas Clarkson Papers, HL; Horatio Bridge, *Journal of an African Cruiser*, ed. Nathaniel Hawthorne (New York, 1853), 33–43 (quotes 37, 43), 46.

21. *Examination of Mr. Thomas C. Brown, a Free Colored Citizen of S. Carolina [. . .]* (New York, 1834), 7–10, 15 (quote); MacGregor Laird, *Narrative of an Expedition into the Interior of Africa* (London, 1837), 39–42; Bridge, *Journal*, 33–43 (quotes 37, 43); Jacob Rambo journal, 1849–1852, HL; and Frederick Clark to Lincoln Clark, October 11, 1856, May 15, 1857; Charlotte Clay to Lincoln Clark, August 20, 1857; and Frederick and Charlotte Clark to Lincoln Clark, January 14, 1861, all in box 6, Lincoln Clark Papers, HL.

22. *Charleston (SC) Mercury*, March 10, 1853, 3. Though Crowe's original sketch does not survive, two versions of the information that Crowe recorded in it have survived. Other than the painting, a later etching made from the same sketch also removes those two men and the book and repositions other figures. Alonzo J. White's name is in the painting on a banner in the middle ground toward the left center. White was listed as a broker and auctioneer, with his place of business at 27 Broad Street and his residence at the corner of Tradd and Market Streets, in *Directory of the City of Charleston, for the Year 1852* (Charleston, SC, 1851), 135. In the image, a sign on the side of a building across the street to the left says "Atlantic Wharf." On an 1855 map of Charleston there is an Atlantic Wharf and a North Atlantic Wharf. The former was at the end of Broad Street. The ship masts seen in the image would be at the wharf. Jeff Strickland, *All for Liberty: The Charleston Workhouse Slave Rebellion of 1849* (New York: Cambridge University Press, 2022), 73, 127, 189.

23. *Charleston Mercury*, March 10, 1853, 3; *City Gazette and Daily Commercial Advertiser*, February 7, 1822, 3.

24. Vincent Brown, *Tacky's Revolt: The Story of an Atlantic Slave War* (Cambridge, MA: Belknap Press of Harvard University Press, 2020), 162–63.

25. On the politics of the memory of the 1822 uprising movement, see Ethan J. Kytle and Blain Roberts, *Denmark Vesey's Garden: Slavery and Memory in the Cradle of the*

Confederacy (New York: The New Press, 2018); and Ashleigh Lawrence-Sanders, "The Many Uses of Denmark Vesey: Exploring the Evolving Memory of Slavery through Interpretations of Vesey's Insurrection Plot," *Journal of African American History* 107, no. 2 (2022): 185–211. In 1936, one elderly former slave in the Charleston area still remembered the 1822 uprising and claimed others had long spoken of it, see Jeff Strickland, *All for Liberty: The Charleston Workhouse Slave Rebellion of 1849* (New York: Cambridge University Press, 2022), 23, 213n54.

Afterword

1. The epigraphs for this chapter come from, respectively, *City Gazette*, August 21, 1822, 2; and "Account of the Contingent Fund of Gov. Thomas Bennett," 1822, Governor's Messages, S165009, SCDAH. There are about a dozen committee reports from Lionel Kennedy in the legislative papers held at the South Carolina Department of Archives and History in Columbia that can be used as writing samples and examples of Kennedy's clerical habits. See, e.g., Lionel Kennedy, "Special Committee Report Concerning the Report and Petition of the Quarter Master General Relative to His Compensation," December 3, 1824, Committee Reports, S165005, SCDAH.

2. See "Confession of Monday Gell," July 13, 1822, House Copy, SCDAH; and "Confession of Monday Gell," July 13, 1822, Senate Copy, SCDAH.

3. This identification hopefully helps settle a recurring debate about the "reality" of the movement and especially the reliability of the tribunal's records. The movement was real and the records are not a fabrication. However, the resolution is also partly to admit the usefulness of Michael P. Johnson's contention that the problems in the records, which many historians have recognized over time, are more significant than has been allowed. Fully acknowledging the limits changes our understanding of the events. Michael P. Johnson, "Denmark Vesey and His Co-Conspirators," *William and Mary Quarterly*, 3rd ser., 58, no. 4 (2001): 915–76; Bennett to Robert Y. Hayne, Esq., July 1, 1822, in Douglas R. Egerton and Robert L. Paquette, *The Denmark Vesey Affair: A Documentary History* (Gainesville: University Press of Florida, 2017); Thomas Bennett, Governor's Message 2, November 28, 1822, Governors' Messages, SCDAH; Thomas Bennett, "Circular of Governor Thomas Bennett Jr.," August 10, 1822, in Egerton and Paquette, *Denmark Vesey Affair*, 467–71; Mary Lamboll Beach to Eliz. Gilchrist, July 5, 1822, Mary Lamboll Thomas Beach Papers, SCHS (new enemies).

4. For Jeannerett's signature on the 1823 receipt, see "Louisa Martindale and Charles O'Neale, executors of James C. Martindale, Petition and Supporting Papers Asking to be Paid back Money Expended by James Martindale to Arm the Charleston Neck Rangers," series S165015, Petitions to the General Assembly, SCDAH. See also Giles Bergel, "Authorship in Script and Print: The Example of Engraved Handwriting Manuals of the Eighteenth Century," in *Pen, Print, and Communication in the Eighteenth Century*, ed. Caroline Archer-Parré and Malcolm Dick (Liverpool, UK: Liverpool University Press, 2020), 38–40; and L. C. Hector, *The Handwriting of English Documents* (London: Edward Arnold, 1966), 63–64.

5. The 1822 *City Directory* locates Jeannerett at 21 Bull Street and Vesey at 20 Bull Street. Jeannerett was a clerk, bookkeeper, and teacher who had lived and worked in

Charleston for many years. Born in 1764, he died in 1849. He was sued repeatedly as a representative of the State Bank of South Carolina. In 1830 he owned four enslaved Black people and six white people in his household. *Directory and Stranger's Guide* [...] (Charleston, SC, 1824); *The Directory and Stranger's Guide for the City of Charleston* [...] (Charleston, SC, 1822), 25, 50, 109; *The Directory and Stranger's Guide* (Charleston, SC, 1819); *Directory of the City and District of Charleston* [...] (Charleston, SC, 1813); *Directory of the City and District of Charleston* [...] (Charleston, SC, 1809); *Negrin's Directory* [...] (Charleston, SC, 1807); *Negrin's Directory and Almanac* [...] (Charleston, SC, 1806); *A Directory and Stranger's Guide* [...] (Charleston, SC, 1803); *New Charleston Directory* [...] (Charleston, SC, 1802); United States, Fifth Census of the United States, 1830, City of Charleston, South Carolina, Records of the Bureau of the Census, RG 29 (Washington, DC: National Archives and Records Administration); Christopher Jeannerett record, South Carolina, 1821–1849, Charleston City Death Records, 1821–1965, Charleston County Public Library, Charleston; "Relatives and Friends of Mr. Christopher Jeannerett... ," *Charleston (SC) Courier*, February 7, 1849.

6. Egerton and Paquette (*Denmark Vesey Affair*, xv–xvi, 336n1) speculate that the tribunal record transcripts were created at Governor Bennett's direction and that two unidentified clerks hired by each of the legislature's branches made the copies.

7. "Examination of Joe La Roche," House Copy, SCDAH; "Examination of Joe La Roche," Senate Copy, SCDAH.

8. There is also a blank space in both the House and Senate copies in the July 13 proceedings, where the date for Julius Forrest's hanging was apparently intended to be. Lionel H. Kennedy and Thomas Parker, *An Official Report of Sundry Negroes, Charged with an Attempt to Raise an Insurrection* [...] (Charleston, SC, 1822), 127. Paper and copyedit evidence suggests that the original of Bennett's cover letter for the tribunal records seems also to have been lost. In the cover letter, the "Governor's Message no. 2" appended to each document packet for the House and Senate, there are emendations to both copies, which were probably made from an original (now lost). That conclusion is based on a few features. There is a sentence-length cut-and-paste error in the Senate copy—deleted with tick marks and reinserted at the correct location—that does not appear at all in the House copy, where the same text appears but in clean form, without edits. Shortly after making this edit, Jeannerett appears to have run out of the paper he used for all of the June and July House and Senate tribunal records copies and the House copy of the governor's message. The last two leaves of the Senate copy are on smaller sheets (shorter and narrower).

9. The Senate copy starts with ten pages of randomly organized examinations and a full page break and then begins on a new sheet of paper with the first trials (June 19) and one of the few copyist page numbers: page 1. Kennedy and Parker probably shared the originals with the governor only after they had published their *Official Report* in October. Jeannerett got the originals from them sometime in late October or early November. He had just a few weeks to make both copies. Thomas Cooper, ed., *The Statutes at Large of South Carolina* [...] *1682 to 1716, Inclusive* (Columbia, SC: A. S. Johnston, 1837), 2:428 (illegal to alter court records); Egerton and Paquette, *Denmark Vesey Affair*, 280–83.

10. Joe Nickell, *Pen, Ink, and Evidence: The Study of Writing and Writing Materials for the Penman, Collector, and Document Detective* (Lexington: University Press of Kentucky,

1990), 35–37; *City Gazette and Daily Commercial Advertiser*, February 10, 1821, 1 ("1 trunk Ink Powder" for sale in Charleston).

11. Measurements of the paper stock of the 1822 investigatory records are consistent with the theory that one person (Jeannerett) made both the House and Senate copies of the June and July investigatory records, while others with different paper supplies made copies of "Governor's Message 2" and the August investigatory records. When cut in half, the common foolscap size formed leaves about the size of Jeannerett's pages:

House copy paper dimensions
Jeannerett's June/July pages measured 33.3 × 19.7 cm.
"Governor's Message 2" pages (not Jeannerett's) measured 32.4 × 20.3 cm.

Senate copy
Jeannerett's June/July pages measured 33.4 × 19.6 cm.
August 3 records pages measured 31.7 × 19.6 cm and later pages measured 33.8 × 20.7 cm.
"Governor's Message 2" pages (not Jeannerett's) measured 32.7 × 20.1 cm, except for two items that measured 33.3 × 19.6 cm.

Very minor differences of about a millimeter in the dimensions of the House and Senate copies of the June/July investigatory records may have been caused by uneven wear on the edges of the sheets from storage over time. Of three common paper types—royal, demy, and foolscap—the latter was the smallest (and cheapest). It typically measured about 40.6 × 33 cm and would yield pages about 33 × 20.3 cm when cut in half. This confirms that Jeannerett had likely used foolscap paper that was cut in half. Nickell, *Pen, Ink, and Evidence*, 45–47.

12. Page numbers appear early in the Senate copy but commence only after the first ten unnumbered pages, which are out-of-place pages unfortunately added to the front permanently by the technician who laminated the collection in the twentieth century. In the Senate copy, pagination begins only with the dated section starting June 19, which is where the House copy begins its incomplete pagination. But the numbering is ultimately not the same as in the House copy—information on a given page number in one copy is not on the same page number in the other because of line spacing and character size changes between the two copies. The page numbers therefore must be the copyist's and not in the original. In his cover letter, "Governor's Message 2," Bennett cited page numbers from the House copy, which he probably used to write the cover letter while Jeannerett made the Senate copy from the (now lost) originals.

13. The foolscap paper stock for the Enslow confession held at the South Carolina Historical Society was 33.3 × 20.6 cm, whereas the Jeannerett copies in the legislative papers are on foolscap of about 33.3 × 19.7 cm.

14. The evidence for this comes from the routing notations for document management in the House and the Senate. One notation provides labels for the exhibits. The tribunal's investigatory records exhibit is labeled "Document B" in the Senate (and "Evidence B" in the House), and the subsequent exhibits are labeled documents C, D, E, F, and G. These notations were written between the folds on the back side of the last page of each exhibit, perpendicular to the main text. Some of the A–G exhibits are still missing.

15. There are no other binding marks before the mid-twentieth-century application of William J. Barrow's acetate lamination process.

16. The history of the South Carolina Department of Archives and History begins with the Fireproof Building in Charleston, which was commenced about the time of the Vesey affair in the early 1820s. State and district records were to be housed there. Several efforts to gather and save records were made before the Civil War. And a massive effort to move the entire archive to North Carolina ahead of the Union advance took place in 1865. Nonetheless, officials succeeded only in rescuing "most" of the records, and a fire in Columbia on February 17, 1865, may have destroyed Vesey-related materials. Never in a bound volume, the papers remained loose or almost loose in bundles and stacks. They have had at least three organizational methods applied to them. The physical condition of the surviving items clearly indicates wear and damage, such as minor water stains, significant tears, dust and smoke stains, folding-induced breakage, and at least one possible burn mark. A program of using the "Barrow method" for deacidification and lamination of the pages began in the 1950s. By sometime in the 1970s, probably, the Vesey records in possession of the state were bathed and laminated. Charles Lesser, *The Palmetto State's Memory: A History of the South Carolina Department of Archives and History, 1905–1960* (Columbia: South Carolina Department of Archives and History, 2009), 2–4, 78–79. See also *South Carolina Department of Archives and History Report, 1980–1981* (Columbia: South Carolina Department of Archives and History, 1981), 19–24; and *South Carolina Department of Archives and History Report, 1971–1972* (Columbia: South Carolina Department of Archives and History, 1972), 23.

Index

Page numbers in italics refer to illustrations.

Adam (free man), 194n62
Africa, 1, 15–19, 31–32, 47, 60, 134–36;
  Akan states, 5, 166n19, 168n33, 169n35;
  Asante, 21; Dakar, 5, 20; Gold Coast,
  15, 20–21, 168nn33–34, 169n35; Goree
  Island, 20; Igboland, 5; Kongo, 5, 15,
  167n25; Kormantse, 20; Liberia, 39,
  41, 67, 135–36, 181n48; Mrima Coast,
  15, 16, 45; Mozambique, 15, 166n21;
  Sierra Leone, 39, 41, 67, 135, 174n83,
  178n13; Tanzania, 5, 15–16, 17, 45, 108,
  166nn21–22, 175n1; Zanzibar, 15–16,
  166n21
African Church: on Anson Street, 9, 37;
  on Cow Alley, 27, 37, 39; on Hanover
  Street, 9, 37, 39–41
Africans, 1, 2, 4–5, 13, 14–24, 61–64, 104,
  166n21; indigenous knowledge of, in
  Charleston, 15–19, 31–32, 45–46, 53–54,
  67–68
Akan states, 5, 166n19, 168n33, 169n35
Allen, William, 123–24
American Colonization Society, 178n13.
  See also settler colonialism
Anderson, Smart, 47, 70, 108, 187n7,
  191n29, 193n56, 194n62
arrivant, 162n1
arson, 54–55, 79
Asante, 21
Ashley River, 8, 9, 10, 11, 12, 14, 28, 42, 61,
  71–72, 73, 110, 165n13

Ball, Paris, 70, 194n62, 201n19
banishment, 84, 85, 86, 116, 118, 127, 135,
  201n19; as tool to divide Black community, 122–23

Bennett, Batteau, 12, 87, 98, 99, 180n17
Bennett, Mathias, 12, 87, *101*
Bennett, Ned, 55, 84, 93, *101*, 103, 179n17;
  among first hanged, 98; named in
  Monday Gell's statement, 194n62
Bennett, Rolla, 5, 7, 37, 55, 56, 60, 82, 84;
  among first hanged, 98, 106, 121, 138;
  named in Monday Gell's statement,
  179n22, 194n62; statement by, 95,
  178n17, 180n34, 185n77; trial of, 89–94,
  101–2, *101*, 120
Bennett, Thomas, 7, 8–9, 12, 82, 98–99,
  122–23, 129, 143–45, 157; hiring of
  clerk to copy tribunal's manuscript records by, 87–89; during Rolla Bennet's
  trial, 89–94
Bennett's Mills, 8, 9, 12, 31, 50, 54, 59, 71,
  72, 73, 76, 78, 79, 125, 143, 165n13
Blackwood, Jesse, 24, 96–99, *101*, 101–3,
  104, 106, 120, 121, 192n40
Brown, Morris, 39, 49, 98, 123; cleared by
  Monday Gell, 110–11
Brown, Thomas C., 135
Brown Fellowship Society, 16, 44
Bulkley's Farm, 9, 65, 69, 76–77; indigenous ceremony at, 67–68. *See also*
  Payne's Farm; Thayer's Farm
burials, 98, 125–26; tribunal records
  likened to, 128. *See also* public burial
  ground
Bussacre, Prudence, 24, 34, 57–58, 66, 84,
  101; statement by, 102–4

Calypso, 52, 54–55, 178n13
Cannon's Bridge, 9, 71, 72, 73, 78–79
capitalism. *See* racial capitalism

207

Charleston Bridge Ferry, 11, 73
Chieffel's Steam Mill, 13
Christ Church Parish, SC, 35, 56, 58, 62, 64, 183n62
churches: African Church on Anson Street, 9, 37; African Church on Cow Alley, 27, 37, 39; African Church on Hanover Street, 9, 37, 39–41; Circular Church, 27, 37, 39, 40, 43, 49, 64, 95; Second Presbyterian, 13, 40, 54, 115, 116, 174n81. *See also* community organizing; Vesey, Denmark
Circular Church, 27, 37, 39, 40, 43, 49, 64, 95
clerks. *See* Jeannerett, Christopher; Rouse, James W.; Stevens, Jervis Henry; Strobel, Martin
Coats' and West's Steam Mill, 13
Colcock, William, 70, 121, 153, 154, 194n62
Columbia (steamboat), 42–43
community organizing, 1, 11, 38, 48, 49, 53–71, 93, 100, 101–3; mobilization technique of, 53–54, 61–64; and naming of movement, 46; and revolutionary counterstructure to slavery's racism, 46–47; and social networks, 44, 57–58, 61–64. *See also* fugitive ethics; plan of attack; targets of insurrection
Cooper River, 9, 13, 26, 28, 30, 37, 54, 57, 67, 72, 73, 80
court cases. *See* tribunal proceedings
crab claws, 16, 17, 45–46, 63, 105, 167n22, 181n37
Crafts Wharf, 27, 79
Creighton, James, 41, 52
Cross, Yorick, 17, 61–64, 70, 75, 98, 101, 102, 180n34, 181n37; statement by, 104–7, 171n51, 178n17, 183n62, 187n7
cullah. *See* crab claws

Dakar, 5, 20
Daniel Island, SC, 35

Douglass, Frederick, 5–6, 29, 48, 80, 86, 182n50; on love in shaping resistance, 120, 197n84
Drayton, Charles, 70, 98–99, 101, 104, 106, 109, 111, 169n36, 194n66; banishment of, 122, 201n19; and betrayal of Monday Gell, 107–8; named in Monday Gell's statement, 179n22, 194n62; statement by, 112, 117, 121, 133
Du Bois, W. E. B., 123, 131–34
Duncan's Mills, 9, 12, 25, 31, 54, 73, 89, 170n44
Duquercron's Store, 62, 73, 75, 183n62

Egleston's Steam Mill, 13
Emanuel African Methodist Episcopal Church. *See* African Church
Enslow, John, 58, 70, 108, 109, 156, 187n7, 194n62, 195n73–74, 204

Ferguson, Adam, 96, 101, 194n62
Ferguson, Frank, 70, 77, 96, 101, 179n17, 194n62
Ferguson, John O., 101
Ferguson, Pompey, 101
Ferguson plantation, 56, 70, 75
financial panic of 1819, 12, 26, 50
fire, 54–55, 79
Forrest, Julie, 101
Forrester, Lot, 101, 194n62
Fredensborg (slaving vessel), 20–21, 22, 168nn33–34
freedom, 1–3, 29, 32, 52, 53–54, 59, 80, 83, 84, 120, 122, 134–35; buying, 11, 21–23, 31, 51–52, 132; and Haitian example, 67, 80, 133–34; and intimate relationships, 6, 36, 52, 82, 106; ongoing struggle for, 140; and rebel leaders' ideologies, 46–48, 52, 56, 60, 82, 106, 134; and rhetorical resistance to tribunal, 124; smothered by slavery's racism, 98, 124, 129–30
fugitive ethics, 2, 6–7, 34, 44, 48, 57, 59, 81–85, 95, 99, 111, 116, 119–24, 128

fugitives. *See* fugitive ethics; maroon communities
fugitivity, 16, 164n4. *See also* fugitive ethics; maroon communities

Gadsden's Wharf, 13, 26, 27, 42, 70, 79, 165n16, 183n67
Gaillard, Saby, 70, 97–98, 108, 131, 188n10, 193n56, 194n62
Garner, William, 11–12, 36, 52, 70, 110; named in Monday Gell's statement, 110, 194n62
Gell, Monday, 1, 14–15, 18–19, 29–32, 58, 65–66, 85, *101*, 130, 137; banishment of, 122, 201n19; on freedom, 130, 134; and Igbo politics, 19, 30, 68, 83; and letter to Haitian president, 66–67; location of residence of, 27, 171nn50–51; named in other people's statements, 104, 115, 143, 181n45; and racism and violence, 152; recruiting efforts of, 48, 55–56, 62–64, 84; reportedly overall leader of rebellion, 53, 76, 77, 95, 96–97; shop of, as place of indigenous political knowledge, 68–71, 83; on slavery, 47, 176n5, 179n17; silence of, 99, 106–7; statement by, 108–12, 117, 121, 133, 143, 158, 179n22, 191n25, 192n30, 194n58, 194n62, 194n66, 197n86
Gibbs and Harper's Wharf, 25, 26, 27, 28, 64, 170n46, 175n46
Glen, Jack, 70, 194n62
Gold Coast, 15, 20–21, 168nn33–34, 169n35
Goree Island, 20
guardhouses: Main Guardhouse, 9, 27, 32, 59, 64, 72, 74, 75, 79, 98, 179n17; Piquet Guard House, 62, 63, 73, 75
Gullah language, 16, 44, 53, 59
Gullah people, 16, 17–18, 46, 56, 67–68, 83, 95

Hadden, Jim, 35
Hadden, Robert, 98

Haig, Harry, 98, *101*, 103–4, 108–9, 180n34; banishment of, 122, 201n19
Haig, Nero, 115–16
Haiti, 5, 66–68, 70, 75–76, 80, 133–34, 139; Haitian Revolution, 4, 60, 176n4. *See also* Saint-Domingue
Hamilton, James H., 81, 87, 142; *Negro Plot*, 93, 94, 121, 143, 189n15, 191n30
Hammett, Bacchus, 32, 70, 71, 73, 107–8, 193n56; named in Monday Gell's statement, 194n62; statement by, 94, 156, 163, 194nn69–70, 195nn73–74; trial of, 112–15
handwriting identification. *See* methods
hangings, 47, 98, 108, 111, 113, 114, 116, 119, 176n4. *See also* banishment; tribunal proceedings
Harth, Isaac, 193n56, 194n62, 201n19
Harth, Mingo, 70, 95, *101*, 103, 194n62
Harth, Robert, 84, 94–95, *101*, 102, 104, 187; statement by, 179n17
Hibben's Ferry, 27, 28, 64, 65, 170n46, 175n86
hiring out. *See* labor
Horry, John, *101*
Howard, Sally, 24, 66, 84, *101*; statement by, 99–101

Igboland, 5
Igbo politics, 19, 30, 68, 83
Inglis, Albert, 194n62

Jack, Gullah, 1, 13, 14–18, 19, 64–65, 69, 71, 75–76, 77, *101*, 130, 166nn20–21, 181n37; belief in English support, 180n34; burial of, 125–26; fire possibly set by, 54–55; on freedom, 134; hanging of, 121; location of residence of, 27, 28–30, 171n51; named in other people's statements, 103–5, 113, 116, 194n58, 194n62; and *ngoma*, 45, 56, 67–68, 83, 167n22, 167n25, 181n49; and racism and violence, 20, 32, 132, 158; reportedly overall leader of rebellion, 46, 53, 62, 95–96, 178n17, 193n48;

Index 209

Jack, Gullah (*continued*)
    sentencing of, 108, 189n15, 192n34;
    silence of, 120, 138; and tribunal proceedings, 93, 94, 98, 99, 106–7, 109, 122
Jacobs, Harriet, 6, 38, 48, 80, 86, 120
Jeannerett, Christopher, 87–89, *88*, 95, 128, 141–45, 152–58, 188n13, 189n15, 202n5, 203n8, 203nn8–9, 204n12; handwriting of, 146–51, 204n11
Johns Island, 61, 183n62
Johnson, Edward, 70, 97, 194n62
Jore, Joe, 70, 194n62

Kennedy, Lionel H., 88, 89, 90, 97, 106–7; *The Official Report*, 87, 92–93, 94, 97, 102, 106, 114–15, 116, 124, 129, 131, 143, 189n15; and tribunal proceedings, 93, 110, 121, 123, 142–43, 156–57
Kongo, 5, 15, 167n25
Kormantse, 20

labor, 2, 4, 7, 22; and children, 5, 29; crabbing and oystering, 14; in crafts, 7, 8–10, 12, 13; hiring out surplus, 28–29, 50; and learning geography, 14; as recession buffer, 25–27, 50; as social reproduction, 5, 23; and women, 5, 23–24; in yards, 15, 23. *See also* mills
La Roche, Amaritta, 90–92, *101*, 103; providing safe space, 102; statements about, 102–3; as uprising messenger, 101–2
La Roche, Joe, 5–6, 60–61, 63, 65, 85, 90–93, 101–3, *101*, 104, 152–53, *153*, 190n22; statement by, 95, 152–53, 187n7, 191n30
La Roche, Sambo, 91–92, 101–2, *101*
leadership coalition, 52–56, 83, 124, 134, 139; disagreement among, 56, 83; and indigenous ceremony, 67. *See also* Gell, Monday; Jack, Gullah; Poyas, Peter; Vesey, Denmark
Liberia, 39, 41, 67, 135–36, 181n48
love, 1–2, 3, 5–6, 77, 33, 35, 41–44, 46, 4, 50, 2, 89–119, 125, 132, 134, 136, 138, 139, 140, 158, 162n1, 164n4; and attachment to place and people, 5–6, 42, 57; and belonging, 44, 140; and flight to places and people, 35, 43, 57; and revolution, 3, 43–44, 48, 82, 140, 162n1, 164n4; role of, in shaping statements to investigators, 83, 86, 89–119; and slaving capitalism's contradictions, 7, 41, 134; and social networks, 5, 89–119. *See also* fugitive ethics
Lucas, Bram, 11, 78–79, 187n7
Lucas, Jonathan, 9, 11–12, 72, 73, 78–79, *78*
Lucas, Richard, 11, 78–79, 187n7
Lucas's Mill, 9, 11–12, 72, 73, 79, 125

Main Guardhouse, 9, 27, 32, 59, 64, 72, 74, 75, 79, 98, 179n17
manufacturing. *See* labor; mills
manumission, 51–52, 113. *See also* freedom
mapping, 73–74, 75, 77–79
maroon communities, 33, 92–93, 184n69. *See also* fugitive ethics
Martin, Denbow, 70, 110, 194n62
meeting places: Bulkley's Farm, 9, 65, 67–68, 69, 76–77; Payne's Farm, 9, 76–77, 98, 184n70; Thayer's Farm, 65, 69
methods, 60; handwriting identification, 88, 141–58; italics instead of quotes, 163n3, 176n6; mapping, 73–74, 75, 77–79; naming, 46, 53; social networks, 38, 40, 44, 56, 59, *101*, 121; testimony credibility test, 85, 186n7
mganda, 181n49
Miles, Tiya, 3
mills, 11–13; Bennett's Mills, 8, 9, 12, 31, 50, 54, 59, 71, 72, 73, 76, 78, 79, 125, 143, 165n13; Chieffel's Steam Mill, 13; Coats' and West's Steam Mill, 13; Duncan's Mills, 9, 12, 25, 31, 54, 89, 170n44; Egleston's Steam Mill, 13; Lucas's Mill, 9, 11–12, 72, 73, 79, 125; Steele's Saw Pit, 12, 31, 54. *See also* targets of insurrection

Monrovia, 41, 178n13
Mount Pleasant, SC, 28, 64, 170n46
Moten, Fred, 125, 198n1
movement. *See* community organizing
Mozambique, 15, 166n21
Mrima Coast, 15, 16, 45

Negro Plot (Hamilton), 93, 94, 121, 143, 189n15, 191n30
ngoma practices, 16–17, 45, 56, 67–68, 181n49
Ngoni people, 16, 166n21

obeah, 17, 18
Obia religion, 18, 168n29
Official Report (Kennedy and Parker), 87, 92–93, 94, 97, 102, 106, 114–15, 116, 121, 124, 129, 131, 143, 189n15

Palmer, Benjamin, 49
Palmer, Billy, 70, 194n62, 201n19
Paul, Edwin, 101
Paul, Sarah, 6, 23, 84, 101; statements about, 66, 103; stepdaughter of Denmark Vesey, 24, 164n6
Paul, William, 66, 80–81, 84, 85, 95, 101, 102, 104; list of uprising participants of, 110; statement by, 92, 94, 103, 164n6, 191n30
Parker, Thomas, 88, 89, 90; *The Official Report*, 87, 92–93, 94, 97, 102, 106, 114–15, 116, 124, 129, 131, 143, 189n15; and tribunal proceedings, 93, 110, 121, 123, 142–43, 156
Payne, Daniel, 31, 39–40, 42, 49–50, 57
Payne, William, 77, 184n70
Payne's Farm, 9, 76–77, 98, 184n70. *See also* Bulkley's Farm; Thayer's Farm
Perry, Agrippa, 116–19
Perry, Doll, 119
Perry, Kit, 118–19
Perry, Liddy, 117–19
Piquet Guard House, 62, 63, 73, 75

plan of attack, 64, 71–80. *See also* community organizing; targets of insurrection
potter's field. *See* public burial ground
Poyas, Mingo, 101
Poyas, Peter, 1, 14, 43, 48, 84, 93, 101, 105, 181n37; among first hanged, 98, 116, 121; and belief in English support, 180n34; burial of, 126; evading arrest, 81, 85; first discussion of rebellion, 54; named in other people's statements, 94, 85, 92, 103, 104, 179n17, 182n49, 183n62, 194n62; and *ngoma* ceremonies, 67–68; and racism and violence, 47, 49, 52, 132, 158; recruiting efforts of, 56, 58, 61–62, 96; reportedly overall leader of rebellion, 53, 95, 125; silence of, 93–94, 106, 109, 120, 138; trial of, 94–95; and uprising, 74–75
Prince, Mary, 6, 50, 86
Prioleau, Peter, 32, 80, 101; statement by, 187n7
Pritchard, Jack. *See* Jack, Gullah
Pritchard's Wharf, 27, 79, 105, 179n21; suspicious fire on, 54–55
public burial ground, 125–26, 127, 139–40
Purcell, Jack, 55, 110, 111, 179n17, 194n62

racial capitalism, 7–8, 134–35; as problem without solution, 39. *See also* racism
racism, 22, 39, 42, 44, 86, 97–98, 99, 116, 118, 126, 128, 133–34; and slavery institution, 2, 41–43, 42–44, 48–49, 89–90, 97–98, 112–13, 118–19, 128, 131–33, 196n83; and tribunal's presumptions about gender, 124; and uprising movement's counterstructure, 47; and Denmark Vesey, 47, 52, 132, 158; and David Walker, 42–43
rebellion. *See* community organizing; targets of insurrection
Remoussin, Luis, 70, 194n62
rivers: as sources of medicine and food, 14, 16–18, 30, 35, 45, 63; as routes, 8, 14,

rivers (*continued*)
    72; in uprising plans, 72–75. *See also* Ashley River; Cooper River
Robertson, Robert, 67, 68, 178n17, 193n48, 193n56
Rouse, James W., 144, *146–51*
runaways. *See* fugitive ethics; maroon communities
Russell, Tom, 67, 70, 107, 112, 191n29, 193n56; named in other people's statements, 194n58, 194n62; trial of, 112, 115

Saint-Domingue, 21, 166n19, 168n33. *See also* Haiti
Schubrick, Charles, *101*
Second Presbyterian Church, 13, 40, 54, 115, 116, 174n81
settler colonialism, 7–8, 43, 135–36; American Colonization Society, 178n13; and term *arrivant*, 162n1
ships: *Fredensborg*, 21, 22, 168nn33–34; *Columbia*, 42–43; *Calypso*, 52, 54–55, 178n13
Sierra Leone, 39, 41, 67, 135, 174n83, 178n13
Sims, Dick, 193n56
Sims, Scipio, 70, 110, 116–19, 193n56, 194n62, 196n77
slavery. *See* racial capitalism; racism
Smith, Ceasar, 13, 113
Smith, Stephen, 70, 194n62
Smith, William, Jr., 26, 183n67
Smith's Warf, 26, 27, 34, 75, 79, 170n45, 183n67
Steele's Saw Pit, 12, 31, 54
Stevens, Jervis Henry, 144, 145, *146–51*
St. John's Island, SC, 102
Strobel, Martin, 144, *146–51*
Strohecker, Perrault, 13, 14–15, 20, 34, 53, 58, 59, 66, 70, 71, 76, 193n56, 194n62; and racism and violence, 158; trial of, 108–9, 112, 114, 115, 116–17, 121, 133, 183
Sullivan's Island, SC, 28, 35

Tanzania, 5, 15–16, 17, 45, 108, 166nn21–22, 175n1
targets of insurrection, 71–72, 76, 79; banks, 8, 27, 64, 75; Cannon's Bridge, 9, 71, 72, 73, 78–79; Duquercron's Store, 62, 73, 75, 183n62; powder magazines, 9, 72, 73, 76–78, 88; US Arsenal, 62, 73, 75, 126; Wharton's Store, 62. *See also* plan of attack; Workhouse
Thayer's Farm, 65, 69. *See also* Bulkley's Farm; Payne's Farm
Thompson, Pharo, 69–70, 193n56, 194n62
trials. *See* tribunal proceedings
tribunal proceedings, 85–87, 89, 108, 142–44; against William Allen, 123–24; against Rolla Bennett, 90–94; against free Black people, 97–98; against Nero Haig, 115; against Bacchus Hammett, 112–15; against Agrippa Perry and Scipio Sims, 116–19; against Peter Poyas, 94–95; against Tom Russell, 112; against Denmark Vesey, 95–97; statements about Amaritta La Roche, 102–3; statements about Sarah Paul, 66, *101*, 103; statement by Monday Gell, 108–11; statement by Prudence Bussacre, 102–4; statement by Sally Howard, 99–101, *101*. *See also individual names of uprising participants*

uprising. *See* community organizing
US Arsenal, 62, 73, 75, 126

Vanderhorst, George, *101*
Vanderhorst's Wharf, 27, 67, 79, 109–10
Vesey, Denmark, 1, 14–15, *101*; among first hanged, 6, 98; birth in Africa of, 14–15, 20–21, 22, 168nn33–34; burial of, 98; children of, 24, 36, 194n62; church memberships of, 40–41, 174n81; and family members enslaved, 6, 22; and Igbo politics, 19; knowledge of local area of, 14, 26; marriages of,

23, 162n3; as member of uprising leadership coalition, 1, 52–54; as movement leader, 1–2; purchase of freedom by, 21, 22, 23, 51; and racism and violence, 47, 52, 132, 158; recruitment efforts of, 48; residence of, 31; as sole leader of uprising, 46, 53; trafficked to St. Thomas, 21; trial of, 95–97. *See also* leadership coalition

Vesey, Sandy, 70, 102, 193n40, 194n62

Vesey, Susan, 1–2, 6–7, 23, 66, 84, 125, 134, 135, 136, 162n3

Vincent, John, 70, 79, 194n62, 201n19

Walker, David, 42–43

wharves, 8, 9, 11, 12, 13, 26, 64–65, 66–67, 79, 134; as center of Black life, 26–28, 37–38; Crafts Wharf, 79; as fugitive refuge, 28, 30, 34–35, 37–38, 57–59; and James Creighton, 41, 52; Gadsden's Wharf, 13, 26, 27, 42, 70, 79, 165n16, 183n67; Gibbs and Harper's Wharf, 25, 26, 27, 28, 64, 170n46, 175n46; Hibben's Ferry, 27, 28, 64, 65, 170n46, 175n86; individual locations of, 27; as meeting place, 70; as part of Black neighborhoods, 30–31; Pritchard's Wharf, 54–55, 79, 105, 179n21; as site of organizing, 66; Smith's Wharf, 26, 34, 75, 170n45, 183n67; Vanderhorst's Wharf, 67, 79, 109–10. *See also* community organizing; ships

Wilson, George, 85, 90–91, 92, 101–2, *101*, 120, 187n7, 190n22

women, 5, 6, 32, 34, 52, 65–66, 68, 83, 84, 89, 92, 127–28; and labor, 22–24; speaking to tribunal, 99–105, *101*, 117–19. *See also* Bussacre, Prudence; fugitives; Howard, Sally; labor; Paul, Sarah; Perry, Doll; Perry, Kit; Perry, Liddy; Vesey, Susan

Woods, Mary, 4, 6, 58

Workhouse, 32–34, 43–44, 59, 89, 95, 98, 106–8, 113, 115, 116, 119–20; as site of rhetorical fighting retreat, 89

Zanzibar, 15–16, 166n21. *See also* Tanzania

www.ingramcontent.com/pod-product-compliance
Lightning Source LLC
Chambersburg PA
CBHW032024230426
43671CB00005B/189